AWS
Certified SysOps Administrator
Practice Tests

AWS
Certified SysOps Administrator
Practice Tests
Associate SOA-C01 Exam

Sara Perrott

Ben Piper

A Wiley Brand

I dedicate this book to my husband for his patience and encouragement throughout the writing process. Getting this book finished meant many missed nights in Azeroth. It's a labor of love for sure!
—Sara Perrott

I dedicate this book to my family and Jesus Christ, the Creator and Sustainer of all things (Colossians 1:16).
—Ben Piper

Acknowledgments

While a book may be a labor of love for an author, there is a fantastic team of people behind the author or authors that makes the book a reality. First off, a shoutout to our team at Wiley who put in a lot of hard work to take the book from a manuscript to the finished book in front of you now. My gratitude to our editor Kelly Talbot, who kept us on task and helped to polish the text. Another shoutout to my co-author Ben Piper for stepping in to co-author this book so that I could assist on the study guide that this book complements.

My personal thanks also to my agent Carole Jelen, and my coworkers who put up with my need to take extra personal days to finish the book.

—Sara Perrott

Special thanks as always to Kenyon Brown, Senior Content Acquisitions Editor, for the opportunity to contribute to this work. Thanks also to Sara Perrott for the invitation to co-author this book. To everyone at Wiley who patiently read and edited my questions— I know it's not always easy! Your efforts don't go unnoticed, so thank you. Last but not least, a big thank you to our readers for trusting us and allowing us to assist you on your learning journey.

—Ben Piper

About the Authors

Sara Perrott   is an Information Security professional with a Systems and Network Engineering background. She shares her passion for all things Information Technology by teaching classes related to Windows Server, Amazon Web Services, Networking, and Virtualization as well as other classes when needed at a local community college. She enjoys speaking at public events and presented most recently at the RSA Conference in 2019. Sara also enjoys technical editing and technical proofreading and has had the pleasure to work on a few projects doing this type of work.

When Sara is not working or writing, she enjoys spending time with her husband playing *World of Warcraft*, building robots, and playing with her ham radio. She also loves playing with her two pugs. Sara has a website where you can see some of the things she has been up to: www.saraperrott.com. You can also follow her on Twitter (@PerrottSara) and Facebook (@PerrottSara).

Ben Piper   is a cloud and networking consultant who has authored multiple AWS study guides, including the *AWS Certified Solutions Architect Study Guide: Associate SAA-C01 Exam, Second Edition* (Sybex, 2019) and the *AWS Certified Cloud Practitioner Study Guide: CLF-C01 Exam* (Sybex, 2019). He's also created more than 20 technology training courses covering Amazon Web Services and Cisco routing and switching. You can contact Ben by visiting his website: https://benpiper.com.

About the Technical Editor

Todd Montgomery has been in the networking industry for over 35 years. Todd is AWS Certified Sysops Administrator Associate certified and holds a total of five AWS certifications. Todd has spent most of his career out in the field working on-site in datacenters throughout North America and around the world. He has worked for equipment manufacturers, systems integrators, and end users of datacenter and cloud computing in the public, service provider, and government sectors. Todd currently works as a datacenter network automation engineer in Austin, Texas. He is involved in network implementation and support of emerging datacenter technologies and AWS public cloud services. Todd lives in Austin, Texas, and in his free time enjoys auto racing, general aviation, and Austin's live music venues. He can be reached at toddmont@thegateway.net.

Contents at a Glance

Contents

Introduction

If you've taken an AWS certification exam before, we're sure you know that they aren't easy. AWS certification exams test you to ensure that you have obtained the knowledge needed to work in AWS.

To pass the AWS Certified SysOps Administrator - Associate exam, you are going to need to understand the various services across the AWS ecosystem that enable you to do system administration and system operations work. This book is an excellent resource for your certification journey. In addition to this book, there is an AWS Certified SysOps Administrator - Associate exam Study Guide book that goes into detail with the content that you are expected to know to ensure that you are well prepared to sit the exam. Other materials that we would recommend would be the AWS documentation (typically available as HTML and PDF) and the FAQs.

You should absolutely have hands-on experience with AWS before sitting for this exam. When you first sign up for an AWS account, you get 12 months of free tier access. This means that so long as you stick to free tier eligible items, and you don't exceed the hours or usage specified, you can practice building out your infrastructure in AWS. Practice with the console, but also practice with the AWS CLI. You don't have to be an AWS CLI expert to pass the exam, but you should be familiar enough with it to know the format of some of the more common AWS CLI commands.

We highly recommend setting aside study time to focus on a chunk of questions each night. Don't try to get through an entire domain in one sitting (especially Domain 1, it's huge!). Instead, set a goal for yourself to get through 20 to 30 questions a night and stick to it. When you have gone through the book, make sure that you register and take the free practice exams available online. This is mentioned in the section, "Interactive Online Learning Environment and Test Bank" later in this introduction.

Last but not least, take a break the night before the exam and give your brain a rest. You're almost there!

Registering and Taking the Exam

When you register for the exam, you have your choice of either PSI or Pearson Vue for your testing center. At the time of this writing, the cost for the associate exam is $150 USD. The questions will be in either multiple-choice or multiple-answer format. You have a total of 130 minutes to finish the exam.

You should arrive at the testing center early. It's a good idea to be at least 20 minutes early in case there are others checking in ahead of you. You will need to take some form of ID with you, and remember that you may not take your notes or your cell phone into the exam room with you.

Once you finish the exam, you will be given immediate feedback as to whether you passed or failed. Within a few days, you will get a more detailed message showing you which domains you did well on and which domains you didn't do as well on. If you passed, then congratulations! If not, use the feedback in the email to focus on the areas in which you didn't do as well.

Interactive Online Learning Environment and Test Bank

There are tools that have been developed to aid you in studying for the Amazon Certified SysOps Administrator - Associate exam. These tools are all available for no additional charge at

https://www.wiley.com/go/sybextestprep

Just register your book to gain access to the practice test resources in the following list.

- **Chapter Questions:** These are presented to you in an electronic format so that you can run through the questions on your computer or tablet.

- **Practice Exams:** There is one 60-question practice exam available to test your knowledge. The questions in this exam are completely different from the questions in each chapter.

Exam Objectives

The AWS Certified SysOps Administrator - Associate exam is designed with system administrators who have been working with AWS in an operational capacity for at least one year in mind. The exam candidate should have experience in deploying resources and managing existing resources as well as basic operational day-to-day tasks like troubleshooting, monitoring, and reporting.

As a general rule, before you take this exam, you should meet the following conditions:

- Have at least one year of experience in system administration in AWS.

- Have hands-on experience with AWS management, including the AWS Management Console, AWS CLI, and AWS SDK.

- Understand networking concepts and methodologies in relation to AWS networking infrastructure.

- Know how to monitor systems for performance and availability.

- Understand basic security and compliance requirements and the tools within AWS that can help with auditing and monitoring.

- Have the ability to translate an architectural document in a functional AWS environment.

The exam is organized into different domains, and each domain has its own chapter. In each chapter, there will be questions that focus on the various subdomains. Let's take a quick look at the chapters and what is covered in each.

- **Chapter 1: Monitoring and Reporting (Domain 1):** This chapter may include questions on Amazon CloudWatch, AWS CloudTrail, Amazon Inspector, AWS Organizations, AWS Trusted Advisor, and AWS Cost Explorer.

- **Chapter 2: High Availability (Domain 2):** This chapter may include questions on managed services, Auto Scaling groups and elastic load balancers and other questions related to High Availability.

- **Chapter 3: Deployment and Provisioning (Domain 3):** This chapter may include questions on Amazon CloudFormation, AWS Elastic Beanstalk, Amazon Elastic Compute Cloud (EC2), Amazon Relational Database Service (RDS), and Amazon Elastic Container Service (ECS).

- **Chapter 4: Storage and Data Management (Domain 4):** This chapter may include questions on S3, Glacier, storage gateways, lifecycle management, and encryption.

- **Chapter 5: Security and Compliance (Domain 5):** This chapter may include questions on Identity and Access Management (IAM), users, groups, roles, policies, Key Management Service (KMS), resource policies, CloudTrail, CloudWatch, and service control policies (SCPs).

- **Chapter 6: Networking (Domain 6):** This chapter may include questions on Virtual Private Cloud (VPC), subnets, routing, VPC peering, security groups, network access control lists (NACLs), and Direct Connect.

- **Chapter 7: Automation and Optimization (Domain 7):** This chapter may include questions on Amazon CloudFormation, AWS Elastic Beanstalk, Simple Systems Manager (SSM), AWS CodeCommit, CodeDeploy, and CodePipeline.

Objective Map

This table provides you with a list of each domain on the exam, the weights assigned to each domain, and the chapters where content in the domains is addressed.

Domain	Exam Percentage	Chapter
Domain 1: Monitoring and Reporting	22%	1
1.1 Create and maintain metrics and alarms utilizing AWS monitoring services		
1.2 Recognize and differentiate performance and availability metrics		
1.3 Perform the steps necessary to remediate based on performance and availability metrics		
Domain 2: High Availability	8%	2
2.1 Implement scalability and elasticity based on use case		
2.2 Recognize and differentiate highly available and resilient environments on AWS		
Domain 3: Deployment and Provisioning	14%	3
3.1 Identify and execute steps required to provision cloud resources		
3.2 Identify and remediate deployment issues		

Domain	Exam Percentage	Chapter
Domain 4: Storage and Data Management	12%	4
4.1 Create and manage data retention		
4.2 Identify and implement data protection, encryption, and capacity planning needs		
Domain 5: Security and Compliance	18%	5
5.1 Implement and manage security policies on AWS		
5.2 Implement access controls when using AWS		
5.3 Differentiate between the roles and responsibility within the shared responsibility model		
Domain 6: Networking	14%	6
6.1 Apply AWS networking features		
6.2 Implement connectivity services of AWS		
6.3 Gather and interpret relevant information for network troubleshooting		
Domain 7: Automation and Optimization	12%	7
7.1 Use AWS services and features to manage and assess resource utilization		
7.2 Employ cost optimization strategies for efficient resource utilization		
7.3 Automate manual or repeatable process to minimize management overhead		

Reader Support for This Book

How to Contact the Publisher

If you believe you've found a mistake in this book, please bring it to our attention. At John Wiley & Sons, we understand how important it is to provide our customers with accurate content, but even with our best efforts an error may occur.

In order to submit your possible errata, please email it to our Customer Service Team at wileysupport@wiley.com with the subject line "Possible Book Errata Submission."

Domain

1

Monitoring and Reporting

1. You are a system administrator and you need to view the metrics that are available in the Amazon EC2 instance namespace. What command can you type into the Amazon CLI?

   A. `aws cloudwatch list-instances --namespace AWS/EC2`

   B. `aws cloudwatch list-metrics --name AWS/EC2`

   C. `aws cloudwatch list-metrics --namespace AWS/EC2`

   D. `aws cloudwatch list-instances --name AWS/EC2`

2. Where can you look up metrics that are available in Amazon CloudWatch?

   A. EC2 Console

   B. CloudWatch Console

   C. CloudTrail Console

   D. Trusted Advisor Console

3. How can you access Amazon CloudWatch?

   A. Amazon CloudWatch Console

   B. AWS CLI

   C. CloudWatch API

   D. All of the above

4. Which service can use Amazon CloudWatch alarms to increase or decrease capacity based on compute load (CPU utilization, etc.)?

   A. AWS Lambda

   B. Amazon S3

   C. Amazon EC2 Auto Scaling

   D. Amazon VPC

5. Which of the following are valid alarm states for Amazon CloudWatch? (Choose three.)

   A. ALARM

   B. OK

   C. READY

   D. INSUFFICIENT_DATA

   E. OFFLINE

   F. WARNING

6. You have been asked to create Amazon CloudWatch alarms for each of your organization's 600 servers, which all reside within the same region. Assuming you create five alarms per server, will you be able to create alarms for each of the servers?

   A. Yes, because the limit is 5000 alarms per region.

   B. Yes, because the limit is 3500 alarms per region.

   C. Yes, because the limit is 10,000 alarms per region.

   D. No, you can't create that many alarms in a single region.

7. You are a system administrator at your company, and you have been asked to check why an existing Amazon CloudWatch alarm is showing INSUFFICIENT_DATA for one of your established servers. What is the best explanation for why this is occurring?

   A. CloudWatch is experiencing an outage.

   B. Not enough data is available for the metric to determine whether it should be OK or ALARM.

   C. The alarm has only just been started, so it doesn't have enough data to determine if the state should be OK or ALARM.

   D. The server is offline so no metrics are available.

8. You are a system administrator at your company, and you have been asked to check why a new Amazon CloudWatch alarm is showing INSUFFICIENT_DATA for one of your established servers. What is the best explanation for why this is occurring?

   A. CloudWatch is experiencing an outage.

   B. Not enough data is available for the metric to determine whether it should be OK or ALARM.

   C. The alarm has only just been started, so it doesn't have enough data to determine if the state should be OK or ALARM.

   D. The server is offline so no metrics are available.

9. Your bosses have come to you and have asked you if there is a way for them to get real-time notifications if a certain Amazon CloudWatch alarm is triggered. What should your bosses do to ensure that they can get real-time notifications? The answer should minimize administrative overhead.

   A. Subscribe to an SNS topic that will send an SMS text message when the Amazon CloudWatch alarm is triggered.

   B. Write a custom AWS Lambda function that will send an email when the Amazon CloudWatch alarm is triggered.

   C. Use an SQS queue to deliver messages when an Amazon CloudWatch alarm is triggered.

   D. Use a third-party solution to send notifications via SMS text message when an Amazon CloudWatch alarm is triggered.

10. You need to set up an Amazon CloudWatch alarm that will trigger after four failed evaluations of the alarm metrics in a 5-minute period. What do you need to set the evaluation period and the data points to alarm to so that you get the desired result?

   A. Data points to alarm should be set to 5. Evaluation period should be set to 1 minute.

   B. Data points to alarm should be set to 4. Evaluation period should be set to 5 minutes.

   C. Data points to alarm should be set to 5. Evaluation period should be set to 5 minutes.

   D. Data points to alarm should be set to 4. Evaluation period should be set to 1 minute.

11. Your boss has asked you to ensure that the 5-minute data points from CloudWatch are available for at least 60 days. What do you need to change within Amazon CloudWatch to ensure that you have at least 60 days' worth of 5-minute data points?

    A. Nothing, Amazon CloudWatch can't retain data points that long.

    B. Nothing. By default, Amazon CloudWatch keeps 5-minute data points for 63 days.

    C. Create an archive to maintain 5-minute data points for at least 60 days.

    D. Set Amazon CloudWatch to never delete the 5-minute data points.

12. What is a namespace in Amazon CloudFront?

    A. A logical grouping of Amazon CloudWatch metrics

    B. A logical grouping of Amazon CloudWatch alerts

    C. A logical grouping of Amazon CloudWatch logs

    D. A logical grouping of report names for Amazon CloudWatch

13. In which Amazon CloudWatch namespace would the metrics for EC2 be located?

    A. AWS/ELB

    B. AWS/EBS

    C. AWS/EC2

    D. AWS/Auto Scaling

14. In which Amazon CloudWatch namespace would the metrics for an Application Load Balancer be located?

    A. AWS/ELB

    B. AWS/ApplicationELB

    C. AWS/EBS

    D. AWS/Auto Scaling

15. You have been asked to retrieve some statistics from Amazon CloudWatch for a production server that is having issues. Your organization uses dimensions to further identify custom metrics. You know that the published dimension for the metric contains the following:

Dimensions: Server=Production, Site=Location1

Which of the following could be used to retrieve the statistics that you need?

    A. Server=Production

    B. Server=Production, Site=Location

    C. Server=Prod

    D. Server=Production, Site=Location1

16. Which of these Amazon EC2 metrics require that an agent be installed on the server so that Amazon CloudWatch can gather the statistics for the system?

   A. Disk performance

   B. Network utilization

   C. Memory utilization

   D. CPU utilization

17. When using Amazon CloudWatch, there are two types of health checks used for EC2 instances. Which of the following options are valid status checks? (Choose two.)

   A. Performance status check

   B. System status check

   C. Health status check

   D. Virtual machine status check

   E. Instance status check

18. You are a system administrator for a mid-size financial institution. You are checking the health of your company's assets when you notice that CloudWatch is indicating that one of your EC2 instances has failed its instance status check. Which of the following is a possible cause?

   A. Exhausted memory

   B. Incompatible application installed

   C. Software license key has expired.

   D. Wrong OS is installed.

19. You are a system administrator for a mid-size financial institution. You are checking the health of your company's assets when you notice that CloudWatch is indicating that one of your EC2 instances has failed its instance status check. Which of the following is a possible cause?

   A. Wrong OS is installed.

   B. The filesystem is NTFS.

   C. Corrupted filesystem

   D. The filesystem is ext4.

20. You are a system administrator for a mid-size financial institution. You are checking the health of your company's assets when you notice that CloudWatch is indicating that one of your EC2 instances has failed its instance status check. Which of the following is a possible cause?

   A. IPv4 is enabled.

   B. Subnet is too large.

   C. Wrong OS is installed.

   D. Incorrect network configurations

21. You want to check the status of your Amazon EC2 instances. What is the command that you would enter into the AWS CLI to check the status of your instances?

    A. `aws cloudfront check-instance-status`

    B. `aws cloudfront describe-instance-status`

    C. `aws ec2 check-instance-status`

    D. `aws ec2 describe-instance-status`

22. You have been asked to ensure that some of your organization's junior system administrators can access Amazon CloudWatch to look at metrics. They have very limited credentials currently. Which policy can they be given that will enable them to view CloudWatch metrics without granting them additional access to the other AWS services?

    A. CloudWatchReadOnlyAccess

    B. CloudWatchMetricsAccess

    C. MetricsReadOnlyAccess

    D. AmazonEC2ReadOnly

23. Your boss has asked you to ensure that your Amazon EC2 instances have metrics being measured every 5 minutes. What type of monitoring should you use?

    A. Standard

    B. Basic

    C. Advanced

    D. Detailed

24. Your boss has asked you to ensure that your Amazon EC2 instances have metrics being measured every minute. What type of monitoring should you use?

    A. Standard

    B. Basic

    C. Advanced

    D. Detailed

25. You want to be able to store all of your log files from on-premises systems and AWS systems. Which AWS solution will allow you to store all of your log files in one place that will allow Amazon CloudWatch to monitor them?

    A. Amazon S3

    B. Amazon CloudWatch Events

    C. Amazon CloudWatch Logs

    D. Amazon EBS

26. You are wanting to move some Solaris servers to AWS from your on-prem datacenter and you would like to take advantage of CloudWatch Logs. Will you be able to install the agent for Linux on your Solaris servers?

    A. Yes. All versions of Unix and Linux support the Amazon CloudWatch Logs agent.

    B. Yes. Solaris is supported with the Amazon CloudWatch Logs agent.

    C. No. Solaris doesn't support Python, which is a requirement of the Amazon CloudWatch Logs agent.

    D. No. Solaris isn't supported with the Amazon CloudWatch Logs agent.

27. You want to ensure that you are able to update your Amazon CloudWatch Logs agent on your Red Hat Linux servers without having to manually copy and install the update package. How can you accomplish this task with the least amount of administrative overhead?

    A. Use wget to copy the package to the server then run it.

    B. Use the Red Hat Package Manager to install awslogs.

    C. Copy the package via FTP with an automated file transfer service.

    D. You can't update the CloudWatch Logs agent automatically.

28. You have chosen to update an existing server's Amazon CloudWatch agent using the Red Hat Package Manager (RPM). When the agent was first installed, a Python script was used. Since the update through RPM, you are no longer receiving logs in Amazon CloudWatch. When you check the server, you find that the configuration has changed. What is the most likely cause?

    A. Configuration issues are caused by updating the agent with Red Hat Package Manager because RPM has technical limitations.

    B. The Linux server needs to be restarted for the updated agent installation to take effect and start sending logs to Amazon CloudWatch.

    C. Configuration issues are caused by updating the agent with Red Hat Package Manager when it was installed by Python initially.

    D. The wrong agent installation package was used; you mistakenly ran the Debian package instead of the RPM package.

29. Which is a type of log that you can get from the Amazon CloudWatch Logs agent for Windows?

    A. Firmware log

    B. Proprietary logs

    C. Website

    D. IIS logs

30. Which is a type of log that you can get from the Amazon CloudWatch Logs agent for Windows?

   A. Firmware log

   B. System logs

   C. Website

   D. Boot diagnostics logs

31. The Amazon CloudWatch Logs agent for Windows has been installed on an EC2 instance running Windows Server 2016. You look for the EC2Config service but can't find it running. Logs are flowing into Amazon CloudWatch, but why do you not see the EC2Config service as you would on other older servers?

   A. EC2Config service is not supported for Windows Server 2016.

   B. There is an issue with the CloudWatch Logs Agent for Windows.

   C. Your installation of Windows Server 2016 needs to be updated.

   D. The CloudWatch Logs Agent didn't actually install; the logs are getting to Amazon CloudWatch another way.

32. You work for a hospital and must ensure that your log data is encrypted at all times. Does Amazon CloudWatch meet this requirement?

   A. Yes, but you have to configure it when you install the log agent.

   B. No. Log data is only encrypted in transit.

   C. Yes. Log data is encrypted at rest and in transit.

   D. No. Log data is only encrypted at rest.

33. Your supervisor has asked you if there is a way to create reports with billing data so that they can view billing by usage, or the cost per individual log group. What should you tell your boss?

   A. Yes. AWS allows you to get this information with detailed billing.

   B. Yes. AWS allows you to get this information with basic billing.

   C. No. AWS does not allow you to get this information.

   D. No. AWS does not give you the ability to create reports in this way.

34. How many tags can you have in an Amazon CloudWatch log group?

   A. 35

   B. 50

   C. 100

   D. 500

35. Your accounting department wants to know if there is a way to identify resources in Amazon CloudWatch so that they can bill back to the individual departments that are utilizing AWS resources. What is the best method you can tell your accounting department to use?

    A. Accounting will need to manually track which department needs to get billed for various resources.

    B. You can add a prefix to all of the alert names and resource names and Accounting can search on the prefix.

    C. Tags can be used for resources and log groups in order to identify which department to bill.

    D. There is no way to track which department is using which resources.

36. Your security team has contacted you with concerns regarding the activity of a user in the AWS Management Console. Which service allows you to view all of the activity that was generated under their account?

    A. AWS IAM

    B. AWS Trusted Advisor

    C. Amazon CloudWatch

    D. AWS CloudTrail

37. By default, where are AWS CloudTrail trails stored?

    A. S3

    B. EBS

    C. EFS

    D. Glacier

38. How do Amazon CloudWatch and AWS CloudTrail work together?

    A. Amazon CloudWatch and AWS CloudTrail don't work together at all; they are two separate products.

    B. Amazon CloudWatch monitors performance and availability, and AWS CloudTrail feeds API activity into Amazon CloudWatch.

    C. Amazon CloudWatch uses AWS CloudTrail to send alerts to end users when a security event occurs.

    D. Amazon CloudWatch uses AWS CloudTrail to monitor costs related to alerting and monitoring.

39. Which type of monitoring is free and updates in 5-minute periods in Amazon CloudWatch?

    A. Detailed

    B. Advanced

    C. Basic

    D. Simple

40. Which type of monitoring updates in 1-minute periods for an additional charge in Amazon CloudWatch?

   A. Detailed

   B. Advanced

   C. Basic

   D. Simple

41. How would you enable Amazon CloudWatch detailed monitoring via the AWS CLI?

   A. `aws ec2 monitor-instances --instance-ids <instance-id>`

   B. `aws ec2 watch-instances --instance-ids <instance-id>`

   C. `aws cloudwatch monitor-instances --instance-ids <instance-id>`

   D. `aws cloudwatch watch-instances --instance-ids <instance-id>`

42. How would you disable Amazon CloudWatch detailed monitoring via the AWS CLI?

   A. `aws cloudwatch unmonitor-instances --instance-ids <instance-id>`

   B. `aws cloudwatch nomonitor-instances --instance-ids <instance-id>`

   C. `aws ec2 unmonitor-instances --instance-ids <instance-id>`

   D. `aws ec2 nomonitor-instances --instance-ids <instance-id>`

43. Your boss wants to know how many read operations are happening across your Amazon EC2 instances. Which type of statistic will be most useful to give your boss the information they want?

   A. Average

   B. Maximum

   C. Minimum

   D. Sum

44. Your boss wants to know the average number of read operations that are happening across your Amazon EC2 instances. Which type of statistic will be most useful to give your boss the information they want?

   A. Average

   B. Maximum

   C. Minimum

   D. Sum

45. Your boss wants to know the highest number of read operations that have occurred across your Amazon EC2 instances within a set span of time. Which type of statistic will be most useful to give your boss the information they want?

   A. Average

   B. Maximum

   C. Minimum

   D. Sum

46. Your boss wants to know the lowest number of read operations that have occurred across your Amazon EC2 instances within a set span of time. Which type of statistic will be most useful to give your boss the information they want?

    A. Average

    B. Maximum

    C. Minimum

    D. Sum

47. Your boss wants to know the total number of read operations metrics that have been gathered from across your Amazon EC2 instances within a set span of time. Which type of statistic will be most useful to give your boss the information they want?

    A. SampleCount

    B. Sample

    C. Number

    D. Sum

48. Which steps are necessary to be able to aggregate statistics across multiple instances? (Choose two.)

    A. Choose the Amazon EC2 namespace and select Across All Instances.

    B. Enable basic monitoring.

    C. Choose the Amazon CloudWatch namespace and select Across All Instances.

    D. Enable detailed monitoring.

    E. Enable standard monitoring.

49. Which are ways that you can choose to filter which statistics you want to view? (Choose three.)

    A. By specific trails

    B. By specific instance

    C. By Auto Scaling group

    D. By Elastic Load Balancer

    E. By AMI

    F. By application load balancer

50. When an alarm is triggered in Amazon CloudWatch, your boss wants the Amazon EC2 instance to self-heal. How can you automatically reboot an Amazon EC2 instance when it is having issues?

    A. Set an alarm action to trigger a reboot.

    B. Set an alarm action to stop the instance.

    C. Set an alarm action to terminate the instance.

    D. Set an alarm action to recover the instance.

51. When an alarm is triggered in Amazon CloudWatch that appears to be reporting hardware failure, your boss wants the Amazon EC2 instance to recover itself. How can you recover an Amazon EC2 instance when it is on a host that is having hardware issues?

    A. Set an alarm action to trigger a reboot.

    B. Set an alarm action to stop the instance.

    C. Set an alarm action to terminate the instance.

    D. Set an alarm action to recover the instance.

52. Your organization has development workloads that run on Amazon EC2 instances. Your boss has asked you to determine the best method to ensure that the development instances are not left running when they are not in use. What is the best method to accomplish this goal?

    A. Use Amazon CloudWatch to watch for low CPU utilization. Set the alarm action to stop the instance when the alarm is triggered.

    B. Use Amazon CloudWatch to watch for low CPU utilization. Set the alarm action to terminate the instance when the alarm is triggered.

    C. Use Amazon CloudWatch to watch for high CPU utilization. Set the alarm action to stop the instance when the alarm is triggered.

    D. Use Amazon CloudWatch to watch for high CPU utilization. Set the alarm action to terminate the instance when the alarm is triggered.

53. When is a good time to use the Terminate alarm action?

    A. When an Amazon EC2 instance is currently not needed anymore but will be needed later.

    B. When an Amazon EC2 instance needs to be running 24x7.

    C. When an Amazon EC2 instance is not needed after finishing a job.

    D. You should never use the Terminate alarm action.

54. Your boss would like to view previous Amazon CloudWatch alarms. Where can these be viewed?

    A. The Alarms tab in the AWS Management Console

    B. The Alarms tab in the Amazon EC2 Management Console.

    C. The History tab in the AWS Management Console

    D. The History tab in the Amazon CloudWatch Console

55. Your boss has come to you asking if there is an easy way to view the usage each month to see how much their assets in AWS are going to cost. Where can they go to see this information?

    A. They can view this information in the AWS Management Console.

    B. They can view this information in AWS Billing and Cost Management.

    C. They can view this information in AWS Trusted Advisor.

    D. They can't; there is no way to monitor for this in AWS.

56. Your security team has asked you if there is a way to report on anyone who made changes in AWS Billing and Cost Management using the root credentials. What should you tell them?

    A. No. There isn't a way to tell if a change was made as the root account.

    B. No. You can tell that a change was made, but you can't tell who made the change.

    C. Yes. You can make a report in Amazon CloudWatch that will tell them if the root user was used to make changes in the AWS Billing and Cost Management Console.

    D. Yes. You can make a report in AWS CloudTrail that will tell them if the root user was used to make changes in the AWS Billing and Cost Management Console.

57. Your organization is just getting started using AWS. It has opted to use the AWS Free Tier to do a proof of concept. Your boss wants to ensure that they will get an alert if they will exceed what the AWS Free Tier provides. What is the best way to give them the alert they need with the least amount of administrative overhead?

    A. Set up an AWS Free Tier alert in AWS Budgets.

    B. Set up an AWS Free Tier alert in Amazon CloudWatch.

    C. Set up an AWS Free Tier alert in AWS CloudTrail.

    D. Set up a manual billing alert utilizing Amazon CloudWatch.

58. You are the system administrator in charge of getting your organization's AWS environment set up. You want to enable billing alerts, but when you log in with your IAM account, you are unable to do so. Why can't you create the billing alert?

    A. Your IAM account doesn't have the necessary permissions; you need more access.

    B. You can't set up billing alerts in AWS; you have to arrange them with your technical account manager.

    C. You need to be signed in with the AWS account's root user credentials to enable billing alerts.

    D. It is not possible to set up billing alerts in AWS.

59. What are the valid statuses you can get from the Amazon EC2 health checks? (Choose two.)

    A. Pass

    B. Fail

    C. OK

    D. Impaired

    E. Offline

60. You don't like the status checks and the alerting done from the status checks that exist on Amazon EC2. You want to disable the status checks in favor of another solution. How can you disable the Amazon EC2 status checks?

A. You can disable them by turning off the monitoring in the Amazon EC2 instance.

B. You can disable them by installing the Amazon CloudWatch Logs agent and then disabling them through the agent.

C. You can't disable them; they are part of Amazon EC2.

D. You can't disable them; they are part of Amazon EC2. You can disable the alerts that trigger off of the status checks.

61. How can you view the status checks for your organization's Amazon EC2 instances? (Choose two.)

A. Amazon EC2 Console

B. AWS Management Console

C. Command Line

D. Amazon CloudWatch Console

E. AWS CloudTrail Console

62. Where should you create an alarm for a failed Amazon EC2 status check failure?

A. Amazon EC2 Console

B. Amazon CloudWatch Console

C. AWS CloudTrail Console

D. AWS Management Console

63. How long are statistics retained in Amazon CloudWatch?

A. 6 months

B. 12 months

C. 15 months

D. 30 months

64. Which product would you use to monitor all API calls including activities performed on the AWS Management Console against Amazon EC2 and Amazon EBS?

A. Amazon CloudWatch

B. AWS CloudTrail

C. Amazon API Gateway

D. AWS Lambda

65. Where do the trails from AWS CloudTrail store their data?

A. Amazon EBS

B. Amazon EFS

C. Amazon EC2 instance

D. S3 bucket

66. Your boss has asked you if there is a way to validate that all of the AWS services that you rely on are up and operational. What should your answer be?

    A. Yes, we can check the Service Health Dashboard.

    B. Yes, we can check Amazon CloudWatch.

    C. Yes, we can check AWS CloudTrail.

    D. No, there is no way to check the AWS services.

67. Your boss has asked you if there is a way to get a personalized view of all the AWS services that you rely on to confirm that they are up and operational. What should your answer be?

    A. Yes. We can check the Service Health Dashboard.

    B. Yes. We can check AWS CloudTrail.

    C. Yes. We can use the Personal Health Dashboard.

    D. Yes. We can check Amazon CloudWatch.

68. You log into the Personal Health Dashboard. You see a notification that there is a "Route 53 operational issue." You begin getting calls saying that customers aren't able to reach your website. Could these two issues be related?

    A. Yes. Amazon Route 53 provides DNS services. If DNS is not working properly, then customers may not be able to reach your resources.

    B. Yes. Amazon Route 53 provides caching services. If it can't cache content, then customers may not be able to reach your resources.

    C. No. Amazon Route 53 errors wouldn't show up in the Personal Health Dashboard.

    D. No, the issues couldn't be related.

69. Your boss has approached you about giving access to only a specific set of Amazon EC2 instances in Amazon CloudWatch. How would you accomplish this in AWS IAM?

    A. You specify which Amazon EC2 instances can be accessed in an AWS IAM policy.

    B. You give permissions to the individual Amazon EC2 instances, and those permissions will carry over into Amazon CloudWatch.

    C. You can't grant access in Amazon CloudWatch for specific resources with AWS IAM.

    D. You can create a role that will define granular permissions for individual Amazon EC2 instances in Amazon CloudWatch.

70. You have been tasked by your boss to ensure that you receive alerts when a particular event ID occurs on both your on-premises systems and your Amazon EC2 instances. Which product would allow you to collect the logs in a single place, filter on the event ID, and send an alert?

    A. AWS CloudTrail

    B. Amazon CloudWatch Logs

    C. Amazon EC2 Logs

    D. Amazon SNS

71. Your boss wants to leverage your existing investment in AWS as much as possible and has asked you to implement a real-time performance and availability monitoring solution that will cover both your on-premises systems and your resources in the AWS cloud. What should you suggest?

   A.   A third-party tool like SolarWinds

   B.   AWS CloudTrail

   C.   Amazon SNS

   D.   Amazon CloudWatch Logs

72. You have strict regulatory requirements on log retention. You need to find a solution that will allow you to collect logs and store them at a lower cost. What would be the best solution to meet this need?

   A.   Amazon SNS

   B.   AWS CloudTrail

   C.   Amazon CloudWatch Logs

   D.   Amazon EBS

73. Your security team has mandated that you need to avoid using service accounts unless absolutely necessary because of the overhead in managing password rotation. You want to deploy the Amazon CloudWatch Logs agent. What could you use to authenticate the agent that is not a service account?

   A.   Access keys

   B.   AWS IAM

   C.   Active Directory

   D.   There isn't any option other than a service account.

74. Your security team has mandated that you need to avoid using service accounts unless absolutely necessary because of the overhead in managing password rotation. You want to deploy the Amazon CloudWatch Logs agent. What could you use to authenticate the agent that is not a service account?

   A.   Active Directory

   B.   AWS IAM

   C.   IAM roles

   D.   There isn't any option other than a service account.

75. Your operations center has asked if there is a better way to analyze and visualize the data that has been made available to them with Amazon CloudWatch. What would you recommend?

   A.   Amazon CloudWatch Logs agent

   B.   AWS CloudTrail

C. Amazon Redshift

D. Amazon CloudWatch Logs Insights

76. Your security team wants to minimize the amount of metrics that are kept in Amazon CloudWatch. They have asked you to delete the older metrics. How will you accomplish this?

A. You can't delete metrics; they are retained for the life of the account.

B. You can't delete metrics, though metrics do expire according to a schedule.

C. Log into the AWS Management Console with your IAM account and delete the metrics.

D. Log into the AWS Management Console with the root account and delete the metrics.

77. You have an application that you need to monitor. As it is critical to the business, you have been asked if you can create a metric that can record data every second. You also need to be able to retrieve it every second. How can you accomplish this?

A. Create a custom metric with a fast resolution.

B. Create a custom metric with a standard resolution.

C. Create a custom metric with a high resolution.

D. Create a custom metric with a detailed resolution.

78. Your boss has asked you if you can get pre-built metrics at a 1-second sampling rate as you can with your custom metrics. What should your response be?

A. Yes, you can use high resolution on pre-built metrics.

B. Yes, you can use high resolution on all metrics.

C. Yes, you can use standard resolution on all metrics.

D. No, you can't use high resolution for pre-built metrics.

79. How would you set a custom metric to use high resolution?

A. Set MetricResolution to 1 using the PutMetricRequest API.

B. Set StorageRetention to 1 using the PutMetricRequest API.

C. Set StorageResolution to 1 using the PutMetricRequest API.

D. Set MetricRetention to 1 using the PutMetricRequest API.

80. Your boss wants to use high-resolution metrics because they want to be able to get data every 15 seconds. They are concerned about additional cost from using high-resolution metrics. What should you tell your boss?

A. High-resolution metrics are more expensive.

B. High-resolution metrics are less expensive.

C. High-resolution metrics cost the same as standard.

D. You can't do 15-second periods with high resolution.

81. You have installed the Amazon CloudWatch Logs agent on a set of Amazon EC2 systems. They are sending logs to Amazon CloudWatch every 5 seconds, but you would prefer that happened every 15 seconds instead. What can you do?

    A. Adjust the Amazon CloudWatch Logs agent to send logs every 15 seconds.

    B. You can't adjust the 5-second time; it is the default setting.

    C. Set Amazon CloudWatch to pull the data every 15 seconds.

    D. Set AWS CloudTrail to pull the logs every 15 seconds.

82. You have begun sending system logs into Amazon CloudWatch. You want to ensure that you see any logs that contain the word *error* in them. How would you achieve this?

    A. Statistic filters

    B. Log filters

    C. Metric filters

    D. Error filter

83. You work for a financial institution and you need to parse your log data for account numbers. You have a regex query built that has been used in other solutions. How can you parse your log data for the regex that will find account numbers?

    A. Amazon CloudWatch Metric Filters

    B. AWS Management Console

    C. Amazon CloudWatch

    D. Amazon Kinesis

84. You have created some high-resolution custom metrics and want to ensure that Amazon CloudWatch will trigger an alarm no more than 10 seconds after an incident occurs. How can this be accomplished?

    A. Create a high-resolution Amazon CloudWatch alarm.

    B. Create a standard Amazon CloudWatch alarm.

    C. Create a detailed Amazon CloudWatch alarm.

    D. You can't set an Amazon CloudWatch alarm for under a minute.

85. You have created an Amazon CloudWatch alarm for your Amazon EC2 instances and it is constantly in the ALARM state. None of your systems are having any issues. How can you resolve the issue?

    A. Delete the alarm and then re-create it.

    B. Adjust the threshold that the alarm is set to so that it is no longer breached.

    C. Reboot the Amazon EC2 instances.

    D. Install the Amazon CloudWatch Logs agent.

86. Your Operations Center would like to create a dashboard to track Amazon CloudWatch alarms. What would be the best solution?

    A. Amazon CloudWatch Logs

    B. AWS CloudTrail

    C. Amazon EC2 with business analytics software

    D. Amazon CloudWatch Dashboards

87. You want to view how well your systems and resources in AWS are doing at any point in time. You have systems in multiple regions. How do you get a dashboard-like experience for your availability and performance data?

    A. You can't set up a dashboard that can monitor across all regions.

    B. Use Amazon CloudWatch Dashboards.

    C. Use Amazon CloudWatch Logs.

    D. Use an Amazon CloudWatch Logs agent.

88. Your security team has asked you to ensure that API calls are being logged. You know that you can use AWS CloudTrail to accomplish this. What do you need to do next?

    A. AWS CloudTrail is enabled, but you need to tell it what type of API calls to log.

    B. AWS CloudTrail is enabled, but you need to configure a trail to start logging API calls.

    C. Nothing; AWS CloudTrail is enabled and configured by default.

    D. You need to enable AWS CloudTrail to begin recording API calls.

89. Your security team has asked you to ensure that *all* API calls are being logged. You know that you can use AWS CloudTrail to accomplish this. What do you need to do next?

    A. AWS CloudTrail is enabled, but you need to tell it what type of API calls to log.

    B. AWS CloudTrail is enabled, but you need to configure a trail to start logging all API calls.

    C. Nothing; AWS CloudTrail is enabled and configured by default.

    D. You need to enable AWS CloudTrail to begin recording API calls.

90. Your security team wants to ensure that all activity within the AWS Management Console is recorded. What is the best solution that meets this goal?

    A. AWS Trusted Advisor

    B. Amazon CloudWatch Logs

    C. AWS CloudTrail

    D. Amazon CloudWatch

91. You are the system administrator for a rapidly growing company. While you only have resources in one region currently, you know that you will expand into other regions soon. How can you ensure that API calls are captured automatically for any new regions that are added? (Choose two.)

    A. Select Global from the region drop-down, then create the trail.

    B. Select the existing region in the trail configuration page.

    C. Select Yes to apply to all regions in the trail configuration page.

    D. In the CLI, you set the parameter IsMultiRegionTrail to True.

    E. You can't automatically add new regions to an AWS CloudTrail trail.

92. Your boss wants you to create two separate trails in Amazon CloudWatch, one for management and one for data. Can you create the trails in the way that your boss wants you to?

    A. Yes, you can create two separate trails and separate management activity from data activity.

    B. No, you can't put management and data traffic into separate trails or create multiple trails.

    C. No, you can't put management and data traffic into separate trails, though you can create multiple trails.

    D. No, you can't create multiple trails, though you can separate management and data activity.

93. Your security team has required that you encrypt your AWS CloudTrail log files. What do you need to do to ensure that they are encrypted and only accessible to those who need to review them?

    A. Nothing; you can't encrypt AWS CloudTrail log files.

    B. Nothing; they are encrypted with S3 SSE by default.

    C. They are encrypted by default using S3 SSE; you can use S3 bucket policies or IAM to control access.

    D. You need to enable encryption in S3 so that the AWS CloudTrail log files are encrypted.

94. Your security team has made the requirement that controls need to be implemented to prevent accidental deletion of AWS CloudTrail log files. What is the best solution for this?

    A. Restrict access to the S3 bucket.

    B. Enable MFA Delete.

    C. Enable versioning.

    D. Use lifecycle policies to archive deleted objects.

95. Your legal team has asked you to ensure that AWS CloudTrail log files are only retained for 90 days. What can you do to meet their needs?

    A. You can't adjust the retention time frame on AWS CloudTrail log files.

    B. You make the change in AWS CloudTrail to reflect the 90-day rule.

C. You make the change in Amazon CloudWatch to reflect the 90-day rule.

D. You make a lifecycle rule in S3 to delete log files older than 90 days.

96. Your developers are checking an AWS CloudTrail log file troubleshooting their work. They are complaining that API calls they are making are not showing up until 15 minutes later. What can you do to remediate this issue?

A. The AWS CloudTrail trail is not configured properly; you need to reconfigure it to log items faster.

B. There is nothing to remediate; AWS CloudTrail log files typically get an event around 15 minutes after the API call.

C. You should change the timing between the delivery of the event and the occurrence of the event to 5 minutes.

D. You should change the timing between the delivery of the event and it occurring to 1 minute.

97. You look in your S3 bucket where AWS CloudTrail stores its log files and you notice that there are no log files during the late evening hours. What is the most likely cause for the missing log files?

A. There was no API activity during this time frame.

B. There was a misconfiguration in AWS CloudTrail.

C. You don't have permissions to view the log files.

D. AWS CloudTrail doesn't have the access it needs to write the log files.

98. Your security team has asked for you to provide a way to validate that AWS CloudTrail log files have not been modified since being placed in the S3 bucket. What can you do to prove that the files have not been changed with the least amount of administrative effort?

A. Enable encryption in Amazon S3.

B. Create an AWS Lambda function to check the hashes every hour and compare against a database of the original hashes.

C. Enable AWS CloudTrail log file integrity validation.

D. Manually hash the files and check against known hashes.

99. Your security team wants to ensure that AWS resources are built according to the organizational standards that have been set. How can you prove to your security team that your systems are using the desired configurations?

A. Use Amazon CloudWatch.

B. Use AWS CloudTrail.

C. Use AWS Config.

D. Use AWS Lambda.

100. Your legal department wants to know anytime a configuration change is made on one of their systems. They want to receive a notification when the change is made. How can you ensure that the legal department is aware of any changes made to their server?

   A. Enable Amazon CloudWatch and create an SNS topic; subscribe them to the topic.

   B. Enable AWS CloudTrail and create an SNS topic; subscribe them to the topic.

   C. Enable AWS Config and create an SNS topic; subscribe them to the topic.

   D. Enable AWS Config and create an SMS topic; subscribe them to the topic.

101. One of your critical applications just suffered an outage. It is suspected that a change caused the outage but there is no scheduled change in your change management calendar. How can you figure out who made the change and what the change was?

   A. Use Amazon CloudWatch to check for events that happened around the time of the outage.

   B. Use AWS CloudTrail to look at any of the API calls made around the time that it is believed the change occurred to see who made the change and what the change was.

   C. Setup AWS Config to send a message to an SNS topic when any config changes are made.

   D. Use AWS Config to view the configuration history of the resource that suffered the outage and AWS CloudTrail to see who made the change.

102. You are the system administrator in charge of your organization's AWS resources. You work for a hospital and have been asked by the internal audit team for a report that proves that you have implemented the proper controls to maintain HIPAA compliance. How can you do this within AWS?

   A. Create rules that evaluate your systems for the desired controls in AWS Config.

   B. Use AWS CloudTrail to check for inappropriate API calls.

   C. Use Amazon CloudWatch to monitor for compliance.

   D. There is no automated tool; you must do it all manually.

103. You are the system administrator for your organization in charge of its AWS infrastructure. You have configured the desired configurations for your systems. You want to ensure that systems are never out of compliance. Can you prevent users from making changes with AWS Config?

   A. Yes, select the Enforce option when you set up AWS Config.

   B. Yes, it does it automatically without any further interaction.

   C. No, AWS Config is only able to monitor configurations, not change them.

   D. No, AWS Config doesn't monitor configuration drift.

104. You have multiple accounts under AWS Organizations. You want to combine the results of AWS Config under AWS Organizations. How can you do this?

   A. Create an aggregator in one of the regions that you want to monitor.

   B. Create an aggregator in AWS Organizations.

    C. You can't view the AWS Config data from multiple regions, though you can view it for multiple regions.

    D. You can't view the AWS Config data from multiple regions or accounts in one area.

105. You have multiple accounts under AWS Organizations. You want to combine the results of AWS Config under one of the regions that most of your resources reside in. How can you do this?

    A. Create an aggregator in one of the regions that you want to monitor.

    B. Create an aggregator in AWS Organizations.

    C. You can't view the AWS Config data from multiple regions, though you can view it for multiple regions.

    D. You can't view the AWS Config data from multiple regions or accounts in one area.

106. You want to ensure that AWS Config is enabled for all three regions that your organization is using. How would you enable AWS Config for all three regions?

    A. It is automatically enabled for all regions.

    B. You need to enable it once for all regions.

    C. You need to enable it once per region.

    D. You can't use AWS Config for that many regions.

107. Your security team has asked you to make sure that any changes to the desired configurations in AWS Config are monitored so that they know who made the change. Which product can be used to achieve this request?

    A. AWS Config

    B. Amazon CloudWatch

    C. AWS CloudTrail

    D. AWS IAM

108. You currently have 145 individual AWS Config rules built for your organization's environment. You need to make 10 more rules for new criteria that your legal team wants you to monitor for. Will you be able to create 10 more rules?

    A. Yes, you can create unlimited rules.

    B. Yes, but you will need to request an increase on the limit from AWS.

    C. No, because you can't have more than 150 rules.

    D. No, because you can't add more rules.

109. Your boss wants you to set up a periodic rule in AWS Config, and they want it to run every 6 hours. How should you respond to this request?

    A. Set up the periodic rule for 3 hours because you can't set it to 6.

    B. Set up the periodic rule to run every 6 hours.

    C. Set up the periodic rule to run every 12 hours because you can't set it to 6.

    D. Tell your boss that AWS Config can only do change-triggered rules.

110. You are not using AWS Organizations, but you want to aggregate your AWS Config data from all of your other accounts. Besides setting up AWS Config and the aggregator, what else do you need to do?

A. There is nothing else to set up; once the aggregator is created it will work.

B. Create a role and assign it to the aggregator account.

C. Add an AWS IAM account for the aggregator to use in each individual AWS account.

D. Authorize the aggregator account in each individual AWS account.

111. A resource has been reported as noncompliant by AWS Config and a notification has been sent. When the rules are run again, the resource is still noncompliant, but you didn't get a notification. Why is this?

A. AWS Config is having a service outage.

B. AWS Config is misconfigured so it is not sending messages properly.

C. This behavior is by design; notifications are sent when the status changes.

D. You will only get one notification when it fails.

112. You have AWS Config configured in your AWS account. You have added a security group to an Amazon EC2 instance. Which resources will have changes recorded in AWS Config?

A. Amazon EC2 instance

B. The security group

C. Primary resource and related resources

D. All of these

113. Your Operations Center team would like to know what kinds of things AWS Config can record. What should you include in your response?

A. All of the following options

B. OS patches

C. Application installations

D. Network configurations

114. Which account is used in AWS Organizations to create an organization, invite new AWS accounts, and remove AWS accounts?

A. root

B. master

C. An IAM user with sufficient access

D. A shared access key

115. You have a new person in Accounting who is in charge of paying for your AWS account charges. They have asked you if there is a way to see what the charges are so far. Where should you tell them to go?

A. AWS Budgets

B. AWS Management Console

    C. AWS Billing and Cost Management Dashboard

    D. AWS Trusted Advisor

116. You have been asked by your manager to create a report that will forecast how much AWS is going to cost your organization over the next three months. You have been using AWS for six months. Which tool will provide this information?

    A. AWS Organizations

    B. AWS Trusted Advisor

    C. AWS Budgets

    D. Cost Explorer

117. Your accounting department likes the view that the Billing and Cost Management Dashboard gives them, but they don't want to have to go to each individual AWS account to view billing for the entire organization. What should you implement to allow them to view billing for the entire organization?

    A. AWS Trusted Advisor

    B. AWS Organizations

    C. AWS Management Console

    D. AWS Budgets

118. Your boss wants to view the current amount due on your AWS account. Where should you tell your boss to look?

    A. AWS Management Console

    B. AWS Trusted Advisor

    C. AWS Budgets

    D. AWS Cost Explorer

119. Your boss wants to view the forecasted amount due on your AWS account. Where should you tell your boss to look?

    A. AWS Cost Explorer

    B. AWS Trusted Advisor

    C. AWS Management Console

    D. AWS Budgets

120. Your accounting department wants to know if there are ways to save on costs for EC2 instances. When they view the Reservation Recommendations screen in AWS Cost Explorer, they get a message saying that there are no recommendations available at this time. What is a possible cause of this error?

    A. You are using instance types that can't be set as reserved instances.

    B. Your instances haven't run long enough to generate recommendations.

    C. They don't have permissions to view cost and budget items.

    D. You are using instance sizes that can't be used with reserved instances.

121. Which services does AWS Trusted Advisor not provide?

    A. Cost savings recommendations

    B. Performance recommendations

    C. Security recommendations

    D. Alarms for going over budget

122. You want to use AWS Trusted Advisor to monitor how well you are setting things up in your organization's AWS account. When you log in, you are disappointed to see only seven checks. How can you get access to all of the checks within AWS Trusted Advisor? (Choose two.)

    A. Upgrade to Developer-level support.

    B. Upgrade to Enterprise-level support.

    C. Upgrade to Teams-level support.

    D. You can't upgrade; there are only seven checks.

    E. Upgrade to Business-level support.

123. Which of the following is a category that AWS Trusted Advisor checks?

    A. Security

    B. Cost monitoring

    C. Budgeting

    D. System vulnerabilities

124. Which of the following is a category that AWS Trusted Advisor checks?

    A. Network intrusions

    B. Application configurations

    C. Service limits

    D. Conflicting security groups and NACLs

125. Which of the following is a category that AWS Trusted Advisor checks?

    A. Vulnerability scanning

    B. Budgeting

    C. Cost reporting

    D. Performance

126. Which of the following is a category that AWS Trusted Advisor checks?

    A. Network intrusions

    B. Cost optimization

    C. Security scans

    D. Cost budgeting

127. Which of the following is a category that AWS Trusted Advisor checks?

    A. IOPS optimization

    B. Budgeting

    C. Fault tolerance

    D. Available IP space

128. Trusted Advisor continuously alerts on one of your resources and your boss has asked you to ensure that AWS Trusted Advisor no longer alerts on that resource. How can you accomplish this?

    A. Add an exclusion for reporting the resource at the resource level.

    B. Add an exclusion for reporting the resource at the check level.

    C. Add an exclusion for reporting the resource in Amazon CloudWatch.

    D. There is no way to disable the alerts from occurring in AWS Trusted Advisor.

129. You have remediated an issue that was being reported by AWS Trusted Advisor. You have hit refresh multiple times in the past minute but nothing has changed. What is the most likely cause?

    A. You did not properly remediate the issue that AWS Trusted Advisor was reporting.

    B. You have to wait for 15 minutes to refresh a check from the last time it was checked.

    C. You have to wait for 10 minutes to refresh a check from the last time it was checked.

    D. You have to wait for 5 minutes to refresh a check from the last time it was checked.

130. You try to create an elastic IP address and you get a message that states that your service limit has been reached. Where can you go to verify that this is the case?

    A. Amazon CloudWatch

    B. AWS Trusted Advisor

    C. AWS CloudTrail

    D. AWS Config

131. You try to create an elastic IP address and you get a message that states that your service limit has been reached. You have verified in AWS Trusted Advisor that the service limit has indeed been reached. How can you resolve the issue? (Choose two.)

    A. Increase your service limits from the AWS Management Console.

    B. Increase your service limits from the AWS CLI.

    C. Contact AWS to request a service limit increase.

    D. Deprovision old resources to free up unused elastic IP addresses.

    E. Increase your service limits from the AWS SDK.

132. Your organization's accounting department is looking at reservation recommendations but is not seeing any. You use spot instances to support batch jobs that can be easily interrupted. How can you explain to your accounting department why they are not seeing any recommendations?

    A. AWS Trusted Advisor uses on-demand rates to calculate savings with reserved instances.

    B. Spot instances aren't up long enough to generate recommendations in AWS Trusted Advisor.

    C. Spot instances don't show up in AWS Trusted Advisor.

    D. The accounting department doesn't have permissions to view the reserved instance recommendations.

133. Your security department wants an easy way to monitor the overall security posture of your AWS environment. Which tool should you recommend to them?

    A. AWS WAF

    B. AWS Systems Manager

    C. Amazon Inspector

    D. Amazon GuardDuty

134. Your security department wants to know which processes are running on open ports. How can you give them this information? (Choose two.)

    A. Run a scan from Amazon Inspector.

    B. Run a scan with Amazon GuardDuty.

    C. Use AWS WAF.

    D. Install the Amazon Inspector agent.

135. Your security department has asked you for a report that includes how well your systems are lining up with CIS benchmarks. How can you provide them with this report?

    A. Use Amazon Inspector to run an assessment template that contain the CIS rules package desired.

    B. Use AWS Config to run an assessment template that contains the CIS rules package desired.

    C. Use AWS Systems Manager to run an assessment template that contains the CIS rules package desired.

    D. You can't; there isn't a report like this.

136. You have just begun using Amazon Inspector to analyze your systems. You get a call stating that Amazon Inspector is causing performance impacts; however, you do not have the agent installed, and you don't currently have an assessment running. What should your response be?

    A. Amazon Inspector couldn't be the cause since you are not currently scanning the environment.

    B. Amazon Inspector is probably the issue because the agentless configuration is known to cause performance impacts.

C.   Amazon Inspector is not likely to be the cause of the performance issue as the agentless configuration is not supposed to cause performance issues.

D.   Amazon Inspector is the cause of the performance issue as the agentless configuration has been known to cause performance issues.

137.   You have been asked to create your own rules packages for Amazon Inspector assessment templates to use. How do you create a rules package?

A.   You can't create rules packages.

B.   Create the rules package inside of the Amazon Inspector Dashboard.

C.   Create the rules package inside of the AWS Config Dashboard.

D.   Create the rules package inside of the AWS Systems Manager Dashboard.

138.   You have been asked to scan your application servers for a vulnerable version of software. The software was installed using Ansible. When you look at the scan, you don't see the application listed. What is the most likely cause?

A.   Ansible is not supported for use in AWS.

B.   Amazon Inspector can only find applications installed by the operating system's package manager.

C.   The application is not supported in Amazon Inspector.

D.   Amazon Inspector can't tell you application version numbers.

139.   You have been asked to provide a basic report based on the findings of Amazon Inspector for the executives of your organization. What type of report should you run from Amazon Inspector?

A.   Full report

B.   Executive report

C.   Findings report

D.   Basic report

140.   You have been asked to provide a detailed report based on the findings of Amazon Inspector for the members of the security team in your organization. What type of report should you run from Amazon Inspector?

A.   Full report

B.   Executive report

C.   Findings report

D.   Basic report

141.   Your security team has come to you and asked if AWS has a solution that will allow them to monitor network traffic for threats. How should you respond?

A.   Yes, Amazon GuardDuty.

B.   Yes, Amazon Inspector.

C.   Yes, but it's only available via a third party.

D.   No, there is no built-in way to do this.

142. Which AWS service identifies threats throughout your AWS account by analyzing VPC Flow Logs, DNS logs, and CloudTrail events?

   A. Amazon CloudWatch

   B. Amazon Inspector

   C. Amazon GuardDuty

   D. Amazon Macie

143. Which AWS services classifies data in S3 and catalogs the normal behaviors from users who are accessing that data?

   A. Amazon CloudWatch

   B. Amazon Inspector

   C. Amazon GuardDuty

   D. Amazon Macie

144. Which of these is not something that Amazon GuardDuty monitors for?

   A. Instance compromise

   B. Account compromise

   C. Reconnaissance activity

   D. DDoS

145. Your security team wants to be notified when Amazon GuardDuty finds a threat on the network. Which products can be used with Amazon GuardDuty to send them alerts? (Choose two.)

   A. Amazon CloudWatch Logs

   B. Amazon CloudWatch Events

   C. Amazon SNS

   D. Amazon SQS

   E. Amazon Inspector

146. You have been asked by your organization's CISO how long Amazon GuardDuty will retain the findings that it has alerted on as your organizational standard is 90 days. What should you tell the CISO?

   A. 90 days

   B. 180 days

   C. 45 days

   D. 30 days

147. You have a lot of sensitive data in your S3 buckets and you have been asked if there is a solution to classify sensitive data and then monitor it for usage. Which product would fit the criteria?

   A. Amazon Inspector

   B. Amazon Macie

C. Third-party product

D. There is no product that will meet these requirements.

148. You want to see how well your environment compares to the five pillars of the Well-Architected Framework. Which tool could you use to get a report regarding how well your workloads fit into the AWS Well-Architected Framework?

A. AWS Well-Architected Tool

B. Amazon CloudWatch

C. AWS CloudTrail

D. Amazon Inspector

149. You want to be able to monitor what software is installed and add licenses to installed software across your on-prem systems and your AWS systems. Which products will allow you to do this? (Choose two.)

A. Amazon Inspector

B. AWS Systems Manager

C. AWS License Manager

D. AWS Config

E. Amazon CloudWatch

150. You are using AWS License Manager to monitor license usage in your account. You want to be able to manage licensing in all of the AWS accounts in your organization. What is the most efficient way to manage your licenses?

A. Have your IAM account added to each AWS account.

B. Set up the AWS accounts in AWS Organizations.

C. Have individual account owners report license usage.

D. You can't centrally manage your license for all AWS accounts.

151. Which of these is a use case for Amazon CloudWatch?

A. Infrastructure automation and orchestration

B. Infrastructure security and privacy

C. Infrastructure patching and updates

D. Infrastructure monitoring and troubleshooting

152. Which of these is a use case for Amazon CloudWatch?

A. Resource management

B. Resource optimization

C. Resource allocation

D. Resource security

153. Which of these is a use case for Amazon CloudWatch?

  A. Application load balancing

  B. Application routing

  C. Application monitoring

  D. Application geolocation

154. Which of these is a use case for Amazon CloudWatch?

  A. Log storage

  B. Log retention

  C. Log rotation

  D. Log analytics

155. Your boss wants to be able to search for specific data from an event field and have those queries appear on an Amazon CloudWatch Dashboard. Since you have queries built in regex already, how would you use the regex queries to search for the data from an event field?

  A. Amazon CloudWatch Logs Insights

  B. Amazon Kinesis

  C. Amazon Athena

  D. Amazon RedShift

156. Which product allows you to take Amazon CloudWatch logs and use interactive queries and visualizations with the data in addition to creating Amazon CloudWatch Dashboards?

  A. Amazon CloudWatch Logs

  B. Amazon CloudWatch Events

  C. Amazon CloudWatch Logs Insights

  D. Amazon CloudWatch

157. Which open-source solutions are popular for gathering custom application metrics for Amazon CloudWatch?

  A. REST

  B. Solarwinds

  C. collectd

  D. dmesg

  E. StatsD

158. Your monitoring team has asked you if there is a way to integrate Amazon CloudWatch graphs into their existing solution so that they can see on-prem and AWS systems from the same source. What should you tell them to use?

  A. Amazon CloudWatch Logs

  B. Amazon CloudWatch Logs agent

  C. Amazon CloudWatch snapshot graphs

  D. Amazon CloudWatch APIs

159. What is a common use case for AWS CloudTrail?

    A. Firewalling

    B. Compliance aid

    C. API management

    D. Monitoring logs

160. What is a common use case for AWS CloudTrail?

    A. Monitoring logs

    B. Detecting application issues

    C. Detecting data exfiltration

    D. Detecting HTTP response codes

161. What is a common use case for AWS CloudTrail?

    A. Installing software

    B. Installing patches

    C. Monitoring for installed software

    D. Security analysis

162. What is a common use case for AWS CloudTrail?

    A. Operational issue troubleshooting

    B. Installing security updates

    C. Monitoring logs

    D. Monitoring for HTTP response codes

163. Which data event type in AWS CloudTrail allows you to see when an AWS Lambda function was executed and who executed it?

    A. Invoke API

    B. Management events

    C. AWS Lambda logs

    D. Log

164. For regulatory purposes, you need to ensure that AWS CloudTrail trail data is stored for one year with easy access, and then you want the trail data to be deleted. Which solution provides the correct response with the least amount of administrative effort?

    A. Save trails to S3 and manually delete data after one year.

    B. Save trails to S3 and create a script that runs daily and deletes trails older than one year.

    C. Save trails to S3 and use lifecycle policies to delete trails older than one year.

    D. There is no way to accommodate this request in AWS.

165. Name one of the benefits of using AWS Systems Manager?

   A. Monitoring logs

   B. Monitoring API calls

   C. Monitoring vulnerabilities in your environment

   D. Detecting problems more quickly

166. Name one of the benefits of using AWS Systems Manager?

   A. API Management

   B. Automation

   C. Federated access

   D. Log monitoring

167. Name one of the benefits of using AWS Systems Manager?

   A. Improve network accessibility

   B. Improve visibility and control

   C. Improve security assessments

   D. Improve API management

168. Name one of the benefits of using AWS Systems Manager?

   A. Manages hybrid cloud environments

   B. Improves visibility into logs

   C. Makes security assessments more accessible

   D. Provides visibility into API calls

169. Name one of the benefits of using AWS Systems Manager?

   A. Manage API calls

   B. Perform security assessments

   C. Maintain security and compliance

   D. Monitor logs

170. What is the benefit of the Run Command in AWS Systems Manager?

   A. Provides console access to the system without the need for remote access ports to be open

   B. Provides console access to Linux hosts via SSH

   C. Provides automation of tasks so long as remote access ports are open

   D. Provides automation of tasks without the need for remote access

171. What is the benefit of the Session Manager in AWS Systems Manager?

   A. Allows remote console sessions via an interactive web browser with no need to open inbound ports

   B. Allows remote console sessions via an interactive web browser once the necessary ports are open

    C. Allows configuration management and tracking

    D. Allows management of APIs

172. What is the benefit of the Patch Manager in AWS Systems Manager?

    A. Patch management and reporting for Windows systems only

    B. Patch management and reporting for Linux systems only

    C. Patch management and reporting for AWS systems only

    D. Patch management and reporting for on-prem and AWS systems

173. What is the benefit of the State Manager in AWS Systems Manager?

    A. Backs up system state for on-prem and AWS resources

    B. Backs up system state for AWS resources only

    C. Provides configuration management for on-prem and AWS resources

    D. Provides configuration management for AWS resources only

174. What is the benefit of the Parameter Store in AWS Systems Manager?

    A. Centralized storage of license keys, database stings, and secrets

    B. Used only to store secrets for AWS KMS

    C. Used only to store secrets for AWS IAM

    D. Used only to store parameters for AWS Lambda

175. Your boss would like to have a single "source of truth" to run queries against the data from the AWS services you use. Is there a way to accomplish this within AWS?

    A. Yes, you can query data from the other AWS services with Amazon CloudWatch.

    B. Yes, you can query data from the other AWS services with Amazon Athena.

    C. Yes, you can query data from the other AWS services with AWS CloudTrail.

    D. No, there is not a way to accomplish this in AWS.

176. Which AWS product allows you to analyze the data within Amazon S3 and run queries against it?

    A. Amazon CloudFront

    B. Amazon RDS

    C. Amazon Athena

    D. AWS Lambda

177. Your boss wants to be able to not only analyze the data from the various services you use in AWS but also visualize that data. Which two services will allow you to analyze the data from the AWS services and visualize the data as well? (Choose two.)

    A. Amazon Athena

    B. Amazon QuickSight

    C. AWS CloudTrail

    D. AWS Lambda

    E. Amazon Inspector

178. You need a location where you can store persistent metadata related to Amazon S3. Which AWS service will allow you to accomplish this task?

    A. Amazon Athena

    B. AWS Glue Data Catalog

    C. Amazon RDS

    D. Amazon Elasticache

179. Your boss wants to be able to use visualizations within Amazon QuickSight, and to be able to use Active Directory security groups with the least amount of administrative effort. You are using AWS Directory Service already. Which edition of Amazon QuickSight should you choose?

    A. Developer

    B. Standard

    C. Basic

    D. Enterprise

180. How is Amazon QuickSight billed?

    A. Pay-per-session

    B. Pay-per-transaction

    C. Pay-per-minute

    D. Pay-per-hour

181. What is one of the benefits of Amazon Athena?

    A. Amazon Athena is available for a flat monthly rate.

    B. Amazon Athena is free.

    C. Amazon Athena is a serverless solution.

    D. Amazon Athena only requires one server.

182. What is one of the benefits of Amazon Athena?

    A. Supports standard SQL

    B. Supports proprietary SQL

    C. Uses EBS as its data store

    D. Needs input to be in JSON or CSV

183. How is Amazon Athena billed?

    A. Per session

    B. Per transaction

    C. Per query, $1/TB scanned

    D. Per query, $5/TB scanned

184. What is one of the benefits of Amazon Athena?

    A. Uses SQS to queue queries

    B. Uses parallel query execution

    C. Uses Elasticache to speed up query execution

    D. Uses DynamoDB to speed up query execution

185. What is a common use case for AWS Config?

    A. Security assessments

    B. Continuous monitoring of API calls

    C. Continuous monitoring of logs

    D. Continuous monitoring of configuration changes

186. What is a common use case for AWS Config?

    A. Help troubleshoot issues related to configuration changes.

    B. Help troubleshoot issues related to permissions.

    C. Help troubleshoot issues related to storage space.

    D. Help troubleshoot issues related to processor usage.

187. What is a common use case for AWS Config?

    A. Audit configurations for vulnerabilities.

    B. Audit configurations for compliance with organizational baselines.

    C. Audit configurations for best practices.

    D. Audit configurations for bad AMI IDs.

188. What is a common use case for AWS Config?

    A. View compliance status of API calls made in the environment.

    B. View compliance status of services based on logs.

    C. View compliance status for configurations across multiple AWS accounts.

    D. View compliance status of password policy in AWS IAM.

189. What is a common use case for AWS Config?

    A. Improve change management capabilities and tracking.

    B. Improve security assessment capabilities.

    C. Improve monitoring of logs.

    D. Improve monitoring of APIs.

190. What is a common use case for Amazon Inspector?

    A. Identify exploits on the network.

    B. Identifying vulnerabilities in applications

    C. Identifying best practices according to the Well-Architected Framework

    D. Identifying configuration changes in your environment

191. What is a common use case for Amazon Inspector?

   A.   Assess configurations for changes to your environment.

   B.   Assess the API calls in your environment for API usage that is not secure.

   C.   Alert you to a misconfiguration on a NACL that would prevent outbound traffic.

   D.   Assess your AWS environment against security best practices.

192. What is a common use case for Amazon Inspector?

   A.   Identify attack traffic on the network.

   B.   Monitor API calls being used in your environment.

   C.   Perform assessments within the CI/CD pipeline.

   D.   Identify configuration changes that have occurred.

193. What is a common use case for Amazon Inspector?

   A.   Validate security best practices during application development.

   B.   Validate that current patch levels are correct and patch if they are not.

   C.   Validate that user access for AWS services is appropriate.

   D.   Validate that configurations meet your organization's baselines.

194. What is a common use case for Amazon Inspector?

   A.   Support development shops that use Waterfall methodology.

   B.   Support development shops that use Agile methodology.

   C.   Monitor API calls for insecure requests.

   D.   Monitor for unauthorized configuration changes.

195. What is a common use case for Amazon Inspector?

   A.   Patch machines that are not on the current patch level.

   B.   Monitor your network for intrusions.

   C.   Define the standards or best practices that your applications must adhere to.

   D.   Compare best practices of the Well-Architected Framework to the current state.

196. Which of these responses is a benefit of Amazon GuardDuty?

   A.   Compare the environment to the best practices laid out in the Well-Architected Framework.

   B.   Perform security assessments.

   C.   Identify threats on the network.

   D.   Maintain patch levels for systems.

197. Which of these responses is a benefit of Amazon GuardDuty?

   A.   Automated responses to identified threats

   B.   Identification of stale user accounts

   C.   Identification of users/groups with excessive permissions

   D.   Automated security assessments

198. Which of these responses is a benefit of Amazon GuardDuty?

    A. Maintain desired patch levels.

    B. Manage encryption keys for your AWS environment.

    C. Support a single AWS account.

    D. Support multiple AWS accounts.

199. Your security department has approached you wanting to have a centralized view of all identified network threats in your AWS environment. What would be the best product to give them that visibility?

    A. Amazon Inspector

    B. AWS Trusted Advisor

    C. Amazon GuardDuty

    D. Amazon QuickSight

200. Your security department has approached you about monitoring suspicious user activity in AWS. What would be the best product to give them that visibility?

    A. Amazon GuardDuty

    B. AWS IAM

    C. AWS Directory Service

    D. AWS Organizations

201. Which product provides the fastest performance when you need to run a large report that includes complex queries?

    A. Amazon EMR

    B. Amazon RedShift

    C. Amazon Athena

    D. Amazon RDS

202. Which AWS product is best suited to replace an on-premises data lake using Hadoop?

    A. Amazon EMR

    B. Amazon RedShift

    C. Amazon Athena

    D. Amazon RDS

203. You need to be able to run ad hoc queries against data in Amazon S3. Which product is best suited for this task?

    A. Amazon EMR

    B. Amazon RedShift

    C. Amazon Athena

    D. Amazon RDS

204. You are using Amazon Kinesis Firehouse to collect a large amount of data in real time. How can you analyze the data if it is stored in Amazon S3 in a cost-effective manner?

    A. Amazon RDS

    B. Amazon CloudWatch

    C. AWS Lambda

    D. Amazon Athena

205. What is a benefit provided by Amazon Macie?

    A. Performing security assessments in AWS

    B. Visibility into the locations where you store data

    C. Running ad hoc queries against Amazon S3

    D. Management of storage encryption keys

206. What is a benefit provided by Amazon Macie?

    A. Monitor API usage for storage access.

    B. Manage storage versioning in S3.

    C. Integration with Amazon CloudWatch Events

    D. Manage the storage lifecycle in S3.

Domain

2

High Availability

1. Your website has been suffering performance issues, and you have been able to determine that this is due to a spike in traffic to your servers. The servers are behind an ELB and the CPU on both Amazon EC2 instances hovers around 95% during this time frame. Your boss has asked you to find a way improve performance without impacting cost any more than is absolutely necessary. What should you do?

   A. Create an EC2 Auto Scaling group and have Amazon CloudTrail trigger an autoscale event to scale up when the CPU reaches 80% and scale down when the CPU drops to 40%.

   B. Create an EC2 Auto Scaling group and have Amazon CloudWatch trigger an autoscale event to scale up when the CPU reaches 80% and scale down when the CPU drops to 40%.

   C. Create an EC2 Auto Scaling group and have Amazon CloudWatch trigger an autoscale event to scale up when the CPU reaches 95% and scale down when the CPU drops to 40%.

   D. Create an EC2 Auto Scaling group and have Amazon CloudWatch trigger an autoscale event to scale up when the CPU reaches 80% and scale down when the CPU drops to 75%.

2. You are trying to set up EC2 Auto Scaling groups. What must you do before you can set up an Auto Scaling group?

   A. Create an ELB.

   B. Create an Amazon EC2 instance.

   C. Create a launch configuration.

   D. Set up monitoring in Amazon CloudWatch.

3. Your EC2 Auto Scaling group is being monitored by Amazon CloudWatch. When the CPU goes over 80%, Amazon CloudWatch enters an alarm state. Amazon CloudWatch sends a message to the Auto Scaling group containing instructions on what to do. This set of instructions is referred to as what?

   A. Amazon Machine Image

   B. Config file

   C. Launch configuration

   D. Policy

4. Your boss has heard that EC2 Auto Scaling groups can scale based on metrics monitored in Amazon CloudWatch. However, the traffic to your web servers follows very predictable patterns, so your boss would like to know if you can schedule a scaling event instead. What should your response be?

   A. Yes, scaling events can be triggered on a schedule.

   B. No, scaling events can't be triggered on a schedule.

   C. Yes, you can schedule scaling events through Amazon CloudWatch.

   D. No, scaling events can only be triggered based on Amazon CloudWatch metrics.

5. You want to be able to automatically scale your resources but you don't want to have to specify scaling policies or schedule scaling. What should you do?

    A. Use analytics scaling.

    B. Use behavioral scaling.

    C. Use predictive scaling.

    D. There are no other options.

6. You have just set up your EC2 instances and have configured an Auto Scaling group that uses predictive scaling. Scaling events are not occurring. What is the most likely reason why the scaling events are not occurring?

    A. Predictive scaling needs at least two weeks of data.

    B. Predictive scaling needs at least one month of data.

    C. Predictive scaling needs at least one week of data.

    D. Predictive scaling doesn't support EC2 instances.

7. Which of these cannot take advantage of Auto Scaling groups?

    A. Amazon Elastic Container Service (ECS)

    B. Amazon DynamoDB

    C. Aurora replica in Amazon Aurora

    D. Oracle database in Amazon RDS

8. You have created your Auto Scaling group but you notice that you have no EC2 instances within the group. What is the most likely cause?

    A. You didn't set a desired capacity.

    B. Minimum capacity is set to 0, and there is no load.

    C. Maximum capacity is set to 1.

    D. Autoscaling is not available in your region.

9. Which of these options are valid states for an EC2 instance in an Auto Scaling group? (Choose two.)

    A. Active

    B. Online

    C. Pending

    D. Starting

    E. InService

10. Which of these is a valid reason for an Amazon EC2 instance in an Auto Scaling group to be terminated?

    A. It is getting hit by too many requests and the CPU is nearing 90% utilization.

    B. It is getting hit by too many requests and the memory is nearing 85% utilization.

    C. It is exceeding the threshold set in AWS Budgets.

    D. The instance has failed a defined number of health checks.

11. To create an Auto Scaling group, you must first create a non-versioned template that defines what the EC2 instances should be configured to do. That template is called what?

    A. Launch configuration

    B. Launch template

    C. Autoscaling template

    D. EC2 template

12. You have an EC2 instance that has been in your environment for six months. You would like to create an Auto Scaling group to put it in, and you want to ensure that the other instances are configured exactly the same. What should you do that will involve the least amount of administrative effort?

    A. Attach the EC2 instance to the Auto Scaling group after manually creating the Auto Scaling group.

    B. Attach the EC2 instance to a security group.

    C. Manually create a launch configuration with the same settings as the EC2 instance.

    D. Create a launch configuration using the EC2 instance as a template.

13. You have an EC2 instance that you have used as a template for a launch configuration. After creating the launch configuration for the Auto Scaling groups and deploying them, you decide that you need another EBS volume added to the instances. You add the volume. What do you need to do next? (Choose two.)

    A. You need to manually create a new launch configuration.

    B. Change the Auto Scaling group to use the new launch configuration.

    C. You don't need to do anything…when you update the EC2 instance, the launch configuration is automatically updated.

    D. Use the EC2 instance to create another launch configuration.

14. You have assigned a new launch configuration to your Auto Scaling group. You need to refresh all of your instances, but you can't have downtime. What is the best option?

    A. Set the desired capacity to 0, then once they are all terminated, set it back to its previous setting.

    B. Manually terminate the old instances so they are relaunched using the new configuration.

    C. Choose each instance and assign the new launch configuration.

    D. Let the instances age out over time.

15. You've been using launch configurations, but as part of a DevOps model, you want to begin using versioning to track changes to your launch configurations. How can you enable versioning for launch configurations?

    A. Create a launch template from your launch configurations.

    B. Enable versioning on your launch configurations.

    C. Manually name your launch configurations with a version number.

    D. There is no way to set up versioning for launch configurations.

16. You currently have a MySQL database running in RDS. You want to ensure that the database is highly available. How can you accomplish this?

    A. Take frequent snapshots of your database.

    B. Create a read replica.

    C. Create multiple read replicas.

    D. Set the database to be multi-AZ.

17. You notice that your multi-AZ deployment is running out of a different availability zone than normal. Looking through the logs, you notice that a failover occurred two days prior. What could be the cause of the failover?

    A. Your database became corrupt.

    B. Your database became too big.

    C. The primary availability zone became unavailable.

    D. The database in the primary AZ ran out of memory.

18. You notice that your multi-AZ deployment is running out of a different availability zone than normal. Looking through the logs, you notice that a failover occurred two days prior. What could be the cause of the failover?

    A. Network connectivity in the primary AZ was interrupted.

    B. Network connectivity was slow but online.

    C. The IP address of your RDS instance changed.

    D. Your database became unresponsive due to resource constraints.

19. You notice that your multi-AZ deployment is running out of a different availability zone than normal. Looking through the logs, you notice that a failover occurred two days prior. What could be the cause of the failover?

    A. Your database became corrupt.

    B. Your RDS instance ran out of disk space.

    C. Your RDS instance ran out of memory.

    D. The host your RDS was running on suffered a hardware failure.

20. You notice that your multi-AZ deployment is running out of a different availability zone than normal. Looking through the logs, you notice that a failover occurred two days prior. What could be the cause of the failover?

    A. Your RDS instance ran out of space.

    B. Your RDS instance ran out memory.

    C. The storage your RDS instance was using suffered a failure.

    D. You encrypted the storage for your RDS instance.

21. What is a region?

    A. AWS uses regions to create datacenters in countries.

    B. AWS uses regions to create datacenters in whole continents.

    C. A region is a geographic area, not necessarily bound to country boundaries.

    D. A region is a geographic area bound by country boundaries.

22. What is an availability zone?

    A. One or more isolated datacenters connected with low-latency links

    B. A single isolated datacenter connected with a low-latency link

    C. A datacenter that spans multiple regions

    D. A datacenter that spans multiple countries

23. You need to ensure that your application is highly available. It runs on two EC2 instances that are part of an Auto Scaling group. What is the simplest way to make your application highly available while still using the same AMI?

    A. Ensure that your EC2 instances are using a Windows AMI.

    B. Ensure that your EC2 instances are using a Linux AMI.

    C. Ensure that the EC2 instances are in different regions.

    D. Ensure that the EC2 instances are in different availability zones.

24. You have been asked to make your application more highly available. What would be a good recommendation to make?

    A. Use loose coupling whenever possible.

    B. Add more memory to your EC2 instances.

    C. Add more CPU to your EC2 instances.

    D. Create more frequent backups.

25. You need a highly available solution to manage the passing of messages from your application to another application. The messages must be delivered at least once…your application can tolerate receiving messages more than once. What should you use to manage the messages between these systems?

    A. Simple Notification Service (SNS)

    B. Simple Workflow Service (SWF)

    C. Simple Queue Service (SQS)

    D. Email

26. What is Amazon Simple Queue Service?

    A. Highly available message queueing service that offers FIFO at-least-once delivery

    B. Highly available message queueing service that offers LIFO at-least-once delivery

    C. Highly available message queueing service that offers FILO at-least-once delivery

    D. Highly available message queueing service that offers FIFO only-once delivery

27. You have a backend system that has been having issues lately. You need to ensure that messages sent to this system will be saved if it goes offline. What is the best option?

    A. Simple Notification Service (SNS)

    B. Simple Queue Service (SQS)

    C. Simple Workflow Service (SWF)

    D. Simple Storage Service (S3)

28. Your application is producing more data than your backend systems can handle. Your boss doesn't want to add more backend systems, so what is the best choice to ensure that data isn't lost and backend systems aren't overwhelmed?

   A. Simple Workflow Service (SWF)

   B. Simple Notification Service (SNS)

   C. Simple Storage Service (S3)

   D. Simple Queue Service (SQS)

29. You have decided to implement Simple Queue Service (SQS) to support your application. Your boss wants to ensure that messages sent to the queue can be kept for 7 days before being discarded. What should you tell your boss?

   A. Messages can be kept for up to 7 days, so you can meet their requirements.

   B. Messages can be kept for up to 14 days, so you can meet their requirements.

   C. Messages can be kept for up to 30 days, so you can meet their requirements.

   D. Messages can't be retained for more than 1 day.

30. You have decided to implement Simple Queue Service (SQS) to support your application. Your boss wants to ensure that messages sent to the queue can be kept for 30 days before being discarded. What should you tell your boss?

   A. Messages can be kept for up to 30 days, so you can meet their requirements.

   B. Messages can't be retained for more than 1 day.

   C. Messages can be kept for up to 7 days, so you can't meet their requirements.

   D. Messages can be kept for up to 14 days, so you can't meet their requirements.

31. You have chosen to implement an SQS queuing chain. You notice that often the backend servers are only busy during certain times of the day. Other times they are sitting idle. What should you do with the backend servers that will still allow for high availability but that will also allow you to terminate idle instances?

   A. Configure the backend servers to use an Elastic Load Balancer.

   B. Configure the backend servers to use an Auto Scaling group.

   C. Configure the backend servers to use Route 53.

   D. Configure the backend servers to use a placement group.

32. You have an SQS queue that you haven't used for over 45 days. When you start your application, you find that it is running into failures, and when you check, you find that your SQS queue is no longer there. What could be the cause?

   A. The SQS queue expired and disappeared.

   B. It was a glitch on the AWS side and they will need to restore it.

   C. AWS deleted it as it had been inactive for over 30 consecutive days.

   D. You have the wrong region selected in the AWS Management Console.

33. You notice that messages being fed into your SQS queue are not coming out in the same order they went in. What is the likely cause?

   A. You are using a standard queue rather than a FIFO queue.

   B. You are using a standard queue rather than a LIFO queue.

   C. You are using a standard queue rather than a FILO queue.

   D. You are using a standard queue rather than a LILO queue.

34. Which of these are valid polling methods used with Amazon Simple Queue Service? (Choose two.)

   A. Small polling

   B. Short polling

   C. Tall polling

   D. Fast polling

   E. Long polling

35. How does an SQS queue prevent multiple systems from processing the same message from the queue?

   A. Visibility lockout

   B. Processing lockout

   C. Visibility timeout

   D. Processing timeout

36. You need to configure SQS to be able to route messages to a queue when they have failed to successfully process after a certain number of attempts has been reached. What kind of a queue do you need to create?

   A. Normal

   B. Standard

   C. FIFO

   D. Dead letter queue (DLQ)

37. You are attempting to share an SQS queue across two regions, but you are unable to do so. Why is that?

   A. SQS queues can only be shared within the same region.

   B. You don't have permissions to share an SQS queue.

   C. SQS isn't available in the region you are trying to share the queue with.

   D. You've reached the max limit of SQS queues in your account.

38. You need a highly available messaging service that can send messages when systems and/ or services go down to a select group of cell phone numbers via SMS text. Which AWS service would meet this need?

   A. Amazon Simple Queue Service (SQS)

   B. Amazon Simple Storage Service (S3)

   C. Amazon Simple Notification Service (SNS)

   D. Amazon Simple Texting Service (STS)

39. Which of these can be used to subscribe to an SNS topic?

  A. Amazon Simple Storage Service (S3)

  B. AWS Lambda

  C. Amazon EC2

  D. Amazon Simple Workflow Service (SWF)

40. Which of these can be used to subscribe to an SNS topic?

  A. Amazon Elastic Beanstalk

  B. Amazon IAM

  C. HTTP and HTTPS

  D. Amazon CloudFormation

41. Which of these can be used to subscribe to an SNS topic?

  A. Simple Queue Service (SQS)

  B. Amazon CloudWatch

  C. AWS CloudTrail

  D. Amazon Elastic Beanstalk

42. Which of these can be used to subscribe to an SNS topic?

  A. Amazon EC2

  B. Amazon Simple Storage Service (S3)

  C. Amazon CloudFormation

  D. Email

43. Which of these can be used to subscribe to an SNS topic?

  A. Amazon CloudWatch

  B. AWS CloudTrail

  C. Amazon Route 53

  D. SMS text

44. You need to ensure that systems can reach out for updates but that they are not accessible from the Internet. What is the simplest way to allow this while still remaining highly available?

  A. AWS Direct Connect

  B. Security groups

  C. NAT instance

  D. NAT gateway

45. Your application has been having some availability issues lately due to server issues on the backend. You want to ensure that when an instance becomes unhealthy, there is an automated response that ensures your users are only routed to healthy instances. Which service could provide this ability?

   A. Auto Scaling groups

   B. Elastic Load Balancer

   C. Launch configuration

   D. Amazon CloudWatch

46. You have noticed that when your elastic load balancer removes an unhealthy instance, customers call in and complain, stating that they had to repeat their actions. This is negatively impacting sales. What is the best way to manage this?

   A. Make the application stateless.

   B. Enable sticky sessions on the load balancer.

   C. Use Route 53 to handle the routing instead.

   D. Reboot unhealthy instances.

47. There are two services that make it simple to convert an application to stateless because they can be used to track session state. Which AWS services can be used in this way? (Choose two.)

   A. DynamoDB

   B. Amazon RDS

   C. Elasticache

   D. Amazon Redshift

48. You need to be able to store data in multiple regions. You like that S3 makes it easy to encrypt and apply lifecycles. Will S3 be able to store data across multiple regions?

   A. Yes, but only regions on the same continent.

   B. No, S3 can't replicate data across regions.

   C. Yes, S3 natively replicates data across regions.

   D. Yes, cross-region replication.

49. You currently have one customer gateway set up attached to a virtual private gateway in AWS. You are concerned that the connection is not highly available. How would you ensure that your connection into AWS is highly available?

   A. Create another virtual private gateway and another customer gateway.

   B. Create another customer gateway and enable dynamic routing.

   C. Create another virtual private gateway and enable dynamic routing.

   D. You can't make a VPN connection highly available in AWS.

50. You want to use Amazon SQS to send messages for your application as you want to take advantage of the queuing functionality. The messages on average are 512 KB. Is Amazon SQS a good fit?

    A. Yes, it can handle messages up to 1 MB.

    B. Yes, it can handle messages up to 512 KB.

    C. No, it can't handle messages over 256 KB.

    D. Yes, it can handle messages up to 256 MB.

51. You want to use Amazon SQS to send messages for your application as you want to take advantage of the queuing functionality. The messages on average are 64 KB. Is Amazon SQS a good fit?

    A. Yes, it can handle messages up to 1 MB.

    B. Yes, it can handle messages up to 512 KB.

    C. No, it can't handle messages under 256 KB.

    D. Yes, it can handle messages up to 256 KB.

52. You want to use Amazon SNS to send messages to your users when there is an issue with one of your Amazon EC2 instances. How big can the message be and still successfully be processed through SNS?

    A. 512 KB

    B. 256 KB

    C. 512 MB

    D. 256 MB

53. You want to ensure that customers are directed to the web server that has the least amount of latency for them. What is the best solution for this use case?

    A. Elastic Load Balancing

    B. Latency-based routing with Route 53

    C. Geolocation routing with Route 53

    D. Failover routing with Route 53

54. You want to ensure that customers are directed to the web server that is closest to them in terms of location. What is the best solution for this use case?

    A. Elastic load balancing

    B. Latency-based routing with Route 53

    C. Geolocation routing with Route 53

    D. Failover routing with Route 53

55. You want to ensure that customers are always directed to a healthy system. You have two systems that you want to configure as a primary and a secondary. What is the best solution for this use case?

   A. Elastic load balancing

   B. Latency-based routing with Route 53

   C. Geolocation routing with Route 53

   D. Failover routing with Route 53

56. You need to point Route 53 to one of your elastic load balancers. What type of DNS record should you choose?

   A. A record

   B. CNAME record

   C. SRV record

   D. Alias record

57. Which two engines are available if you choose Elasticache to manage session state when decoupling your applications? (Choose two.)

   A. NoSQL

   B. RDS

   C. Memcached

   D. Redis

58. You want to decouple your application to make it more highly available. As part of this work, you want to manage session state separately from the web servers and the load balancers. You need the solution to be highly available and able to heal itself. What is the best option?

   A. Amazon RDS

   B. Amazon Redshift

   C. Amazon Elasticache

   D. PostgreSQL

59. You have some code that needs to run when a certain event happens. This has historically been hosted on a single server, and recently the server went down. You have been asked to choose the most cost-effective option to make this highly available. What should you choose?

   A. Put the code into AWS Lambda.

   B. Build another Amazon EC2 instance.

   C. Use Elastic Beanstalk to deploy another EC2 instance.

   D. Create an elastic load balancer.

60. You have a Lambda function in the us-east-1 region and you want to also use the function in the us-east-2 region. Can you use the same function or would you need to re-create it?

    A. Yes, you can use the same function.

    B. Yes, but you will need to share the function.

    C. No, you will need to create the function in the other region.

    D. No, you can't use the same function.

61. You have found that you have an AWS Lambda function that occasionally hangs and runs for a very long time. As you are charged for the compute the function takes up, what is the best solution to ensure that the function does not run indefinitely?

    A. Set a lockout value.

    B. Set a timeout value.

    C. Create a CloudWatch monitor.

    D. Manually stop the function.

62. You are building out your new infrastructure in AWS. You have already created your VPC and need to create subnets to support a three-tier application model. You want to ensure that subnets are built with high availability in mind. How should you accomplish this? (Choose two.)

    A. Have at least two subnets for each tier.

    B. Have one subnet for each tier.

    C. Allow AWS to choose the availability zone.

    D. Choose different availability zones for each subnet.

63. You need a highly available method for systems in one of your subnets to reach the Internet. They should also be accessible from the Internet. Which AWS component would meet this requirement?

    A. VPN gateway

    B. NAT gateway

    C. NAT instance

    D. Internet gateway

64. You need to ensure that your Amazon EC2 instances can reach out to the Internet for patches but you don't want to allow inbound traffic. How can you meet this need while maintaining high availability?

    A. Create a NAT instance in two availability zones.

    B. Create a NAT gateway in two availability zones.

    C. Create two customer gateways and one virtual private gateway.

    D. Create one customer gateway and two virtual private gateways.

65. You notice that your web application is not available. When you check to see what is going on, you notice that the elastic load balancer that was servicing traffic has been deleted. How can you find out who deleted it?

   A. AWS Systems Manager

   B. Amazon CloudWatch

   C. AWS CloudTrail

   D. VPC Flow Logs

66. You notice that your web application is not available. When you check to see what is going on, you notice that the elastic load balancer that was servicing traffic has been deleted. What can you do to prevent this from happening again?

   A. Choose an application load balancer and enable deletion protection.

   B. Choose a classic load balancer and enable deletion protection.

   C. Lock down access with IAM.

   D. Turn on MFA Delete.

67. You need a load balancer that can route based on the content of the request that is being made as your web servers house several different services. What kind of load balancer do you need?

   A. Classic Load Balancer

   B. Application Load Balancer

   C. Network Load Balancer

   D. There isn't a load balancer that supports this use case.

68. You are using an application load balancer and you want to route traffic for multiple domains. What type of routing should you set up that will allow the load balancer to do what you need?

   A. Content-based routing

   B. Path-based routing

   C. Host-based routing

   D. There is no way to accomplish this type of routing.

69. You have multiple services running behind an application load balancer. You need the load balancer to route to different servers based on the URL in the HTTP request. What type of routing should you use?

   A. Content-based routing

   B. Path-based routing

   C. Host-based routing

   D. There is no way to accomplish this type of routing.

70. Your web application is written in HTTP/2. You need to put it behind an elastic load balancer. What type of load balancer should you use?

A. Network load balancer

B. Classic load balancer

C. Application load balancer

D. There are no load balancers that support this use case.

71. You have your website hosted in S3 because of the high availability inherent to S3. You would like to use a highly available service to cache content so that end user experience is improved. Which service would be the best fit for this use case?

A. AWS CloudTrail

B. Amazon CloudFront

C. Amazon CloudWatch

D. There isn't a service that would work for this use case.

72. You need to throttle the number of API requests being made against your systems as they are being overwhelmed. Which highly available service is a good fit for this?

A. Amazon API Gateway

B. AWS Lambda

C. AWS CodePipeline

D. AWS CodeDeploy

73. You have an API made available through the Amazon API Gateway. There was a new release last night and you want to ensure that the new version of the API has not caused any issues with the availability to call and consume the API. How would you check to see the error rates for the API? (Choose two.)

A. AWS CloudTrail

B. Amazon CloudWatch

C. Amazon API Gateway Console

D. You can't monitor error rates.

74. You have a simple web application and you want a simple load balancing solution that operates at layer 4. Which is the best load balancer to use?

A. Application load balancer

B. Classic load balancer

C. Network load balancer

D. There is no layer 4 load balancer.

75. You want to use a network load balancer as you are only concerned with layer 4 traffic. You do, however, need to be able to use SNI as you are trying to make several domains highly available with the load balancer. Will you be able to use a network load balancer to make these web applications highly available?

    A. Yes, network load balancers support SNI.

    B. Yes, but you will need to enable SNI on the load balancer.

    C. Yes, but only if your web servers are using Windows AMIs.

    D. No, network load balancers do not support SNI.

Domain

3

Deployment and Provisioning

1. You have been asked to automate the deployment of web servers in your organization to meet demand when the load increases on your existing systems. Which service would meet this need?

    A. AWS CloudFormation

    B. Auto Scaling groups

    C. User data field

    D. Amazon CloudWatch

2. You have been asked to automate the deployment of web servers in your organization to meet demand when the load increases on your existing systems. You need to ensure that each of the EC2 instances is configured the same way each time. How would you accomplish this requirement?

    A. AWS CloudFormation

    B. Auto Scaling groups

    C. User data field

    D. Amazon CloudWatch

3. You have been asked to automate the deployment of web servers in your organization along with all of the components needed to support the web application. They must be configured identically every time. How would you accomplish this requirement?

    A. AWS CloudFormation

    B. Auto Scaling groups

    C. User data field

    D. Amazon CloudWatch

4. Which formats are supported for use with CloudFormation templates? (Choose two.)

    A. JSON

    B. JavaScript

    C. YAML

    D. Text

5. Why might you use a template parameter in a CloudFormation template?

    A. Specify passwords at creation time.

    B. Specify instance type and size at creation time.

    C. Specify IAM roles needed at creation time.

    D. You can't use a parameter in a CloudFormation template.

6. You are trying to use a CloudFormation template, but it keeps rolling back and deleting all of the resources it created. This template has worked for you in the past, and no changes have been made to the template or AMIs in your account. Why might this occur?

    A. The template is trying to use an AMI that is not available in your region.

    B. The template contains incorrect syntax.

    C. You don't have permissions to use the AMI in question.

    D. You have exceeded the default number of elastic IP addresses available to you.

7. You are using a CloudFormation template to build out your development environment. You need to ensure that your web servers do not get created until after your application servers are up. You also need to ensure that your application servers aren't created until your RDS databases are provisioned. What can you use in the CloudFormation template to guarantee that resources will be provisioned properly?

   A. DelayCondition

   B. WaitCondition

   C. SyncCondition

   D. There is no mechanism to ensure resources are created in the right order.

8. You have 200 stacks created using CloudFormation. You are asked to create a new stack from a template that has been used successfully in the past but it is failing. Why is that?

   A. The template has problems and that is why it is failing.

   B. 200 is an account limit; you can't go past it.

   C. 200 is an account limit; however. you can request a higher limit.

   D. You don't have permissions to create stacks.

9. Your boss has asked you how many templates you can have in AWS CloudFormation. What should you tell your boss?

   A. 100 templates

   B. 250 templates

   C. 500 templates

   D. Unlimited templates

10. Describe the relationship between templates and stacks?

   A. Templates are instances of stacks.

   B. Stacks are instances of templates.

   C. Templates and stacks are the same thing.

   D. There is no relationship between the two.

11. The EC2 instances created in one of your CloudFormation stacks is running out of disk space. You have updated the template for future deployments but would like to fix the issue manually on the existing systems. How would you do that?

   A. Increase the size of the disk the way you normally would.

   B. You must use the CloudFormation API to adjust the size of a resource created in a stack.

   C. You must redeploy the stack from the updated template to get the larger disk size.

   D. You shouldn't use disks; you should use S3 for storage instead.

12. The EC2 instances created in one of your CloudFormation stacks is running out of disk space. You have updated the template for future deployments but would like to fix the issue automatically on the existing systems. How would you do that?

   A. Increase the size of the disk the way you normally would.

   B. Use a change set to model and execute the changes.

   C. You must redeploy the stack from the updated template to get the larger disk size.

   D. You shouldn't use disks; you should use S3 for storage instead.

13. When creating a template using JSON in CloudFormation, which template section is required?

   A. Parameters

   B. Mappings

   C. Format Version

   D. Resources

14. When creating a template using YAML in CloudFormation, which template section is required?

   A. Conditions

   B. Resources

   C. Format Version

   D. Metadata

15. You have just been hired to be a system administrator at your organization. When you try to create a stack in CloudFormation, you receive a message saying that you don't have the appropriate permissions. What is the likely cause?

   A. You don't have permissions to create stacks in CloudFormation, and your permissions will need to be fixed to continue.

   B. You are trying to create the stack in the wrong region, and your permissions will need to be fixed to continue.

   C. You don't have permissions to create the underlying resources, and your permissions will need to be fixed to continue.

   D. You need to log in as the root account to create stacks, so you will need access to the username and password.

16. You are a new system administrator and would like a way to visualize your CloudFormation template while you build it out. What is the best way to visualize the template and gain the ability to save your template or create a stack from the same location?

   A. Visio and AWS Management Console

   B. Omnigraffle and AWS Management Console

   C. You can't do all of this from one location.

   D. AWS CloudFormation Designer

17. What is the purpose of the template in CloudFormation?

   A. To define your resources and their settings

   B. To define how resources should connect to services outside of the stack

   C. To define how resources should connect to services inside of the stack

   D. A template is an instance of a stack.

18. What is the best description of a stack in CloudFormation?

    A. A logical grouping of resources that have the same metadata

    B. A logical grouping of resources that can be managed together as a single entity

    C. A logical grouping of resources that operate on the same subnet

    D. A logical grouping of resources that can be managed together as separate entities

19. To create a stack using the AWS CLI, what would you use?

    A. `aws ec2 create-stack`

    B. `aws cloudformation update-stack`

    C. `aws cloudformation stack-create`

    D. `aws cloudformation create-stack`

20. Your developers want to deploy their web applications into their own environments. They would like to be able to control the provisioning and deprovisioning of their development environments, but they don't want to deal with the underlying resources that run their applications. Which service would best meet their needs?

    A. AWS Elastic Beanstalk

    B. AWS Lambda

    C. Amazon CloudFormation

    D. They will need to create their environments manually.

21. Which language is not supported in AWS Elastic Beanstalk?

    A. Go

    B. Python

    C. PHP

    D. These are all supported.

22. Your developers have deployed an application via Elastic Beanstalk. However, the application is not becoming available. They have asked you to take a look at it. What do you need to do to be able to troubleshoot the EC2 instances running the application?

    A. Check CloudWatch logs.

    B. Redeploy the application.

    C. Enable login access.

    D. You can't troubleshoot the EC2 instances.

23. Your security team has required that your Elastic Beanstalk environments be kept up to date automatically. They want to ensure that the operating systems, platforms, languages, and frameworks are all kept up to date. What is the best option to ensure this happens with the least amount of administrative overhead?

    A. Manually update each instance whenever updates are released.

    B. Use your enterprise patching system for the OS and application; update the platform and languages manually.

    C. Enable managed platform updates in the Elastic Beanstalk Console.

    D. You can't ensure that this will happen automatically as it is outside of your usual patch management tools.

24. You have enabled managed platform updates in Elastic Beanstalk. Your security team tells you that some of your environments are running Java 7, and they want you to update to Java 8. You're concerned that managed platform updates are not working. What is the best explanation for why the environments are behind?

    A. Managed platform updates are having technical issues that need to be addressed.

    B. Managed platform updates only update minor versions, not major versions.

    C. You should use managed platform updates for OS updates, not application or language updates.

    D. You need to approve the update for Java 8 in the console before it can install.

25. What is the duration and length of a maintenance window in Elastic Beanstalk when using managed platform updates?

    A. 2 hours every week

    B. 2 hours every other week

    C. 2 hours once a month

    D. 1 hour every week

26. Your supervisor has asked you how much Elastic Beanstalk will cost. What do you tell them?

    A. Elastic Beanstalk costs .50 cents per resource created, and you must pay the normal rate for the resources that were created.

    B. Elastic Beanstalk costs .50 cents per resource created, but the resources created are free.

    C. Elastic Beanstalk is free, as are the resources created with it.

    D. Elastic Beanstalk is free; you just pay for the resources created.

27. You have been asked to support a blue/green deployment in Elastic Beanstalk. You need to create a second environment that is as similar to the primary environment as possible. What is the best way to accomplish this?

    A. Back up the primary environment and then make your changes to it. Use the backup to create a secondary environment afterward.

    B. Create a new environment and build it from scripts.

    C. Clone the primary environment to make the second environment.

    D. Create a new environment and restore from backups of the primary environment.

28. Which type of deployment policy is the fastest but will also require an outage of your Elastic Beanstalk environment?

    A. All at once

    B. Rolling

    C. Rolling with additional batch

    D. Immutable

29. Which type of deployment policy is the fastest and does not require an outage of your Elastic Beanstalk environment?

    A. All at once

    B. Rolling

    C. Rolling with additional batch

    D. Immutable

30. Which type of deployment policy is the least expensive and does not require an outage of your Elastic Beanstalk environment?

    A. All at once

    B. Rolling

    C. Rolling with additional batch

    D. Immutable

31. Which type of deployment policy is the least expensive and does not require running at lower capacity or an outage of your Elastic Beanstalk environment?

    A. All at once

    B. Rolling

    C. Rolling with additional batch

    D. Immutable

32. You are using CloudFormation and your system administrators want to be able to update your application while keeping it up. They tell you that it can run at 50% capacity with no issue later that evening. Your supervisor wants to reduce costs where possible. What is the best deployment policy to use?

    A. All at once

    B. Rolling

    C. Rolling with additional batch

    D. Immutable

33. You are using CloudFormation and your system administrators want to be able to update your application while keeping it available. They tell you that it can run at 50% capacity with no issue later that evening. Your supervisor wants to ensure that you can fail back as quickly as possible should something go wrong; this is the highest priority. What is the best deployment policy to use?

    A. All at once

    B. Rolling

    C. Rolling with additional batch

    D. Immutable

34. You are using CloudFormation and your system administrators want to be able to update your application while keeping it available. They tell you that it can run at 50% capacity with only slight performance degradation later that evening. Your supervisor wants to ensure that performance is not impacted at all but wants to keep costs down. What is the best deployment policy to use?

   A. All at once

   B. Rolling

   C. Rolling with additional batch

   D. Immutable

35. Your system administrators want to be able to update your application while keeping it available. They tell you that it can run at 50% capacity with no performance degradation later that evening. Your supervisor wants to keep costs down. What is the best deployment policy to use?

   A. All at once

   B. Rolling

   C. Rolling with additional batch

   D. Immutable

36. You are using CloudFormation and your system administrators want to update your application to the latest version in the development environment for testing. It is okay for the application to be unavailable for a brief period of time. Your supervisor wants to keep costs down. What is the best deployment policy to use?

   A. All at once

   B. Rolling

   C. Rolling with additional batch

   D. Immutable

37. When using CloudFormation, which setting would need to be modified when using the rolling with additional batch policy to specify that only 50% of your instances should be updated at one time?

   A. Policy size with Percentage

   B. Batch size with Percentage

   C. Batch size with Fixed

   D. Policy size with Fixed

38. When using CloudFormation, which setting would need to be modified when using the rolling with additional batch policy to specify that only 2 of your fleet of 10 instances should be updated at one time?

   A. Policy size with Percentage

   B. Batch size with Percentage

   C. Batch size with Fixed

   D. Policy size with Fixed

39. You are using CloudFormation, and you have a deployment that has failed, but the deployment did not roll back even though health checks are failing. What is a likely explanation for why the rollback did not occur?

- **A.** Elastic Beanstalk service is degraded.
- **B.** The command timeout is set too long.
- **C.** The health checks are incorrect.
- **D.** "Ignore health check" is selected in Deployment preferences.

40. When systems are deployed with CloudFormation, health checks are passing during the deployment; however, it is found that the health checks are marking instances as healthy prematurely before all of the services are running that the application relies on. Given a little more time, the application starts with no issue. What is the most likely cause for this?

- **A.** The health checks are incorrectly marking instances healthy.
- **B.** A health check URL is not configured.
- **C.** The instances are healthy, but the application has issues.
- **D.** This is working by design.

41. Which environmental variables are created by Elastic Beanstalk for tagging AMIs when using Packer to build images? (Choose three.)

- **A.** AWS_EB_PLATFORM_DESCRIPTION
- **B.** AWS_EB_PLATFORM_ARN
- **C.** AWS_EB_PLATFORM_NAME
- **D.** AWS_EB_PLATFORM_RESOURCES
- **E.** AWS_EB_PLATFORM_PROPERTIES
- **F.** AWS_EB_PLATFORM_VERSION

42. You have the AWS CLI installed on your system and you manage your environment with it. You have full administrative permissions. When you try to run the Elastic Beanstalk command, `eb platform logs`, the command is not recognized. What is the most likely reason the command is not being recognized?

- **A.** You don't have the EB CLI installed.
- **B.** You have not typed the command properly.
- **C.** You can't configure Elastic Beanstalk with the AWS CLI.
- **D.** It's an invalid command.

43. You have been asked to come up with a solution for your on-premises databases to be moved to AWS. Your supervisor wants the DBAs to focus on databases rather than on maintaining servers. Your organization uses a combination of Microsoft SQL Server and Oracle SQL. What would your recommendation be?

- **A.** EC2 instances running Microsoft SQL Server and Oracle SQL
- **B.** You can't move Microsoft SQL Server to AWS.
- **C.** Amazon Relational Database Service (RDS)
- **D.** You can't move Oracle SQL to AWS.

44. Which database engine is not supported by Amazon RDS?

   A. MariaDB

   B. MySQL

   C. PostgreSQL

   D. MongoDB

45. You need to move your on-premises NoSQL database to AWS. You don't have any issues with upgrading or changing technology; you just require a NoSQL service that is scalable, and you would prefer that it be a managed service. Which AWS service would you choose?

   A. Amazon RDS

   B. Amazon Elasticache

   C. Amazon DynamoDB

   D. Put your NoSQL database on an EC2 instance.

46. Which of these is not a component of ACID?

   A. Atomicity

   B. Durability

   C. Availability

   D. Consistency

47. Which component of ACID is used to refer to the integrity of a database transaction?

   A. Atomicity

   B. Consistency

   C. Isolation

   D. Durability

48. Which component of ACID is used to ensure that multiple transactions can be processed at the same time without interfering with other transactions?

   A. Atomicity

   B. Consistency

   C. Isolation

   D. Durability

49. Which component of ACID is used to ensure that data is only saved once a transaction is complete?

   A. Atomicity

   B. Consistency

   C. Isolation

   D. Durability

50. Which component of ACID is used to ensure that data is only written if it follows validation rules?

    A. Atomicity

    B. Consistency

    C. Isolation

    D. Durability

51. What would you call databases in a NoSQL implementation?

    A. Tables

    B. Stores

    C. Databases

    D. Indices

52. Which type of NoSQL store pairs a key identifier with a document or key/value pair?

    A. Document stores

    B. Graph stores

    C. Key/value stores

    D. Wide column stores

53. Which type of NoSQL store is optimized for querying really large datasets?

    A. Document stores

    B. Graph stores

    C. Key/value stores

    D. Wide column stores

54. Which type of NoSQL store is designed to hold data that you want to represent in graphs?

    A. Document stores

    B. Graph stores

    C. Key/value stores

    D. Wide column stores

55. Which type of NoSQL store is designed to organize data by a name (key) and a value (key data)?

    A. Document stores

    B. Graph stores

    C. Key/value stores

    D. Wide column stores

56. You currently have 38 RDS database instances on your AWS account. You need to add 10 more. What will you need to do to add the 10 database instances?

   A. You can add them as you normally would.

   B. You will need to contact AWS to raise the soft limit on your account as you can only have 40 RDS database instances on your account.

   C. You will need to contact AWS to raise the soft limit on your account as you can only have 50 RDS database instances on your account.

   D. You can't add any more than 40 to your account; it is a hard limit.

57. Which of the following is not a valid database instance type for Amazon RDS?

   A. T (tiny/burstable)

   B. M (multipurpose)

   C. F (free tier)

   D. R (memory optimized)

58. Which database engine available in Amazon RDS automatically stores data across three availability zones?

   A. Microsoft SQL Server

   B. Amazon Aurora

   C. MySQL

   D. PostgreSQL

59. Which of these is not used by the customer to secure Amazon Aurora?

   A. VPC security groups

   B. database authentication

   C. IAM

   D. Antivirus

60. For which of these database engines are you not able to increase storage when using Amazon RDS?

   A. Microsoft SQL Server

   B. MariaDB

   C. MySQL

   D. PostgreSQL

61. You have a MySQL database that is suffering from performance issues and is currently using Provisioned IOPS storage. What is an option you could try to that could improve performance?

   A. Change your storage type from provisioned IOPS to magnetic storage.

   B. Change your storage type from provisioned IOPS to General Purpose SSD.

   C. Scale up your storage so that it has greater capacity to meet demand.

   D. You are on provisioned IOPS, so there is nothing further you can do.

62. You had to fail over to one of your read replicas in Amazon RDS. You notice that it is missing the last transaction that occurred right around the time of the failure. What is the likely cause?

A. It must have stopped replication before the failure.

B. Read replicas only synchronize once an hour.

C. Read replicas use synchronous replication.

D. Read replicas use asynchronous replication.

63. You are using a MySQL database in Amazon RDS. You have five read replicas and would like another, but you are unable to create another read replica. Why is that?

A. You don't have permissions to create a read replica.

B. With MySQL in Amazon RDS, you can have only five read replicas.

C. You can have five read replicas, but that is a soft limit; you will need to request an increase.

D. Use a multi-AZ configuration instead to get around this limitation.

64. You are using an Amazon Aurora database in Amazon RDS. You have 10 read replicas and would like to add a few more. Will you be able to add more read replicas?

A. Yes, with Aurora in Amazon RDS, you can have up to 15 read replicas.

B. No, with Aurora in Amazon RDS, you can have only 10 read replicas.

C. Yes, you can have 10 read replicas, but that is a soft limit; you will need to request an increase.

D. No, use a multi-AZ configuration instead to get around this limitation.

65. You had a failure in one of your databases recently and when you tried to restore from backup, you found that the last backup available was from several weeks ago when there was a large upload of data. What is the likely reason that this occurred?

A. The last backup was a manual backup and automated backups have never worked.

B. The data transfer overloaded the system and disabled the automated backups.

C. Automated backups were disabled while the large amount of data was loaded.

D. Automated backups were disabled due to a system error.

66. Which of the following is not a valid type of security group used in Amazon RDS?

A. VPC security group

B. EC2 security group

C. Table security group

D. DB security group

67. Your security department has mandated that all information inside of your databases must be encrypted. How will you meet this requirement within your Amazon RDS databases?

A. Create an encrypted database and migrate your data to the new database.

B. Enable encryption on all of your databases.

C. Create an encrypted read replica then promote it.

D. Encryption at rest is not supported in Amazon RDS.

68. You want to be able to get real-time monitoring data for your database clusters in Amazon RDS. What is the best tool to accomplish this?

A. Amazon CloudWatch Events

B. AWS CloudTrail log monitoring

C. Amazon RDS Enhanced Monitoring

D. Amazon RDS events

69. You recently had a database outage because of a change that was made to your database cluster. You want to ensure that you are notified of changes going forward so that you can more easily troubleshoot issues that might arise. What would be the best solution to enable messages related to changes with your RDS clusters?

A. Amazon CloudWatch Events

B. AWS CloudTrail log monitoring

C. Amazon RDS Enhanced Monitoring

D. Amazon RDS events

70. You need to implement an in-memory cache environment. Which of the following are available within Amazon Elasticache for use? (Choose two.)

A. Hazelcast

B. Couchbase

C. Aerospike

D. Memcached

E. Redis

71. You want to be able to run containers in your AWS environment, but you would like to use a managed service to make managing your container fleet a little simpler for you. Which service should you choose?

A. Elastic Kubernetes Service (EKS)

B. Elastic Container Service (ECS)

C. Windows EC2 instance with virtualization capability

D. Linux EC2 instance with Docker installed

72. You have multiple container images stored on Docker Hub and you would like to use them once you migrate to using Amazon ECS. Will you still be able to use Docker Hub as your container registry?

A. Yes, although Docker Hub is the only supported external registry.

B. Yes, you can use container registries outside of AWS.

C. No, you can only use Amazon Elastic Container Registry (ECR).

D. No, you can't use external container registries.

73. You have multiple images currently stored in Docker Hub, but you would like to move these container images into AWS. How would you accomplish this while still being able to use the familiar Docker commands?

   A. Create new container images and use the Amazon EC2 Container Registry (ECR).

   B. Create an AMI and launch the containers as you would a normal EC2 instance.

   C. Use the Amazon EC2 Container Registry (ECR) to store the images from Docker Hub.

   D. Continue to use Docker Hub; there's no way to store the images in AWS.

74. You need to customize an Amazon EC2 instance when it is launched from an AMI. What is the simplest way to customize the instance?

   A. Log in manually and make the changes that are needed.

   B. Use SSM to push a script to the instance once its available.

   C. Run a script once the instance is up.

   D. Use the User data field to customize the instance.

75. How large can the data in the User data field be when provisioning an Amazon EC2 instance?

   A. 16 KB

   B. 32 KB

   C. 64 KB

   D. 128 KB

76. You have a system that will need storage added to support caching. Which type of storage is good for caching?

   A. Instance storage

   B. Elastic Block Storage (EBS)

   C. Elastic File System (EFS)

   D. Simple Storage Service (S3)

77. You need storage that will work really well with APIs as you begin to provision more and more resources using tools like Chef and Puppet. Which type of storage works best when API usage is a determining factor?

   A. Instance storage

   B. Elastic Block Storage (EBS)

   C. Elastic File System (EFS)

   D. Simple Storage Service (S3)

78. You want to create a network file share to replace what you are using a file server in your on-premises datacenter for. You do not want to provision a server specifically for this use case however. Which storage type would be the best fit?

   A. Instance storage

   B. Elastic Block Storage (EBS)

   C. Elastic File System (EFS)

   D. Simple Storage Service (S3)

79. You have a server that has an application that requires a high amount of IOPS, approx. 25,000 IOPS. Which type of storage would be the best fit?

   A. Instance storage

   B. Elastic Block Storage (EBS)

   C. Elastic File System (EFS)

   D. Simple Storage Service (S3)

80. You have been called to troubleshoot issues with some of your instances that use a routing policy in Amazon Route 53. They worked previously but now are not working. You suspect there may be a service issue with Amazon Route 53. Where can you go to verify if the service is experiencing issues in your region? (Choose two.)

   A. Amazon Inspector

   B. Amazon CloudWatch

   C. AWS Service Health Dashboard

   D. AWS Trusted Advisor

   E. AWS Personal Health Dashboard

81. You need to ensure that your Amazon EC2 instances are being monitored, with metric being collected at least once every 5 minutes. With which tool would you be able to meet this goal?

   A. Amazon CloudWatch, basic monitoring

   B. Amazon CloudWatch, detailed monitoring

   C. AWS CloudTrail, basic monitoring

   D. AWS CloudTrail, detailed monitoring

82. You have been using a WSUS server on-premises but would like a more scalable solution that can handle patching in AWS and on-premises and will patch both Windows and Linux operating systems. What should you choose?

   A. Amazon GuardDuty

   B. Amazon Inspector

   C. AWS Trusted Advisor

   D. AWS Systems Manager

83. You have been asked to make a recommendation on the kind of instance to use for large amounts of batch processing at night. It needs to be low cost, and it can tolerate being stopped at any time. Which type of instance would you recommend?

   A. On-demand

   B. Reserved

   C. Spot

   D. Dedicated instance

84. You need to supply your application owners with Amazon EC2 instances that can be shut down at any time. They need to be cost-effective, but they also need to complete their work before they are destroyed. What is the best kind of instance to meet this need?

A. On-demand

B. Reserved

C. Spot

D. Dedicated instance

85. You work in a highly regulated environment and you must keep the security and the privacy of your Amazon EC2 instances in mind. Your supervisor has shared that they don't want to share a physical hypervisor with any other customers. Which type of instance would meet this requirement?

A. On-demand

B. Reserved

C. Spot

D. Dedicated instance

86. You are getting ready to move some of your production systems to the cloud. These will be running 24x7 and they are your primary business systems. Which type of instance will be the most cost-effective in this scenario?

A. On-demand

B. Reserved

C. Spot

D. Dedicated instance

87. You want to begin to use Elastic Container Service (ECS). You have created some Amazon EC2 instances from your organization's standard AMI. What should be your next step?

A. Install the AWS SSM agent.

B. Install antivirus software.

C. Install the Amazon ECS agent.

D. Configure the host firewall.

88. You're are moving your systems to the cloud and are looking at saving money whenever possible. You have a system right now that runs a small application coded in C# that sends a notification when a file is uploaded and then moves that file to another system for processing. What would be the most cost-effective way to move this to the cloud?

A. Amazon EC2 instance

B. AWS Lambda

C. AWS Elastic Beanstalk

D. AWS CloudFormation

89. Your developers have requested the ability to be able to spin up single servers that have the OS and their development stack of choice. Which product will give them that capability with the least amount of administrative overhead?

   A.   AWS CloudFormation

   B.   AWS Elastic Beanstalk

   C.   Amazon Lightsail

   D.   Amazon EC2

90. Which operating systems can you choose from when you use Amazon Lightsail? (Choose two.)

   A.   Amazon Linux

   B.   Unix

   C.   Ubuntu

   D.   Red Hat

   E.   Windows

91. Your developers want to use WordPress and would like to be able to seamlessly build the infrastructure to support the WordPress deployment with a minimal amount of administrative overhead. What is the best way to support this effort?

   A.   AWS Elastic Beanstalk

   B.   Amazon EC2 instance with WordPress installed

   C.   Use the Elastic WordPress Service

   D.   Amazon Lightsail

92. You need to remotely manage an Amazon Lightsail instance but you don't want to install an SSH client on your system. How would you connect to the instance with the least amount of administrative effort?

   A.   Use the Connect option in the Amazon Lightsail Console.

   B.   Connect through Session Manager in AWS Systems Manager.

   C.   Use Remote Desktop to connect.

   D.   You will need to install an SSH client.

93. You need to schedule batch jobs and account for dependencies between jobs. This has historically been accomplished with static timed jobs on virtual machines on-premises. What would be the best way to accomplish this in AWS?

   A.   AWS Lambda

   B.   Amazon EC2 instances

   C.   AWS Batch

   D.   Amazon Simple Queue Service (SQS)

94. In AWS Batch, how do you specify how a job should be run, including resource requirements?

   A. Job

   B. Job definition

   C. Job queue

   D. Scheduler

95. Which component of AWS Batch is responsible for storage jobs until they are ready to be executed?

   A. Job

   B. Job definition

   C. Job queue

   D. Scheduler

96. Which component of AWS Batch is responsible for determining when jobs should be run?

   A. Job

   B. Job definition

   C. Job queue

   D. Scheduler

97. You have been working with other system administrators to move your batch jobs to AWS. You need to ensure that you are all using the same terminology so there is no confusion. What is the appropriate word to describe a single unit of work in AWS Batch?

   A. Job

   B. Job definition

   C. Job queue

   D. Scheduler

98. You need to know how the items in an AWS Batch job queue are processed so that you can make the decision as to whether you need to adjust the algorithm used for processing. In what order are items processed from the job queue by default?

   A. First In, Last Out (FILO)

   B. First In, First Out (FIFO)

   C. Last In, First Out (LIFO)

   D. Last In, Last Out (LILO)

99. You have a job that you want to run with AWS Batch. The job size would be 25 KB. Would this be a good fit for AWS Batch?

   A. Yes, the job size is unlimited.

   B. Yes, the job size is 20 KB by default but can be adjusted.

   C. No, the job size limit is 10 KB and can't be changed.

   D. No, the job size limit is 20 KB and can't be changed.

100. There are two types of compute environments available for use with AWS Batch. You want AWS to manage the infrastructure for your batch jobs. Which type of compute environment should you choose?

    A. Managed Compute Environment

    B. Unmanaged Compute Environment

    C. Elastic Compute Environment

    D. Scheduled Compute Environment

101. There are two types of compute environments available for use with AWS Batch. You want to manage the infrastructure for your batch jobs. Which type of compute environment should you choose?

    A. Managed Compute Environment

    B. Unmanaged Compute Environment

    C. Elastic Compute Environment

    D. Scheduled Compute Environment

102. What must you install on your compute resources to utilize them with AWS Batch?

    A. AWS Batch Agent

    B. Amazon Inspector Agent

    C. Amazon ECS Agent

    D. AWS Systems Manager Agent

103. Which of these are valid launch types for Elastic Container Service (ECS)? (Choose two.)

    A. Elastic Beanstalk launch type

    B. Lightsail launch type

    C. Fargate launch type

    D. EC2 launch type

    E. RDS launch type

104. You are trying to set up your application to run on ECS. You have a task definition file that is using the EC2 launch type, but you want to use the Fargate launch type. Where do you need to define the launch type in the task definition file so that your ECS containers will use Fargate instead of EC2?

    A. `"image": "FARGATE"`

    B. `"requiresCompatibilities": ["FARGATE"]`

    C. `"executionRoleArn": "FARGATE"`

    D. This is not defined in the task definition file.

105. Which of these options is not a valid method to provision and manage Amazon ECS?

    A. Amazon ECS CLI

    B. AWS SDK

    C. Amazon EB CLI

    D. AWS Management Console

    E. AWS CLI

106. You have chosen to use an Amazon EC2 instance to host Docker. You have launched the initial Amazon EC2 instance from an Amazon Linux 2 AMI. What do you need to type to install Docker?

    A. `amazon-linux-extras install docker`

    B. `sudo amazon-linux-extras install docker`

    C. `sudo install Docker`

    D. `sudo install docker`

107. You have installed Docker and started the Docker service. Every time you want to run a docker command, you have to add `sudo` to the beginning of the command. What can you do to remove the need to do this with every command?

    A. There is nothing you can do. You must use `sudo`.

    B. Add `ec2-user` to the root group on the EC2 instance.

    C. Change ownership of the Docker folders to `ec2-user`.

    D. Add `ec2-user` to the docker group on the EC2 instance.

108. You have added the user accounts of your administrators to the docker group so that they no longer have to use `sudo` in front of docker commands. However, when they try to use a simple docker command, they get the error "Cannot connect to the Docker daemon. Is the docker daemon running on this host?" What should you do?

    A. Reboot the host.

    B. Add them to the root group instead.

    C. Restart the Docker service.

    D. Reinstall Docker.

109. You are using a dockerfile to build your containers. Your security team finds that you are opening port 80 on your containers and has asked that you change that to 443 as port 80 is insecure. How would you update the dockerfile to meet the request from your security team?

    A. Add EXPOSE 443 under EXPOSE 80.

    B. Change EXPOSE 80 to EXPOSE 443.

    C. Add EXPOSE 443 above EXPOSE 80.

    D. Remove the EXPOSE 80 line from your dockerfile.

110. During a penetration test on your container, the tester was able to get your authentication string for your Elastic Container Registry (ECR). You were logged in on the container and were pushing an image to ECR. What was the likeliest method used to get your credentials?

A. The pen tester installed a key logger on the container.

B. The pen tester was sniffing the network traffic leaving the system and they captured your username and password.

C. You used an authentication string interactively with docker login using -p, and they ran ps -e.

D. You used an authentication string with docker login and you were prompted for your password, then they ran ps -e.

111. During a penetration test on your container, the tester was able to get your authentication string for your Elastic Container Registry (ECR). You were logged in on the container and pushing an image to ECR. You determined that they got your login by running ps -e, which exposed the authentication string. What can you do to prevent this from happening again?

A. Run the docker login command as the root user.

B. Drop the -p from the docker login command so that it prompts you for the password.

C. Run the docker login command with sudo in front of it.

D. Restart the container.

112. You need a place to store the container images that you have created. Where are container images stored?

A. Registry

B. Repository

C. Authorization token

D. Image

113. You need a place to store the container images that you have created. You know that your container images will be saved in a repository, but before you can create a repository, what do you need to create first?

A. Registry

B. Repository

C. Authorization token

D. Image

114. You want to launch your containers with the base operating system and application dependencies already taken care of so that your application can be run without any further configuration. What should you create to accomplish this goal?

A. Registry

B. Repository

C. Authorization token

D. Image

115. You have created a container image and are ready to push to your Amazon ECR repository. You run the `get-login` command so that you can log into the repository. What does the `get-login` command return?

  A. Registry

  B. Repository

  C. Authorization token

  D. Image

116. You have created a server using Amazon Lightsail. You want to connect it to an RDS instance in your default VPC. How should you configure communication to work between Lightsail and the RDS instance?

  A. Direct Connect

  B. VPN gateway

  C. VPC endpoint

  D. VPC peering

117. You have a virtual private server in Lightsail and you need to add a storage volume to it. What kind of storage drives can you use?

  A. Solid-state drives (SSDs)

  B. Magnetic

  C. Throughput optimized

  D. Cold hard disk drive (HDD)

118. You need to add more storage disks to a system in Amazon Lightsail. How many disks can you add?

  A. Up to 10 disks

  B. Up to 15 disks

  C. Up to 20 disks

  D. Up to 25 disks

119. You are hosting a system in Amazon Lightsail that needs a large amount of storage. What is the maximum amount of storage that you can attach to Amazon Lightsail with a single disk?

  A. 4 TB

  B. 8 TB

  C. 16 TB

  D. 32 TB

120. You need to increase the size of a disk that your Amazon Lightsail instance is using. What are the steps involved to increase the disk size? (Choose two.)

   A. Take a snapshot of all of the disks.

   B. Take a snapshot of the disk you want to enlarge.

   C. Enlarge the disk directly from the Amazon Lightsail Console.

   D. Create a disk of the same size, then restore the snapshot, then enlarge the disk using the AWS CLI.

   E. Create a larger disk from the snapshot.

121. You have a system in Amazon Lightsail that is running your website. You want to build another system in another availability zone to make the site highly available. How will you route traffic between the two instances with the least amount of administrative overhead?

   A. Network Load Balancer

   B. Lightsail load balancer

   C. Application Load Balancer

   D. Route 53

122. Your website in Amazon Lightsail is highly available and is using an Amazon Lightsail load balancer. Your security team has noticed that you are using HTTP and has requested you switch to HTTPS. What is the simplest way to take care of their request?

   A. Manually upload a certificate you have created on-prem and attach it to the load balancer.

   B. Use AWS KMS to create and manage SSL certificates.

   C. Use Amazon Lightsail's built-in certificate management utilities.

   D. Ignore your security team's request and continue to use HTTP.

123. You have built an e-commerce application and you are running it in Amazon Lightsail. You are using a Lightsail load balancer. It is important that users who visit the site are directed to the same server throughout their visit so that they don't have to log in multiple times. How can you accommodate this request?

   A. Enable session persistence on the Lightsail load balancer.

   B. Enable session persistence on the Lightsail instance.

   C. Enable sticky cookies on the Lightsail load balancer.

   D. Enable sticky cookies on the Lightsail instance.

124. You want to use a Lightsail-provisioned SSL certificate for your site. What will you need to do to validate that you are the owner of the domain that you are trying to issue the certificate from?

   A. Add a TXT record to your zone at your DNS hosting provider.

   B. Add an ALIAS record to your zone at your DNS hosting provider.

   C. Add a SRV record to your zone at your DNS hosting provider.

   D. Add a CNAME record to your zone at your DNS hosting provider.

125. Your Amazon Lightsail instance is running multiple websites. When you hosted these sites on-premises, you used a wildcard certificate. You have 5 sites total, and you will add 2 more in the next year. What type of certificate should you use in AWS?

A. Use a Lightsail certificate since it can support up to 10 domains.

B. Use a Lightsail certificate since it can support up to 15 domains.

C. Use a Lightsail certificate since it can support up to 20 domains.

D. Use a wildcard certificate as you have been on-premises.

126. You have been running your web application in Amazon Lightsail for a year now. You want to have more fine-grained control over configuration items for your instances as well as support larger instance sizes. What is your best conversion option that reduces administrative overhead?

A. Create an EC2 instance, and install/configure your web application there.

B. Use the Upgrade to EC2 feature to convert your Lightsail instance to an EC2 instance.

C. Create a CloudFormation template and deploy the new EC2 instance with your web application already installed and configured.

D. There is no conversion option available.

127. When using Elastic Beanstalk, which of the following is not a platform update type used?

A. Patch update

B. Major update

C. Hotfix update

D. Minor update

128. You are using Elastic Beanstalk for application deployments. You have chosen to use application lifecycle settings and have opted to keep the five most recent versions. You notice that the applications are being removed if they are older than the most recent five, but you notice that the application bundles are not being removed from S3. What can you do to ensure that the source bundle is removed when the application version is removed automatically?

A. In the Application Versions settings, set it to delete the source bundle from S3 whenever the application version is deleted.

B. Manually remove the application source bundle from S3.

C. Create a function in AWS Lambda that will delete the S3 source bundle when the application is deleted.

D. You can't remove the S3 source bundles automatically.

129. You are using Elastic Beanstalk for application deployments. You have chosen to use application lifecycle settings and have opted to keep the 5 most recent versions. You need to keep the 10 most recent versions in S3 in case you need to roll back. What is the best method to remove the old source bundles from S3 while ensuring that you have no fewer than 10 versions of the source bundle?

    A. In the Application Versions settings, set it to delete the source bundle from S3 whenever the application version is deleted.

    B. Manually remove the application source bundles from S3.

    C. Create a function in AWS Lambda that will delete the oldest S3 source bundle when an application is deleted.

    D. You can't remove the source bundles from S3.

130. You are on an Amazon Linux instance in Elastic Beanstalk. You want to upgrade the platform to Amazon Linux 2. What is the recommended deployment type to use for this type of upgrade?

    A. Fresh install.

    B. Manually upgrade all instances.

    C. Blue/green deployment.

    D. There is no upgrade path from Amazon Linux to Amazon Linux 2.

131. You have a stand-alone instance in Elastic Beanstalk serving out your web application. You want to ensure that it will only accept traffic over HTTPS. What should you do?

    A. Modify the instance security group to only accept TCP/443.

    B. Modify the instance security group to only accept TCP/80.

    C. Modify the instance security group to only accept UDP/443.

    D. Modify the instance security group to only accept UDP/80.

132. You have a highly available setup with four instances in Elastic Beanstalk serving out your web application. You want to ensure that they will only accept traffic over HTTPS. What should you do?

    A. Use the instance security group and set it to TCP/443.

    B. Use the load balancer security group and set it to TCP/443.

    C. Use the instance security group and set it to TCP/80.

    D. Use the load balancer security group and set it to TCP/80.

Domain

4

Storage and Data Management

1. Which of the following is a good example of block storage?

    A.   Amazon Simple Storage Service (S3)

    B.   Amazon Elastic File System (EFS)

    C.   Amazon Elastic Block Store (EBS)

    D.   None of these

2. Which of the following is a good example of object storage?

    A.   Amazon Simple Storage Service (S3)

    B.   Amazon Elastic File System (EFS)

    C.   Amazon Elastic Block Storage (EBS)

    D.   None of these

3. Which of the following is a good example of a managed file storage service?

    A.   Amazon Simple Storage Service (S3)

    B.   Amazon Elastic File System (EFS)

    C.   Amazon Elastic Block Storage (EBS)

    D.   None of these

4. What type of storage is destroyed when the instance it is attached to is stopped or terminated?

    A.   Amazon S3

    B.   Instance store

    C.   Amazon EBS

    D.   Amazon EFS

5. You have an application that requires a minimum of 25,000 IOPS. Which type of storage should you use to ensure that the application gets what it requires?

    A.   General Purpose SSD

    B.   Provisioned IOPS SSD

    C.   Throughput Optimized HDD

    D.   Cold HDD

6. You need to save the data from an application that is used infrequently, and you have been asked to identify the lowest-cost storage. Which storage type would be the best fit for this use case?

    A.   General Purpose SSD

    B.   Provisioned IOPS SSD

    C.   Throughput Optimized HDD

    D.   Cold HDD

7. You have an application that doesn't need high speed but is frequently accessed, and many of the workloads are throughput intensive. Which storage type would be the best fit for this use case?

    A. General Purpose SSD

    B. Provisioned IOPS SSD

    C. Throughput Optimized HDD

    D. Cold HDD

8. You need to choose a storage type for your developers that will minimize cost but still give them the performance they need to test applications and code against. Which storage type would be the best fit for this use case?

    A. General Purpose SSD

    B. Provisioned IOPS SSD

    C. Throughput Optimized HDD

    D. Cold HDD

9. Which of these is not an important consideration when choosing the right storage tier for S3?

    A. Cost efficiency

    B. Durability

    C. Retrieval times

    D. Granular level of control

10. Which of these storage types is not tied to a specific region?

    A. Amazon S3

    B. Amazon EBS

    C. AWS Snowball

    D. Amazon Glacier

11. You have created three Amazon EC2 instances and you want to attach EBS volumes for additional data storage. You have created the three EBS volumes, but when you select Attach in the EBS Dashboard, only two of your Amazon EC2 instances are displayed. What is the most likely reason that the third EC2 instance is not displayed?

    A. The third EC2 instance is in a public subnet, and the other two EC2 instances are in a private subnet.

    B. The third EC2 instance is encrypted so the EBS volume has to be encrypted to be attached to it.

    C. The third EC2 instance is an instance type that will not allow you to attach an EBS volume.

    D. The Amazon EC2 instance that is not showing up is in a different availability zone than the EBS volume.

12. What is the minimum size drive you would need to provision to be able to get to 7500 IOPS?

   A. 150 GB

   B. 200 GB

   C. 350 GB

   D. 400 GB

13. Which command would you use to mount an EBS volume?

   A. `aws ec2 mount-volume --volume-id <volumeid> --instance-id <instanceid> --device /dev/<drivename>`

   B. `aws ebs mount-volume --volume-id <volumeid> --instance-id <instanceid> --device /dev/<drivename>`

   C. `aws ec2 attach-volume --volume-id <volumeid> --instance-id <instanceid> --device /dev/<drivename>`

   D. `aws ebs attach-volume --volume-id <volumeid> --instance-id <instanceid> --device /dev/<drivename>`

14. You have an instance with an EBS volume that you want to copy to an instance in another availability zone within the same region. What is the best way to make the data available to the other instance?

   A. Copy the drive to the other availability zone.

   B. Download the drive and then upload it into the other availability zone.

   C. Create an AMI from the instance and then use the AMI to build an instance in the other availability zone.

   D. Create a snapshot and restore the snapshot to a volume in the other availability zone.

15. Which of these types of encryption can you use with your EBS volumes? (Choose two.)

   A. Client level

   B. Server level

   C. Instance level

   D. Volume level

16. Your security team has mandated that you keep control of your encryption keys. Which type of encryption should you use for your EBS volumes?

   A. Client level

   B. Server level

   C. Instance level

   D. Volume level

17. You want to simplify the administration of your encryption keys while still ensuring strong encryption. What type of encryption should you use?

   A. Client level

   B. Server level

   C. Instance level

   D. Volume level

18. You want to ensure that you are using strong encryption and that key use is audited. Which service would meet this need?

   A. AWS IAM

   B. AWS KMS

   C. AWS CloudTrail

   D. Amazon CloudWatch

19. You need a storage service that can be shared among multiple EC2 instances. You also want it to act like a filesystem as that is what your users are used to. Which storage service would be the best fit for this role?

   A. Amazon EBS

   B. Amazon EFS

   C. Amazon S3

   D. Instance store

20. You need to create an S3 bucket. You know that the address is to be globally unique, but you are worried that the 50-character name you came up with is too long. What is the maximum allowed length of an S3 bucket name?

   A. 24

   B. 56

   C. 63

   D. 42

21. Which of the following is not a legal character to use in an Amazon S3 bucket name?

   A. Underscores

   B. Lowercase characters

   C. Numbers

   D. Dashes

22. Which of the following are valid access methods for Amazon S3 buckets? (Choose two.)

   A. Bucket-style

   B. Virtual-hosted-style

   C. URL-style

   D. Path-style

23. You need to ensure that you choose the storage class in Amazon S3 with the highest amount of durability. Which storage class should you choose?

   A. S3 Standard

   B. S3 Standard-IA

   C. S3 One Zone-IA

   D. They all have the same durability.

24. You need to ensure that you choose the storage class in Amazon S3 with the highest amount of availability. The data is crucial to your business and is access 24x7x365. Which storage class should you choose?

   A. S3 Standard

   B. S3 Standard-IA

   C. S3 One Zone-IA

   D. Amazon Glacier

25. You need to choose the right storage class for your data, which is being moved to Amazon S3. You want to save money, and the data isn't accessed frequently, but it needs to be available immediately when needed. It also needs to be safe from the failure of the availability zone in which it resides. Which S3 storage class would you choose?

   A. S3 Standard

   B. S3 Standard-IA

   C. S3 One Zone-IA

   D. Amazon Glacier

26. You need to choose the right storage class for your data, which is being moved to Amazon S3. You want to save money, and the data isn't accessed frequently (once per year). However, it needs to be available within five hours of a request. It also needs to be safe from the failure of the availability zone in which it resides. Which S3 storage class would you choose?

   A. S3 Standard

   B. S3 Standard-IA

   C. S3 One Zone-IA

   D. S3 Glacier

27. You need to choose the right storage class for your data, which is being moved to Amazon S3. You want to save money, and the data isn't accessed frequently, but it should be available immediately when needed. If the data is lost, it can be re-created fairly easily, so it does not need to be highly available. Which S3 storage class would you choose?

   A. S3 Standard

   B. S3 Standard-IA

   C. S3 One Zone-IA

   D. Amazon Glacier

28. Which S3 storage class offers 99.99% availability?

   A. S3 Standard

   B. S3 Standard-IA

   C. S3 One Zone-IA

   D. None of them offer 99.99%.

29. Which S3 storage class offers 99.9% availability?

    A. S3 Standard

    B. S3 Standard-IA

    C. S3 One Zone-IA

    D. None of them offer 99.9%.

30. Which S3 storage class offers 99.5% availability?

    A. S3 Standard

    B. S3 Standard-IA

    C. S3 One Zone-IA

    D. None of them offer 99.5%.

31. Which of these options is lowest cost and best for long-term archival, where hours are fine for recovery times?

    A. S3 Standard

    B. S3 Standard-IA

    C. S3 Glacier

    D. S3 Glacier Deep Archive

32. You need to prevent accidental deletions in your S3 bucket from authorized users. What is the best method to protect your data from accidental deletions?

    A. IAM group

    B. IAM role

    C. Enable MFA Delete

    D. Enable versioning

33. You need to ensure that your data is retained for a year, but it is often not accessed much after 30 days and not at all after 90 days. You've decided that you would like to take advantage of a few of the storage classes that S3 offers to save money. Which of these should you do? (Choose two.)

    A. After 30 days, move the data to S3 Standard-IA.

    B. After 30 days, move the data to S3 Glacier.

    C. After 90 days, move the data to S3 Standard-IA.

    D. After 90 days, move the data to S3 Glacier.

34. You want to automatically move data through the various S3 storage classes. You want the data to be moved to S3 Standard-IA after 90 days and then to S3 Glacier after 180 days. You want the data to be retained for five years, at which point it is deleted. What is the best way to automate this process?

    A. Scheduled job in AWS Lambda

    B. Run a script each night in the AWS CLI.

    C. Lifecycle policy in S3

    D. Manually move the data as there is no automated process.

35. You have a website being served out from S3. You would like to store copies of your site closer to your customers around the world. What is the best option?

   A. Store copies of the website on EC2 instances and use Auto Scaling groups to meet demand.

   B. Store copies of the website on EC2 instances running in the appropriate regions for your customers.

   C. Cache copies of the website in Amazon CloudFront.

   D. Store copies in S3 in the appropriate regions for your customers.

36. You currently have snapshots of your EBS volumes going to S3. You need to access the snapshots. How would you access them?

   A. Amazon S3 API

   B. Amazon EC2 API

   C. Amazon EBS API

   D. The AWS Management Console

37. You are moving your on-premises datacenter to AWS. You need a solution that will allow your Linux EC2 instances to access a file share that acts similarly to the file servers you have now. You want to avoid creating file servers in AWS, and you want it to grow automatically as more data is stored. What is the best solution to replace your file servers in AWS?

   A. Amazon S3

   B. Amazon EBS

   C. Amazon EFS

   D. Amazon EC2 file server

38. You need to move the data from your on-premises file servers to Amazon EFS. What is the simplest method for copying data from your file servers to Amazon EFS?

   A. Restore from a backup.

   B. Robocopy.

   C. AWS DataSync.

   D. Manually upload the files.

39. Which of the following are storage classes you can choose from for Amazon EFS? (Choose two.)

   A. Amazon EFS Glacier

   B. Amazon EFS Infrequent Access One Zone

   C. Amazon EFS Standard

   D. Amazon EFS Infrequent Access

40. You are moving files to Amazon EFS from your on-prem file servers. You want to save the company money, and you know that some of the data is stale, but you don't know if it's safe to delete the data. What should you do?

    A. Create an age-off policy to move stale data to EFS IA.

    B. Create an expiration policy to move stale data to EFS IA.

    C. Create an age-off policy to move stale data to Amazon S3 IA.

    D. Create an expiration policy to move stale data to Amazon S3 IA.

41. You have some small text files that are around 100 KB in size. You have enabled Amazon EFS Lifecycle Management and have noticed that these files have not been moved to Amazon EFS IA even though they have not been accessed for a long time. What is the most likely reason these files have not been moved?

    A. The files are smaller than 64 KB.

    B. The files are smaller than 128 KB.

    C. The files are smaller than 256 KB.

    D. The files are smaller than 512 KB.

42. How can you secure your Amazon EFS deployment so that only authorized Amazon EC2 instances can access the file share with the least amount of administrative effort? (Choose two.)

    A. Network access control lists

    B. Security groups

    C. IAM policies

    D. IAM groups

43. You would like to create a shared directory in Amazon EFS and ensure through the operating system that certain users will see the shared directory as their root directory. How can this be accomplished with Amazon EFS?

    A. Amazon EFS Peering

    B. AWS IAM

    C. Amazon EFS Access Point

    D. Amazon EFS Endpoint

44. Your security team has required that data be encrypted while in Amazon S3 and that you maintain control over the keys at all times. As a SysOps administrator, you don't want to implement a client-side encryption library; you want something that will not have a high degree of administrative effort. What should you choose?

    A. SSE-S3

    B. SSE-C

    C. SSE-KMS

    D. Amazon S3 Encryption Client

45. Your security team has required that data be encrypted while in Amazon S3. As a SysOps administrator, you don't want to implement a client-side encryption library; you want something that will not have a high degree of administrative effort. What should you choose?

    A. SSE-S3

    B. SSE-C

    C. SSE-KMS

    D. Amazon S3 Encryption Client

46. Your security team has required that data be encrypted while in Amazon S3 and that you be able to audit key access. As a SysOps administrator, you don't want to implement a client-side encryption library; you want something that will not have a high degree of administrative effort. What should you choose?

    A. SSE-S3

    B. SSE-C

    C. SSE-KMS

    D. Amazon S3 Encryption Client

47. Your security team has required that data be encrypted while in Amazon S3 and that you maintain control of the keys. You want to reduce the overhead of encryption on the server side, so you would like to use a client-side encryption library. What should you choose?

    A. SSE-S3

    B. SSE-C

    C. SSE-KMS

    D. Amazon S3 Encryption Client

48. Your security team wants to be able to discover sensitive data within your S3 buckets and to get alerts if there is suspected unauthorized access. Is there a tool with AWS that can provide this functionality?

    A. Yes, there is Amazon Inspector.

    B. Yes, there is Amazon GuardDuty.

    C. Yes, there is Amazon Macie.

    D. No, there is no native tool that provides this function.

49. Your security team would like to be able to audit who has access to S3 buckets and remediate excessive permissions. Is there a tool in AWS that will allow them to audit permissions?

    A. No, there is no tool built into AWS that provides this function.

    B. Yes, there is Amazon Macie.

    C. Yes, there is Amazon Inspector.

    D. Yes, there is Access Analyzer for S3.

50. You want to use Amazon S3 to store data; however, you don't want to set up lifecycle policies. Your management has requested that you save money on storage whenever possible. What is the best solution?

   A. Use lifecycle policies.

   B. Use S3 Intelligent-Tiering.

   C. Use a Lambda function.

   D. Move objects manually.

51. You have decided to use S3 Intelligent-Tiering to store your data. You notice that some small text files that are around 50 KB have not been transitioned to the infrequent access tier even though they have not been accessed for over 90 days. Why is this happening?

   A. The file is under 64 KB.

   B. The file is under 128 KB.

   C. The file is under 256 KB.

   D. The file is under 512 KB.

52. You put some data into S3 Standard-IA but then decide to delete it 10 days later. When you receive the bill, you see that you were charged for 30 days. Why did this occur?

   A. The minimum storage duration is 20 days.

   B. The minimum storage duration is 15 days.

   C. The minimum storage duration is 30 days.

   D. It was a billing error on the AWS side.

53. You have some data that has been archived in Amazon S3 Glacier. You need to retrieve it within 5 hours. Which retrieval speed should you use to keep the costs down?

   A. Expedited

   B. Standard

   C. Bulk

   D. You can't retrieve data that quickly.

54. You have some data that has been archived in Amazon S3 Glacier. You need to retrieve it as soon as possible. Which retrieval speed should you use to keep the costs down?

   A. Expedited

   B. Standard

   C. Bulk

   D. You can't retrieve data that quickly.

55. You have some data that has been archived in Amazon S3 Glacier. You need to retrieve it within 12 hours. Which retrieval speed should you use to keep the costs down?

   A. Expedited

   B. Standard

   C. Bulk

   D. You can't retrieve data that quickly.

56. You have some data that has been archived in Amazon S3 Glacier. You were told that you needed to retrieve the data within 4 hours so you chose a standard retrieval speed. Your management has just informed you that they now need it as soon as possible. What should you do?

A. Cancel the current restore and make an expedited retrieval request instead.

B. Cancel the current restore and make a bulk retrieval request instead.

C. Keep the current restore going as you can't change or cancel it once it is requested.

D. Use S3 Restore Speed Upgrade to request the expedited retrieval speed.

57. You put some data into S3 Glacier but then decide to delete it 30 days later. When you receive the bill, you see that you were charged an additional 60 days for an early deletion fee. Why did this occur?

A. The minimum storage duration is 60 days.

B. The minimum storage duration is 90 days.

C. The minimum storage duration is 30 days.

D. It was a billing error on the AWS side.

58. You have some data that has been archived in Amazon S3 Glacier Deep Archive. You need to retrieve it within 12 hours. Which retrieval speed should you use to keep the costs down?

A. Expedited

B. Standard

C. Bulk

D. You can't retrieve data that quickly.

59. You have some data that has been archived in Amazon S3 Glacier Deep Archive. You need to retrieve it within 48 hours. Which retrieval speed should you use to keep the costs down?

A. Expedited

B. Standard

C. Bulk

D. You can't retrieve data that quickly.

60. Which of these is not a recommended method for migrating data from magnetic tape to Amazon S3 Glacier Deep Archive?

A. AWS Tape Gateway

B. AWS Snowball

C. Transfer over the Internet

D. Transfer over AWS Direct Connect

61. You put some data into S3 Glacier Deep Archive but then decide to delete it 90 days later. When you receive the bill, you see that you were charged an additional 90 days. Why did this occur?

    A. The minimum storage duration is 90 days.

    B. The minimum storage duration is 120 days.

    C. The minimum storage duration is 180 days.

    D. It was a billing error on the AWS side.

62. You need to query S3 for data and would like to use SQL queries as that is what you are most familiar with. How would you do this in AWS against S3?

    A. Amazon Athena

    B. Amazon Macie

    C. AWS Lambda

    D. You can't query using SQL against Amazon S3.

63. You have an S3 bucket that has sensitive information in it that should not change. You want to be notified anytime there is a potential change to the data. Which of these is not a method that will work for sending notifications when events like this occur?

    A. Amazon SNS

    B. Amazon SQS

    C. AWS Lambda

    D. Amazon CloudWatch

64. You need to ensure that offices around the globe can upload data to your Amazon S3 bucket with the least amount of latency and administrative overhead possible. What is the best way to achieve this goal?

    A. Upgrade the connections at your offices.

    B. Enable S3 Transfer Acceleration.

    C. Use geolocation routing in Amazon Route 53.

    D. Enable Multipart upload.

65. You would like to do an analysis of the data that you have in Amazon S3 to see if the lifecycle policies you have in place are adequate or if you should modify them. What is the simplest way to perform this type of analysis?

    A. Check AWS CloudTrail for the last access dates for each object.

    B. Use Amazon Athena to perform a SQL query for the last access dates greater than 90 days.

    C. Perform a Storage Class Analysis.

    D. Manually review the last access date.

66. You need to replace the tag sets on over 500 Amazon S3 objects. How can you accomplish this with the least amount of administrative effort?

    A. Use S3 Batch Operations.

    B. Use Amazon Athena.

    C. Create a function in AWS Lambda.

    D. Manually replace the tag sets.

67. You have several buckets in Amazon S3 and you have a regulatory requirement to store the data in two locations that are at least 350 miles apart. How can you meet this requirement with the least amount of administrative effort?

    A. Use an AWS Lambda function to copy the data over.

    B. Use Amazon Athena to copy the data over.

    C. Enable Amazon S3 Same-Region Replication.

    D. Enable Amazon S3 Cross-Region Replication.

68. You want to use Amazon CloudFront with your website and you are trying to decide where you want to host your static files. What is the best origin server to host static files?

    A. Amazon S3 bucket

    B. AWS Lambda

    C. Amazon EC2 instance

    D. You can't use Amazon CloudFront with static files.

69. You want to use Amazon CloudFront with your website and you are trying to decide where you want to host your dynamic files. What is the best origin server to host dynamic files?

    A. Amazon S3 bucket

    B. AWS Lambda

    C. Amazon EC2 instance

    D. You can't use Amazon CloudFront with dynamic files.

70. You want to ensure that people trying to access your website get access through Amazon CloudFront, but you want to ensure that they can type the web address that you have advertised. What is the best way to accommodate this need?

    A. Set up an A record for the domain name.

    B. Set up a PTR record for the IP address of CloudFront.

    C. Set up a CNAME record for your domain name.

    D. Set up an ALIAS record for your domain name.

71. How does Amazon CloudFront improve performance for your end users in another country?

    A. Caches content closer to end users in an S3 bucket in their region.

    B. Caches content closer to end users at an Amazon CloudFront edge location.

    C. Caches content into a central location that everyone accesses.

    D. It does not improve performance; it just improves cost.

72. Which of the following is not something that would benefit from being cached on Amazon CloudFront?

    A. Image downloads

    B. Dynamic PHP page

    C. Video downloads

    D. Software downloads

73. You have been asked to ensure that the origin server you are using for Amazon CloudFront is highly available. What is the best solution to meet this requirement?

    A. Enable origin redundancy in Amazon CloudFront.

    B. Create an AWS Lambda function that will point to a different origin server should the primary fail.

    C. Manually point Amazon CloudFront to a new origin server.

    D. Point Amazon CloudFront to an application load balancer.

74. You are using Amazon CloudFront, and you want to ensure that people from certain countries can't access your website as you don't do business in those countries. How can you block the desired countries while making sure that your valid customers can still access your site?

    A. Whitelist the desired countries in Geolocation.

    B. Blacklist the desired countries in Geolocation.

    C. Block the IP ranges of the desired countries in the security group.

    D. You can't block countries from accessing your Amazon CloudFront distribution.

75. You want to ensure that your customers get a customized error page that gives them numbers they can call if they encounter an error on your web page. You had a custom page when the website was on-premises, and you would like to create a similar page now that you have moved your website to S3 and created a distribution in Amazon CloudFront. How could you present a customized error page in AWS?

    A. Configure a customized error page in Amazon CloudWatch.

    B. Configure a customized error page in Amazon S3.

    C. Configure a customized error page in Amazon CloudFront.

    D. You can't use customized error pages in Amazon CloudFront.

76. You changed a file in Amazon S3 that you are using as an origin server. The new file wasn't displayed until the next day. Why did it take so long for the changed file to show up on your website?

   A. Amazon CloudFront checks for new versions every 6 hours.

   B. Amazon CloudFront checks for new versions every 12 hours.

   C. Amazon CloudFront checks for new versions every 18 hours.

   D. Amazon CloudFront checks for new versions every 24 hours.

77. You are hosting your site in Amazon S3 and are using Amazon CloudFront to cache content. You need to remove a new advertisement from your site immediately as it was unintentionally offensive to some of your customers. How can you remove the new advertisement immediately without impacting the site?

   A. Delete the file in Amazon S3.

   B. Invalidate the file in Amazon CloudFront.

   C. Change the file expiration to 1 hour.

   D. Contact AWS to have it removed from Amazon CloudFront.

78. You are using Amazon CloudFront in front of your origin servers to cache content closer to your customers. While you are using HTTPS to encrypt web traffic from your customers to your end systems, your security team has requested that you secure the sensitive fields in your application that are asking for credit card information. They want to ensure that only a request from an authorized application can access the credit card number. What is the best way to accomplish what your security team has asked you to do?

   A. Enable TLS 1.2, but disable the weaker TLS 1.0 and 1.1.

   B. Encrypt the database with transparent data encryption (TDE).

   C. Use field-level encryption.

   D. HTTPS is the only option to secure the web traffic.

79. You are using Amazon CloudFront to cache your website, and are currently using a third-party certificate for HTTPS connections. You would like to make certificate management more automated rather than requiring you to provision a new certificate or renew a certificate from your third-party certificate authority. What would be the best way to automate the process so that administrative overhead is reduced?

   A. Create a script to renew certificates for you.

   B. Use AWS Certificate Manager.

   C. Use AWS KMS.

   D. You have to use third-party certificates.

80. Your security team has requested that you choose controls to provide a greater deal of protection than you have currently through Amazon CloudFront. What protection do you have by default in your AWS account?

   A. AWS Shield Standard

   B. AWS Shield Advanced

   C. AWS WAF

   D. Amazon GuardDuty

81. Your security team has requested that you choose controls to provide a greater deal of protection than you have currently through Amazon CloudFront. What control can you use to protect against web application layer attacks?

   A. AWS Shield Standard

   B. AWS Shield Advanced

   C. AWS WAF

   D. Amazon GuardDuty

82. You want to ensure that requests sent to your origin servers are from Amazon CloudFront. How can you provide this assurance with the least amount of administrative effort and no additional cost?

   A. There is no way to assure that requests for the origin servers came from Amazon CloudFront.

   B. Check all requests to the origin servers for Amazon CloudFront's IP address.

   C. Use the request headers to prove traffic came from Amazon CloudFront.

   D. Have Amazon CloudWatch monitor for source addresses that don't belong to Amazon CloudFront.

83. Your website contains dynamic content as it is customized for every customer that visits with sales recommendations. You want to use Amazon CloudFront for the performance gains your customers would notice, but you have to make sure that the cookies will still work. How can you make sure that the cookies still work after moving to Amazon CloudFront?

   A. Allow the cookies through AWS WAF.

   B. Use a DynamoDB database to track cookies instead of tracking them in Amazon CloudFront.

   C. Allow your origin server to use cookies.

   D. Allow Amazon CloudFront to forward cookies to your origin server.

84. You want to embed a URI query parameter into your Amazon CloudFront address. How do you indicate the start and stop of the URI query?

   A. URI query starts after a & and ends with a ? character.

   B. URI query starts after a ? and ends with a & character.

   C. URI query starts after a ? and ends with a $ character.

   D. URI query starts after a $ and ends with a ? character.

85. You are trying to deliver a 30 GB virtual appliance file through Amazon CloudFront for a customer who needs the latest version. While the file uploads to Amazon S3 with no issues, it is not getting cached by Amazon CloudFront. What is the most likely cause?

    A. The limit for a single file delivery in Amazon CloudFront is 10 GB.

    B. The limit for a single file delivery in Amazon CloudFront is 15 GB.

    C. The limit for a single file delivery in Amazon CloudFront is 20 GB.

    D. The limit for a single file delivery in Amazon CloudFront is 25 GB.

86. You are wanting to make the move from your on-premises datacenter to AWS. You currently have 50 TB of data and are trying to figure out the best way to move the data to AWS. What should you recommend?

    A. AWS DataSync

    B. Manual transfer over AWS Direct Connect

    C. Amazon S3 multipart upload

    D. AWS Snowball

87. You are just starting to work with AWS Snowball. You have ordered the 80 TB unit and you need to start transferring data to it. What do you need to do first to prepare the source host for data transfer?

    A. Install the file server role on the source host.

    B. Install the AWS Snowball client.

    C. Compress the directories that you want to move.

    D. Deduplicate the files on the source host.

88. You need to continually move large amounts of data from your on-premises datacenter to AWS. What is the best way to accommodate large ongoing file transfers?

    A. AWS DataSync

    B. Transfer over AWS Direct Connect

    C. Amazon S3 multipart upload

    D. AWS Snowball

89. You need to transfer data from us-west-1 to us-east-1. What is the best way to facilitate the data transfer?

    A. AWS Snowball

    B. S3 Cross-Region Replication

    C. S3 multipart uploads

    D. Transfer the data through the AWS Management Console.

90. You have decided to use AWS Snowball to do the initial transfer of data to AWS from your on-premises datacenter. Your security team wants assurances that the data on the AWS Snowball device is secure. What should you tell them?

   A. AWS Snowball data is not encrypted but is password protected.

   B. AWS Snowball data is encrypted with a key stored on the AWS Snowball device.

   C. AWS Snowball data is encrypted with a key stored in AWS KMS.

   D. AWS Snowball data is encrypted with a key stored in AWS Certificate Manager.

91. How does AWS Snowball guarantee that your AWS Snowball device has not been tampered with before its arrival at an AWS datacenter? (Choose two.)

   A. Tamper-resistant enclosure

   B. Encryption

   C. TPM chip

   D. Inspection stickers

92. You are the system administrator for a small hospital and are trying to determine the best way to move your data into AWS. Is AWS Snowball a viable option?

   A. Yes, it's HIPAA compliant, so you just need a BAA with AWS.

   B. Yes, it's HIPAA compliant, so you don't need a BAA with AWS.

   C. No, AWS Snowball is not GLBA compliant.

   D. No, AWS Snowball is not HIPAA compliant.

93. Which of these is not needed for AWS Snowball setup?

   A. AWS Snowball client unlock code

   B. Job manifest file

   C. AWS Snowball client

   D. Job manifest unlock code

94. You need to remove a large amount of data from Amazon S3 and bring it back to your on-premises datacenter. The data is approximately 75 TB. What is the best method to transfer the data back to your on-premises datacenter?

   A. Scripted download

   B. AWS Direct Connect

   C. AWS Snowball

   D. Manual download

95. You have a large amount of data in Amazon S3 and Amazon S3 Glacier that you need to move back to your on-premises datacenter. You have decided that you are going to use AWS Snowball to do the export. How will you export the data in Amazon S3 Glacier?

   A. Initiate the request for Amazon S3; Amazon S3 Glacier will be included.

   B. Restore the data from Amazon S3 Glacier and then create the export request.

   C. Initiate the request for Amazon S3 Glacier; it must be done separately from Amazon S3.

   D. You can't export data once it is in Amazon S3 Glacier.

96. Which of the following is not a lifecycle policy available for Amazon EFS?

A. AFTER_7_DAYS

B. AFTER_14_DAYS

C. AFTER_30_DAYS

D. AFTER_45_DAYS

97. Which command is used to enable lifecycle management for Amazon EFS via the AWS CLI?

A. `aws ec2 put-lifecycle-configuration`

B. `aws efs enable-lifecycle-configuration`

C. `aws efs put-lifecycle-configuration`

D. `aws efs create-lifecycle-configuration`

98. You need to protect the data that is stored in your Amazon EFS implementation. Which of the following are methods that will allow you to safeguard the Amazon EFS data? (Choose two.)

A. Enabling lifecycle management

B. AWS Backup Service

C. EFS-to-EFS backup solution

D. EFS-to-S3 backup solution

99. How do you protect your data in Amazon EFS when it is at rest?

A. Use AWS KMS.

B. Use Certificate Manager.

C. Password protect your data.

D. You don't need to do anything; your data is automatically encrypted.

100. How do you protect your data in Amazon EFS when it is in transit?

A. Use AWS KMS.

B. Use Certificate Manager.

C. Password protect your data.

D. You don't need to do anything; your data is automatically encrypted.

101. You have enabled encryption on a new Amazon EFS filesystem. Your users are complaining that they can't access anything on Amazon EFS. What is a likely cause?

A. Their computers don't support encryption.

B. Encryption wasn't enabled properly on Amazon EFS.

C. Your users don't understand how to decrypt data.

D. The CMK is not in an enabled state.

102. You have chosen to delete the CMK you were using for your Amazon EFS deployment. How can you immediately delete the CMK?

    A. You will need root level permissions.

    B. You will need full administrator permissions.

    C. You will need to have permissions in AWS KMS.

    D. You can't immediately delete it.

103. Which of the following is not a logging solution for performance for Amazon EFS?

    A. AWS CloudTrail

    B. Amazon CloudWatch

    C. Amazon CloudWatch Logs

    D. Amazon CloudWatch Events

104. You are using Amazon EFS, and you want to be able to identify which departments have the most data as you want to be able to do chargebacks. How would you accomplish this in Amazon EFS?

    A. Name the folders with the department names.

    B. Use tags to identify departments.

    C. Use folder metadata to identify departments.

    D. Use labels to identify departments.

105. You want to tag a folder in Amazon EFS for data sensitivity. How can you set the tag in the AWS CLI?

    A. `aws efs create-tags`

    B. `aws ebs create-tags`

    C. `aws ec2 create-tags`

    D. `aws efs create-labels`

106. You are curious which tags have been created in Amazon EFS. What is the simplest method to determine the tags that currently exist?

    A. Using the AWS CLI, type `aws ebs describe-tags`.

    B. Using the AWS CLI, type `aws efs retrieve-tags`.

    C. Using the AWS CLI, type `aws efs describe-tags`.

    D. Using the AWS CLI, type `aws efs list-tags`.

107. You want to limit which hosts can access the Amazon EFS filesystem. What is the best way to do this that uses the least amount of administrative overhead?

    A. Use a mount target NACL.

    B. Use a mount target security group.

    C. Block the unwanted hosts from access with IAM permissions.

    D. You can't limit which hosts can access the Amazon EFS filesystem.

108. How can you reduce costs for using Amazon EFS across multiple availability zones?

    A. Create mount points in half of the availability zones.

    B. Create mount points in two availability zones.

    C. Create mount points in each availability zone.

    D. Use one mount point in one availability zone.

109. You want to review the list of mount targets to see if you should create additional mount targets for cost savings. How would you review the mount targets that exist currently using the AWS CLI?

    A. `aws efs list-mount-targets`

    B. `aws efs retrieve-mount-targets`

    C. `aws efs pull-mount-targets`

    D. `aws efs describe-mount-targets`

110. Your security team has requested that you rotate your customer master key at least once every 365 days. How do you enable key rotation using the AWS CLI?

    A. `aws kms enable-key-rotation`

    B. `aws kms use-key-rotation`

    C. `aws kms automatic-key-rotation`

    D. `aws kms enable-key-management`

111. You want to enable the automatic rotation of your CMK. Your security team requires that it be rotated at least once every 365 days. Will the automatic key rotation feature in AWS KMS meet the security team's requirement?

    A. No, key rotation automatically happens every 720 days.

    B. Yes, key rotation automatically happens every 90 days.

    C. Yes, key rotation automatically happens every 180 days.

    D. Yes, key rotation automatically happens every 365 days.

112. You need to prove to an auditor that your CMK is automatically rotated. Which command in the AWS CLI could be used to prove to them that key rotation is enabled?

    A. `aws kms retrieve-key-rotation-status`

    B. `aws kms list-rotation-status`

    C. `aws kms get-key-rotation-status`

    D. `aws kms describe-key-rotation-status`

113. You believe that a CMK is no longer in use. You are cleaning up inactive resources in your AWS environment to reduce costs. What should you do with the CMK that you suspect is not being used?

    A. Delete the CMK.

    B. Disable the CMK.

    C. Revoke the CMK.

    D. Leave it there as it is not incurring additional cost.

Domain

5

Security and Compliance

✓ **Subdomain: 5.1 Implement and manage security policies on AWS**

✓ **Subdomain: 5.2 Implement access controls when using AWS**

✓ **Subdomain: 5.3 Differentiate between the roles and responsibility within the shared responsibility model**

1. In an identity-based policy statement, which of the following values are allowed for the Effect element? (Choose two.)

   A. *

   B. Permit

   C. Allow

   D. Deny

   E. Notify

2. Which of the following AWS services allows using Microsoft Active Directory credentials to authenticate to AWS?

   A. Cognito

   B. AWS Single-Sign On (SSO)

   C. SAML

   D. AWS Organizations

3. Which of the following IAM policies can be applied to only one IAM principal?

   A. Inline policy

   B. Customer managed policy

   C. AWS managed policy

   D. Permissions policy

4. How many versions of a customer managed policy will IAM retain?

   A. One

   B. Two

   C. Three

   D. Four

   E. Five

   F. Six

5. You need to terminate an EC2 Linux instance, but your IAM user doesn't have the permissions to do so. Which of the following will allow you to terminate the instance while posing the lowest security risk?

   A. Use the root user for the AWS account.

   B. Use the `aws ec2 terminate-instances` CLI command.

   C. Assume a role that can perform the `TerminateInstances` action.

   D. Log into the instance and issue the `shutdown -h now` command.

6. Which of the following are the patching responsibilities of AWS? (Choose two.)

   A. Patching the hypervisors running a customer's EC2 instances

   B. Patching the operating systems on a customer's EC2 instances

   C. Patching any applications running on a customer's EC2 instances

   D. Patching the operating system on a customer's RDS instance

7. You have multiple web servers behind an application load balancer in a single VPC. Each web server has a public IP address. You need to explicitly prevent traffic from a particular range of IP addresses from reaching these servers. Which of the following will allow you to accomplish this?

   A. Create an outbound security group rule to deny the range.

   B. Create an inbound security group rule to deny the range.

   C. Create an outbound rule to deny the range using a network access control list.

   D. Create an inbound rule to deny the range using a network access control list.

   E. On each instance configure the operating system's firewall to block the IP address range.

8. You've contracted a third party to perform penetration testing against your own EC2 instances. Which of the following must you do before proceeding?

   A. Nothing

   B. Notify AWS and get permission to proceed.

   C. Ask AWS to patch your instances before the test begins.

   D. Give the third party credentials to access your AWS account.

9. Which of the following is true regarding the encryption of the files stored in an S3 bucket?

   A. The customer is responsible for rotating S3-managed keys.

   B. AWS is responsible for controlling access to customer master encryption keys stored in KMS.

   C. The customer is responsible for ensuring the files are encrypted.

   D. AWS is responsible for ensuring the files are encrypted.

10. Which of the following is true regarding S3 security access controls? (Choose two.)

   A. The customer is responsible for configuring access control lists.

   B. The customer is responsible for configuring bucket policies.

   C. AWS is responsible for configuring access control lists.

   D. AWS is responsible for configuring bucket policies.

11. Which of the following are valid access control methods for granting access to non-public files stored in S3? (Choose three.)

   A. Bucket policies

   B. Security groups

   C. Identity-based policies

   D. Access control lists

   E. Resource groups

12. Which of the following should you do to grant anonymous read access to files stored in an S3 bucket? (Choose three.)

   A. Grant access to the * principal.

   B. Create an IAM policy.

   C. Create a bucket policy.

   D. Apply the policy to the anonymous user.

   E. Apply the policy to the file.

   F. Specify the bucket name in the policy.

13. You need to grant access only to a specific file named `test.txt` stored in an S3 bucket named examplebucket. Which of the following values should you specify for the resource element in the bucket policy?

   A. `["arn:aws:s3:::examplebucket/*"]`

   B. `["arn:aws:s3:::examplebucket/test.txt"]`

   C. `["arn:aws:s3:::*"]`

   D. `*`

14. You have a file stored in an S3 bucket. You want to restrict access such that only a specific IP address can download the file. Which of the following bucket policy elements will allow you to achieve this?

   A. Effect

   B. Principal

   C. Action

   D. Resource

   E. Condition

15. You have an S3 bucket with versioning disabled. You want to allow a particular IAM user to delete files in the bucket only for the next 30 days. You've decided to create an IAM customer managed policy to achieve this. Which of the following actions should you add to the policy?

   A. `s3:DeleteObject`

   B. `s3:DeleteObjectVersion`

   C. `s3:PutObject`

   D. `s3:RemoveObject`

16. You want to allow anonymous users to download files from an S3 bucket only until January 1, 2021. You've decided to use a bucket policy to achieve this. Which of the following values should you put in the condition element of the policy?

   A. `{"DateBefore": {"aws:epochTime": "2021-01-01T00:00:00Z"}}`

   B. `{"DateLessThan": {"aws:epochTime": "2021-01-01T00:00:00Z"}}`

   C. `{"DateBefore": {"aws:CurrentTime": "2021-01-01T00:00:00Z"}}`

   D. `{"DateLessThan": {"aws:CurrentTime": "2021-01-01T00:00:00Z"}}`

17. You need to delete files in an S3 bucket once they reach a certain age. Which of the following allows you to do this in the most secure fashion?

    A. Object lifecycle transition actions

    B. Object lifecycle expiration actions

    C. Bucket lifecycle expiration actions

    D. Lambda functions

    E. CloudWatch Events Rules

18. You have an application running on an EC2 instance. Which of the following represent the most secure way of granting the application access to a DynamoDB table? (Choose two.)

    A. Access key identifier

    B. Secret access key

    C. IAM role

    D. DynamoDB resource-based policy

    E. Instance profile

19. Which of the following services support resource-based policies?

    A. Simple Queue Service (SQS)

    B. Elastic Block Store (EBS)

    C. Elastic Compute Cloud (EC2)

    D. Identity and Access Management (IAM)

20. Which of the following elements is *not* required in an identity-based policy?

    A. Effect

    B. Action

    C. Resource

    D. Principal

21. Which of the following elements is *not* required in a resource-based policy?

    A. Principal

    B. Action

    C. Condition

    D. Effect

22. Which of the following formats are IAM policies stored in?

    A. JSON

    B. YAML

    C. CSV

    D. TSV

23. Which of the following methods can you use to create a customer managed IAM policy? (Choose three.)

    A. Import an AWS managed policy.

    B. Use the AWS CLI to import a JSON policy document.

    C. Use the Visual editor in the AWS Management Console.

    D. Import a JSON policy document from an S3 bucket.

    E. Create an IAM user and copy the user's default policy to a new policy.

24. You have an EC2 instance running an Apache web server on TCP port 80. A public-facing application load balancer is configured to listen for HTTPS traffic and proxy it to the instance. But when you browse to the load balancer's endpoint, you get a "gateway timeout" error. Which of the following should you do to resolve this? (Choose two.)

    A. On the security group attached to the application load balancer, add an inbound rule for HTTP.

    B. On the security group attached to the application load balancer, add an inbound rule for HTTPS.

    C. On the security group attached to the instance, add an inbound rule for HTTP.

    D. On the security group attached to the instance, add an inbound rule for HTTPS.

    E. On the security group attached to the application load balancer, add an outbound rule for HTTP.

25. You have an EC2 instance running a web service with an HTTPS endpoint. The instance has two network interfaces, and the web application listens only on the secondary interface. The primary interface is reserved for SSH management traffic. A public-facing network load balancer is configured to listen on TCP port 443 and forward traffic to the instance. Which of the following is the most secure way to ensure the instance receives HTTPS connections from clients on the Internet? (Choose three.)

    A. Create a new security group with an inbound rule allowing HTTPS access.

    B. Attach the security group to the instance's primary interface.

    C. Attach the security group to the instance's secondary interface.

    D. Create a new security group with an inbound rule allowing SSH access.

    E. Attach the security group to the network load balancer.

    F. Create a new security group with an outbound rule allowing HTTPS access.

26. You've created a new network access control list (NACL) and added a rule to allow inbound SSH access to a public subnet hosting some EC2 instances, but you're unable to SSH to these instances. You've verified that you have the correct SSH key pair, that the SSH service is running on each instance, and that each instance's security group has an inbound rule permitting SSH from your public IP address. What should you do to resolve the issue?

    A. Add an outbound security group rule allowing SSH traffic.

    B. Add an outbound security group rule allowing all traffic.

    C. Add an outbound network access control list rule allowing SSH traffic.

    D. Add an outbound network access control list rule allowing all traffic.

27. When you create an IAM principal, by default it has no permissions. Which of the following is this an example of?

A. Whitelisting

B. Blacklisting

C. Greylisting

D. Blackmailing

28. In IAM, which of the following two compose an example of blacklisting? (Choose two.)

A. Applying an identity-based policy to deny all actions for all services and on all resources

B. Applying an identity-based policy to allow all actions for all services and on all resources

C. Applying an identity-based policy to explicitly deny the `TerminateInstances` action

D. Applying an identity-based policy to explicitly permit the `TerminateInstances` action

29. A user on your organization's AWS account created and subsequently deleted a Simple Notification Service (SNS) policy. Which of the following services may contain the contents of the deleted policy?

A. CloudWatch Events

B. CloudTrail

C. SNS

D. IAM

E. None of these

30. You have an EC2 instance running an application that needs to regularly connect to an IPv6 endpoint on the Internet. Which of the following is the simplest and most secure way to provide outbound-only Internet access to this instance?

A. NAT gateway

B. NAT instance

C. Egress-only Internet gateway

D. NATv6 gateway

31. You've created an unconditional IAM permissions policy allowing access to all EC2 actions and resources. You apply the policy to an IAM user in your account, but several hours later the user is unable to launch any Linux instances. Which of the following could be the cause?

A. The user is using the wrong SSH key pair.

B. An ACL is restricting the user's EC2 permissions.

C. The user is using the wrong region.

D. A permissions boundary is restricting the user's EC2 permissions.

E. The permissions policy restricts the use of Linux AMIs.

32. Which of the following elements of an IAM policy statement is optional?

   A. Sid

   B. Version

   C. Action

   D. Resource

33. Which of the following determines who is allowed to assume an IAM role?

   A. Profile

   B. Trust policy

   C. Group

   D. Permissions policy

34. You need to store data in a relational database. You need to encrypt the data using an encryption key that's rotated every 30 days. Which of the following database services should you use?

   A. MongoDB

   B. KMS

   C. DynamoDB

   D. RDS

35. You're developing a web application that will allow users to upload pictures. The application will run on EC2 instances. Which of the following AWS services will most securely let users upload pictures to an S3 bucket in your account?

   A. Directory Service

   B. Instance profiles

   C. Cognito

   D. Security Ticket Service

36. Which of the following does the Security Token Service provide? (Choose two.)

   A. Secret access key

   B. Short-term credentials

   C. Long-term credentials

   D. An encrypted access key ID

37. While reviewing CloudTrail logs, you notice suspicious activity performed by a principal using an access key ID beginning with AROA. Which of the following principals performed the activity?

   A. Another AWS service

   B. An IAM role

   C. An IAM user

   D. An IAM group

38. What's the maximum number of IAM roles you can have in an AWS account?

    A. 250

    B. 500

    C. 1000

    D. 2000

39. How many concurrent access keys can an IAM user have?

    A. 1

    B. 2

    C. 3

    D. 10

40. You assign an access key to a new IAM user. You then deactivate the key and assign the user a new one. How many *more* keys can you assign to the user?

    A. None

    B. One

    C. Two

    D. Three

41. A large global enterprise with over 10,000 employees in Microsoft Active Directory wants to use a variety of AWS services in different regions. Which of the following approaches will enable them to use AWS in the most secure way and with the least amount of effort?

    A. Use multiple AWS accounts.

    B. Create an IAM user for each employee.

    C. Create an IAM role for each employee.

    D. Automatically assign temporary security credentials to each employee.

42. You run EC2 instances in only the us-east-1 AWS region. These instances use an instance profile role to connect to a DynamoDB database. Which of the following steps will prevent instances only in other regions from using the instance profile role to connect to DynamoDB?

    A. Disable EC2 in all other regions.

    B. Disable the Security Token Service in all other regions.

    C. Delete the instance profile role in all other regions.

    D. Delete the trust policy in all other regions.

43. How many managed policies can be attached to an IAM principal?

    A. 3

    B. 5

    C. 10

    D. 20

    E. 50

44. What is the maximum number of allowed characters in an IAM managed policy?

A. 2048

B. 5120

C. 6144

D. 10,240

45. What is the maximum aggregate inline policy size for an IAM user?

A. 2048 characters

B. 5120 characters

C. 6144 characters

D. 10,240 characters

46. What is the maximum aggregate inline policy size for an IAM group?

A. 2048 characters

B. 5120 characters

C. 6144 characters

D. 10,240 characters

47. What is the maximum aggregate inline policy size for an IAM role?

A. 2048 characters

B. 5120 characters

C. 6144 characters

D. 10,240 characters

48. How many IAM roles can be associated with an instance profile?

A. One

B. Two

C. Three

D. Four

49. What's the maximum session duration for an IAM role?

A. 15 minutes

B. 1 hour

C. 12 hours

D. 24 hours

50. What's the default credential lifetime for an IAM role?

A. 15 minutes

B. 1 hour

C. 12 hours

D. 24 hours

51. You create an IAM group and attach to it a policy that grants access to all read actions against all resources in S3. You then create an IAM user and add the user to the group. Which of the following is true of this user?

   A. The user will be able to read EBS snapshots stored in S3.

   B. The user won't be able to read files encrypted with SSE-S3.

   C. The user will be able to delete an S3 bucket.

   D. The user won't be able to terminate an EC2 instance.

52. A user attempting to log into the AWS Management Console accidentally types their password in the username field. Which of the following will be logged in CloudTrail Events? (Choose two.)

   A. The account ID

   B. The error message text

   C. The password

   D. The username

53. Your organization runs a serverless Lambda application that encrypts data and writes it to a DynamoDB table. Which of the following is responsible for decrypting the data?

   A. The application

   B. KMS

   C. DynamoDB

   D. Lambda

54. Every IAM user in your AWS account has a "department" resource tag with a value that corresponds to their department. You need to grant users different levels of access according to their department. How can you do this with the least amount of effort? (Choose two.)

   A. Create a group for each department.

   B. Create an inline policy for each group.

   C. Create a single managed policy.

   D. Use the Condition policy element to grant access according to the department tag.

55. You use Amazon Certificate Manager (ACM) to create a public TLS certificate. Which of the following can you attach this certificate to?

   A. An RDS instance

   B. An S3 bucket

   C. An EC2 instance

   D. An application load balancer

56. You have a public TLS certificate issued by a third party. You want to use this certificate with a fleet of 100 EC2 instances. How can you do this with the least effort? (Choose two.)

  A. Create an application load balancer.

  B. Create a network load balancer.

  C. Import the certificate into Amazon Certificate Manager.

  D. Import the certificate into each EC2 instance.

57. You take scheduled EBS snapshots of an EC2 instance. Which of the following steps will ensure that the snapshots are always encrypted?

  A. Encrypt the instance's filesystem.

  B. Enable snapshot encryption.

  C. Encrypt the instance's EBS volume.

  D. Store the snapshot in an S3 bucket with encryption enabled.

58. During the process of launching an Amazon Linux 2 EC2 instance, you fail to download the SSH key pair. Which of the following could you do next? (Choose two.)

  A. Terminate the instance and launch a new one.

  B. Log in to the instance using SSM Session Manager.

  C. RDP into the instance.

  D. Import an existing SSH key pair into the instance.

59. Who is responsible for protecting the contents of a KMS master key?

  A. Both the customer and AWS

  B. AWS only

  C. The customer only

  D. Nobody; the master key is intended to be public.

60. Which of the following is true of a KMS data key? (Choose two.)

  A. It's stored unencrypted in KMS.

  B. It's encrypted using a master key.

  C. It can be exported unencrypted.

  D. It can be 256 bits in length.

61. A developer accidentally emailed a copy of an encrypted KMS data key to an overseas vendor. This key is used to encrypt a sensitive organizational database. Which of the following is necessary to protect the database contents?

  A. Rotate the customer master key.

  B. Rotate the data key.

  C. Revoke the developer's decryption access in KMS.

  D. No action is necessary.

62. You just created a customer master key in KMS. What's the earliest you can delete it?

    A. Immediately

    B. 3 days

    C. 7 days

    D. 30 days

63. You've just scheduled a KMS customer master key for deletion in 30 days. Which of the following is true? (Choose two.)

    A. Once the key is deleted, any data encrypted with it will be permanently lost.

    B. You can't use the key during the 30-day waiting period.

    C. You can't cancel the scheduled deletion.

    D. KMS won't delete the key if any AWS services are using it.

64. You just imported a customer master key into KMS. What's the earliest you can delete it?

    A. Immediately

    B. 3 days

    C. 7 days

    D. 30 days

65. You have an application that references a KMS customer master key by its ARN. Which of the following steps do you need to take to immediately rotate the key? (Choose two.)

    A. Update the key's alias to reference the new key's ID.

    B. Update the application to reference the new key's ARN.

    C. Enable automatic key rotation in KMS.

    D. Create a new key in KMS.

66. Your organization requires that all KMS customer master keys be rotated annually. Some of the keys are imported, while others are generated by KMS. Several custom applications use these keys to encrypt data. Which of the following can help ease the burden of meeting the requirement? (Choose two.)

    A. Enable automatic key rotation.

    B. Use key aliases for imported keys.

    C. Perform manual key rotation for all keys.

    D. Set an expiration period on imported keys.

67. You've disabled a customer master key in KMS. Which of the following is true?

    A. The data key is deleted when the customer master key is disabled.

    B. The key can't be rotated automatically.

    C. The key can't be rotated manually.

    D. The key can't be deleted.

68. Your organization runs a web application on EC2 instances. Your processor configured the application to store files in an S3 bucket. The bucket is configured to encrypt data using an imported key stored in KMS. Everything worked fine until today when the application suddenly failed to read files from or write files to the bucket. Attempts to read or write files via the S3 API using your administrative user also failed. After investigating and finding no changes have been made, you've narrowed the problem down to KMS. Which of the following is the most likely cause of the problem?

A. The bucket policy is misconfigured.

B. The key expired.

C. The key was rotated automatically.

D. The EC2 instance role doesn't have the correct permissions to the table.

69. Which of the following are true of keys stored in a KMS custom key store?

A. They can be automatically rotated.

B. They are stored in CloudHSM.

C. They can be imported.

D. They can be managed by AWS.

70. Which of the following do you need to do to export a private key from a CloudHSM cluster? (Choose two.)

A. Export the key using the `exportPrivateKey` command.

B. Export the key using the `exportPubKey` command.

C. Create a wrapping key.

D. Share the private key.

71. What is the monthly service-level agreement for KMS?

A. 99.0 percent

B. 99.5 percent

C. 99.9 percent

D. 99.99 percent

72. What is the monthly service-level agreement for CloudHSM?

A. 99.0 percent

B. 99.5 percent

C. 99.95 percent

D. 99.99 percent

73. Last year you generated a public, email-validated certificate using Amazon Certificate Manager. The certificate expires in 60 days. Which of the following will ensure the certificate is automatically renewed indefinitely? (Choose two.)

A. Associate the certificate with an application load balancer.

B. Revalidate domain ownership using email validation.

C. Revalidate domain ownership using DNS validation.

D. Manually renew the certificate.

74. You're using a TLS certificate generated by Amazon Certificate Manager to encrypt data in-transit between users and an elastic load balancer that terminates HTTPS connections. Which of the following is required to re-create this configuration in another AWS region?

A. Create a network load balancer in the other AWS region.

B. Configure cross-region load balancing in the elastic load balancer.

C. Use the existing certificate in the other region.

D. Create a new TLS certificate in the other region.

75. You've created a customer master key in KMS and configured S3-KMS bucket encryption using the key. You then granted a user full access to KMS and S3 using an IAM identity-based permissions policy. The user, however, is unable to view any objects in the bucket. Which of the following could be misconfigured? (Choose three.)

A. The user's IAM permissions boundaries

B. The bucket policy

C. The object policy

D. The user's IAM permissions policy

E. The key policy

76. Which of the following are options for encrypting data stored in DynamoDB? (Choose two.)

A. Use CloudHSM.

B. Use a customer managed KMS key.

C. Encrypt the data before writing it.

D. Use an AWS managed KMS key.

77. Which of the following is true regarding KMS?

A. KMS keys can be used only with AWS services.

B. It uses CloudHSM to store all keys.

C. It uses FIPS 140-2 validated hardware security modules.

D. KMS is a global service.

78. Which of the following KMS customer master key (CMK) types is used by multiple AWS customers?

A. Customer managed CMK

B. AWS owned CMK

C. AWS managed CMK

D. Data CMK

79. How many customer master keys can be stored in KMS per region?

    A. 10

    B. 100

    C. 1000

    D. 10,000

    E. 100,000

80. You need to review which EC2 instances have used a particular key stored in a custom KMS store. Where will you find this information?

    A. CloudWatch Events

    B. CloudTrail logs

    C. CloudHSM logs

    D. VPC Flow Logs

    E. CloudTrail metrics

81. What's the maximum size of a KMS key policy document?

    A. 1 KB

    B. 6 KB

    C. 9 KB

    D. 32 KB

82. Which of the following will provide high availability for keys stored in a CloudHSM cluster? (Choose two.)

    A. The use of a custom KMS key store

    B. The use of multiple availability zones

    C. The use of multiple regions

    D. The use of duplicate keys

83. You've configured an instance profile role but want to make sure other IAM users can't assume the role. Which of the following actions should you take to ensure this?

    A. Remove the IAM PassRole permission from users' permissions policies.

    B. Remove unnecessary permissions from the role's permissions policies.

    C. Ensure the role's trust policy doesn't allow users to assume the role.

    D. Ensure the user's trust policy doesn't allow users to assume the role.

84. A service-linked role you're trying to use doesn't have the policy permissions you need. Which of the following should you do to resolve the problem with the least effort?

    A. Add the permissions using a managed policy.

    B. Add the permissions using an inline policy.

    C. Modify the trust policy.

    D. Create a new role that duplicates the service-linked role and assign the duplicate role the needed permissions.

85. While using the AWS CLI, you assume a role named Role A. While operating under that role you attempt to assume another role named Role B. Which of the following will occur? (Choose two.)

    A. You'll operate with the permissions of Role B.

    B. You won't be allowed to assume Role B.

    C. You will retain the permissions of Role A.

    D. Your session under Role B will last no longer than one hour.

86. You've configured the AWS CLI with the credentials of root user. Which of the following is true regarding this configuration?

    A. Your CLI session is limited to one hour.

    B. You can't assume an IAM role while operating as root.

    C. You won't have access to certain AWS services.

    D. The root user credentials can't be used with the CLI.

87. An IAM user needs to be able to assume a role named Role X. Which of the following do you need to do to allow this? (Choose two.)

    A. Add Role X's ARN to the user's permissions policy as a resource.

    B. Grant the user the `sts:AssumeRole` permission.

    C. Grant the user the `iam:AssumeRole` permission.

    D. Grant the user the `iam:PassRole` permission.

88. Does an IAM trust policy require specifying a principal? Why or why not? (Choose two.)

    A. A trust policy does *not* require specifying a principal.

    B. It's an identity-based policy.

    C. It's a resource-based policy.

    D. A trust policy does require specifying a principal.

89. Which of the following is true of an IAM trust policy?

    A. The principal must be in the same account as the owner of the trust policy.

    B. The principal can't be a wildcard.

    C. The principal can't be an AWS service.

    D. The effect in a trust policy statement must always be Allow.

90. Which of the following tasks may require logging in as the root user?

    A. Viewing the canonical user ID

    B. Deleting an IAM user

    C. Sending mass email from an EC2 instance

    D. Assuming an IAM role that has unrestricted access to all AWS resources

91. You're using a third-party service provider that needs access to your non-public S3 bucket for backup purposes. The provider has asked for your AWS account number and the ARN of a role that will grant them access. This provider provides similar services for other AWS customers. For security, the provider has given you an external ID of 86730. How should you use this external ID?

  A. Create a CloudWatch Events rule that triggers an alert when anyone assumes the role without specifying the external ID.

  B. Include it in the Condition element of the role's trust policy by specifying it as the value of `sts:ExternalID`.

  C. Include it as a principal in the role's trust policy.

  D. Rename the role 86730.

92. You've created a custom Linux AMI and used it to launch a fleet of EC2 instances. You want to use AWS Simple Systems Manager to manage these instances, but they're not showing up in SSM inventory. You've verified that the SSM agent is installed and running on the instances. What is the most likely cause of the problem?

  A. The instances don't have the proper profile.

  B. The agent is configured with invalid credentials.

  C. The instances' security group don't allow outbound SSH access.

  D. The instances' security group don't allow inbound SSH access.

  E. The instances' security group don't allow inbound HTTPS access.

93. A custom application uses a DynamoDB table to store data. You want to encrypt only particular attributes in the table while leaving the rest unencrypted. How can you achieve this with the least effort?

  A. Have the application encrypt only the attributes that need to be encrypted.

  B. Enable DynamoDB server-side encryption for the table.

  C. Enable DynamoDB KMS encryption for the table.

  D. Enable DynamoDB server-side encryption for only the attributes that need to be encrypted.

  E. Enable DynamoDB KMS encryption for only the attributes that need to be encrypted.

94. You're configuring a relational database Service (RDS) instance to host a database. You want to ensure that only a specific EC2 instance in your VPC can connect to the database. Which of the following should you do?

  A. Place the RDS instance in the same VPC as the EC2 instance.

  B. Configure the EC2 instance's security group to allow inbound access from the database instance.

  C. Configure the database instance's security group to allow inbound access from the EC2 instance.

  D. Place the RDS instance in the same subnet as the EC2 instance.

95. You're building a database-backed application written in Python. You've configured an RDS instance with the MariaDB database engine, but your application is unable to connect to the database instance. Which of the following should you check first?

    A. Ensure the database instance's security group allows outbound traffic on UDP port 1433.

    B. Ensure the database instance's security group allows inbound traffic on TCP port 3306.

    C. Ensure the database instance's security group allows inbound traffic on TCP port 1433.

    D. Ensure the database instance's security group allows inbound traffic on UDP port 3306.

96. Which of the following can log all database queries against an RDS instance running the MySQL database engine?

    A. The pgaudit plug-in

    B. CloudTrail logs

    C. The MySQL audit plug-in

    D. MySQL Workbench

97. What do you need to do to enable SSL encryption for an RDS instance running Oracle? (Choose two.)

    A. Enable transparent data encryption.

    B. Disable native network encryption.

    C. Enable native network encryption.

    D. Add the Oracle SSL option group to the instance.

98. You've created a master RDS instance and a read replica running the MariaDB database engine. Which of the following is true regarding the security of these two instances?

    A. The data on the read replica is always encrypted.

    B. AWS handles all aspects of security between the master and the replica.

    C. If the data on the master is encrypted, the data on the replica can be unencrypted.

    D. You must configure the read replica's security group to enable replication from the master.

99. Which of the following is true regarding in-transit data between a master RDS instance and a read replica?

    A. In-transit data between the master and replica is always encrypted.

    B. In-transit data between the master and replica is encrypted only if the master is encrypted.

    C. In-transit data between the master and replica is encrypted only if you enable SSL/TLS on the master and the replica.

    D. RDS uses KMS to store the encryption keys used to encrypt the in-transit data.

100. Which of the following is an advantage of resource-based policies over identity-based policies?

    A. Resource-based policies are more restrictive.

    B. Resource-based policies restrict the access of users who don't have an AWS account.

    C. Resource-based policies can restrict the permissions of the root user.

    D. Resource-based policies replace identity-based policies for some services.

101. What's the maximum size of an S3 bucket policy?

    A. 2 KB

    B. 6 KB

    C. 10 KB

    D. 20 KB

102. You're working with a third-party vendor that wants to grant you read and write access to an S3 bucket in their AWS account. You plan to store your EBS snapshots in this bucket. The vendor has asked for your AWS account ID so they can add it to the bucket policy, but you're apprehensive about giving it. What's the most secure alternative?

    A. Ask the vendor to use an IAM permissions policy instead of a bucket policy.

    B. Ask the vendor to create an IAM user with access to the bucket.

    C. Provide your canonical user ID.

    D. Create an IAM role and provide them with its ARN.

103. Which version of AWS Signature do all regions support for S3?

    A. Signature version 1

    B. Signature version 2

    C. Signature version 3

    D. Signature version 4

104. When using AWS Signature version 4, which of the following keys is used to sign a request to S3?

    A. Public key

    B. Signing key

    C. Secret access key

    D. Policy key

105. Which of the following AWS CLI commands will list the AWS canonical user ID?

    A. `aws iam list-users`

    B. `aws iam list-account-aliases`

    C. `aws s3 list-buckets`

    D. `aws s3api list-buckets`

106. You need to use IAM database authentication with Amazon Aurora. Which of the following database engines can you use? (Choose two.)

    A. MySQL

    B. PostgreSQL

    C. Oracle

    D. Microsoft SQL Server

107. Which of the following credentials can be used to create a CodeDeploy deployment? (Choose two.)

    A. Root user credentials

    B. Git credentials

    C. IAM user credentials

    D. Anonymous

108. An IAM user is attempting to deploy an application using CodeDeploy but the deployment is failing. You're able to deploy the application using your administrative credentials. Which of the following permissions should you ensure the user has?

    A. `UpdateDeploymentGroup`

    B. `GetDeployment`

    C. `GetDeploymentConfig`

    D. `UpdateApplication`

109. What's the maximum number of GitHub tokens you can have associated with CodeDeploy per region?

    A. 5

    B. 10

    C. 20

    D. Unlimited

110. When trying to deploy a CodeDeploy template using the AWS CLI, you get the error that is required. What can you conclude about the template?

    A. You don't have the appropriate permissions to deploy the template.

    B. The template updates an existing IAM resource.

    C. It creates or modifies an IAM resource without a custom name.

    D. It creates or modifies an IAM resource with a custom name.

111. Which of the following AWS managed policies grants access to create and deploy application revisions to an ECS cluster using CodeDeploy?

    A. AWSCodeDeployDeployerAccess

    B. AWSCodeDeployRole

    C. AWSCodeDeployRoleForECS

    D. AWSCodeDeployRoleForECSLimited

112. You plan to use CodeDeploy to deploy an application to EC2 instances. Which of the following permissions do you need to grant in the instances' IAM profile role? (Choose two.)

    A. `codedeploy:*`

    B. `s3:Get*`

    C. `autoscaling:*`

    D. `s3:List*`

113. You're attempting to use CodeDeploy to deploy an application to an EC2 instance, but the deployment keeps failing with the error "Validation of PKCS7 signed message failed." How should you resolve this?

    A. Attach to the instance an instance profile role with the appropriate permissions.

    B. Restart the instance.

    C. Install the latest version of the CodeDeploy agent.

    D. Add an outbound security group rule to allow HTTPS access to the CodeDeploy service.

114. You used your administrative IAM user to upload an application revision to an S3 bucket. You're attempting to use CodeDeploy to deploy the application revision to an EC2 instance, but the deployment continually fails with the error "UnknownError: not opened for reading error." Your research indicates that this error means the CodeDeploy agent can't read the application revision from the S3 bucket where it's stored. You verify that the permissions of your own IAM user, the instance profile role, and the service role are all configured correctly. You also verify that the latest CodeDeploy agent is installed and running and that you can read the application revision using your IAM user. Which of the following could be preventing access to the revision?

    A. Permissions boundaries

    B. An S3 bucket policy

    C. An S3 ACL

    D. Incorrect permissions in the `appspec.yml` file

115. When attempting to deploy an application revision to an EC2 instance using CodeDeploy, you get the error "InstanceAgent::Plugins::CodeDeployPlugin::CommandPoller: Missing credentials - please check if this instance was started with an IAM instance profile." You check that the instance has an instance profile associated with it. What could be the problem?

    A. The instance is stopped.

    B. The CodeDeploy service role doesn't exist.

    C. The instance profile role doesn't have the correct permissions.

    D. The CodeDeploy service role doesn't have the correct permissions.

116. When attempting to deploy an application to an EC2 instance using CodeDeploy you get the error "InvalidSignatureException – Signature expired." What could be the problem?

    A. The permissions of the instance profile role are incorrect.

    B. The time on the instance is incorrect.

    C. The CodeDeploy agent isn't running.

    D. The application revision is encrypted.

117. Which of the following options can you set in a password policy? (Choose two.)

    A. Password expiration

    B. Maximum length

    C. Require multi-factor authentication (MFA)

    D. Require an administrator to reset expired passwords

118. Your organization has over 500 IAM users in its AWS account. You plan to change the password policy to set a password expiration period of 90 days. Which of the following will occur when you implement this policy?

    A. The password expiration takes effect for each user only after you reset their password.

    B. Users with passwords older than 90 days will be required to change their password at their next sign-in.

    C. All users will be required to change their password immediately, regardless of password age.

    D. All user access keys older than 90 days will expire.

119. Which of the following is *not* an option for an IAM password policy?

    A. Locking a user out after a number of failed login attempts

    B. Requiring the use of lowercase letters

    C. Preventing password reuse

    D. Preventing users from changing their own passwords

120. Which of the following is true regarding a Security Token Service (STS) session token obtained from a regional STS endpoint?

    A. It's valid only in the region from which it was requested.

    B. It's valid in all regions.

    C. It's valid for a longer time than one obtained from the global endpoint.

    D. It's smaller than one obtained from the global endpoint.

121. In which of the following regions can you *not* disable the Security Token Service (STS)?

    A. us-east-1 (N. Virginia)

    B. us-east-2 (Ohio)

    C. Canada (Central)

    D. us-west-1 (N. California)

122. Your organization is terminating operations in the us-west-1 (N. California) region. A colleague has disabled the region, but a month later the organization receives a bill for EC2 instances running in the region. Which of the following do you need to do to avoid incurring additional costs from the EC2 instances? (Choose two.)

  A. Enable the region.

  B. Disable the region.

  C. Disable STS in the region.

  D. Terminate all EC2 instances in the region.

123. You need to grant an IAM user permissions to enable and disable AWS regions. Which of the following actions should you include in the user's IAM policy permissions?

  A. `sts:EnableRegion`

  B. `account:EnableRegion`

  C. `iam:DisableRegion`

  D. `aws-portal:ListRegions`

124. You currently don't use Security Token Service (STS) and want to disable access to as many endpoints as possible. Which of the following STS endpoints can you *not* disable? (Choose three.)

  A. sts.ap-southeast-1.amazonaws.com

  B. sts.ap-east-1.amazonaws.com

  C. sts.us-east-1.amazonaws.com

  D. sts.us-east-2.amazonaws.com

  E. sts.amazon.com

125. You want to grant access to your application running on AWS, but you don't want to provide with them long-term credentials. Instead you'd like them to be able to log in by authenticating to an external identity provider such as Google. What is this called?

  A. Token vending machine

  B. Web identity federation

  C. MFA-protected API access

  D. Web scale identification

126. You want to configure web identity federation for your application running on AWS. Which of the following services can help you easily define and control user permissions?

  A. Security Token Service

  B. Cognito

  C. OpenID Connect

  D. Resource Access Manager

127. You're currently using a token vending machine (TVM) running on a single EC2 instance to provide temporary AWS credentials to users of your mobile application. As your application has grown, the TVM has been unable to keep up with demand and users are occasionally unable to receive credentials. What approach does AWS recommend to resolve this?

   A. Deploy the TVM on more instances and use Auto Scaling.

   B. Upgrade the instance class of the TVM instance.

   C. Replace the TVM with Cognito.

   D. Replace the TVM with web identity federation.

128. You've configured an IAM role that has permissions to terminate any EC2 instances. You want to ensure IAM users can't assume the role unless they provide a valid multi-factor authentication (MFA) token. Which of the following must you do to achieve this?

   A. Configure a password policy to require MFA.

   B. Add the condition `{"Bool": {"aws:MultiFactorAuthPresent": true}` to the role's trust policy.

   C. Disable these users' access keys.

   D. Apply to the users an identity-based policy that requires MFA in order to terminate EC2 instances.

129. You want to allow only specific IAM users to be able to change their own passwords. Other non-administrator users should not be allowed to change their own passwords. Which of the following two steps are necessary to achieve this? (Choose two.)

   A. Create an identity-based policy to grant the specific users permission to perform the `iam:ChangePassword` action.

   B. Implement a password policy that allows users to change their own passwords.

   C. In the policy, specify the resource `arn:aws:iam::account-id:user/${aws:username}`.

   D. Implement a password policy that requires users to create a random password.

130. Several custom Python applications use an AWS SDK to assume a particular IAM role named AppRole. For only one application, you need to limit the permissions granted by this role. What's a secure way to modify the permissions for just this one application?

   A. Use a session control policy.

   B. Use a managed session policy.

   C. Use an IAM permissions boundary.

   D. Use an access control policy.

131. Which of the following policies limit permissions but can't grant them? (Choose two.)

   A. Service control policies

   B. Access control lists

   C. Trust policy

   D. Session policies

132. Several custom Python applications use an AWS SDK to assume a particular IAM role named AppRole. The role's permissions policy grant it write access to all S3 buckets. The application currently writes to a bucket named AppBucket. There's a bucket policy attached to AppBucket that grants write access to the AppRole role. Developers are going to reconfigure the application to write to a new bucket named AppBucketData, and you want to ensure the application can't write any more data to AppBucket. How can you accomplish this?

A.   Modify the role's permissions boundary.

B.   Implement a session policy.

C.   Modify the bucket policy.

D.   Implement a service control policy.

133. You're creating a policy that allows the `TerminateInstances` action against all EC2 instances except for one that's untagged. Which of the following policy elements should you use?

A.   `NotAction`

B.   `NotResource`

C.   `NotPrincipal`

D.   `Condition`

134. Which of the following Security Token Service (STS) API actions support multi-factor authentication (MFA)?

A.   `GetFederationToken`

B.   `AssumeRole`

C.   `AssumeRoleWithWebIdentity`

D.   `AssumeRoleWithSAML`

135. Which of the following Security Token Service (STS) API actions doesn't support session policies?

A.   `GetSessionToken`

B.   `AssumeRole`

C.   `AssumeRoleWithSAML`

D.   `GetFederationToken`

136. Which of the following is required to import a certificate into Amazon Certificate Manager (ACM)? (Choose two.)

A.   Certificate signing request

B.   PEM-encoded certificate body

C.   Certificate private key

D.   Certificate chain

137. Which of the following is required for importing a certificate into Amazon Certificate Manager (ACM)?

A. The public key algorithm must be 2048-bit RSA.

B. The certificate can't be self-signed.

C. The private key must be encrypted.

D. The certificate must contain a public key.

138. Which of the following services can detect whether an EC2 instance has been compromised by malware?

A. Shield Standard

B. GuardDuty

C. Inspector

D. Web Application Firewall (WAF)

139. On an EC2 instance, you're running a legacy application that has a hard-coded SQL connection string in its configuration. The application connects to a self-hosted Microsoft SQL Server in the same VPC. Which of the following can help protect the connection string from exposure? (Choose two.)

A. Use Relational Database Service (RDS) instead of the self-hosted database.

B. Put the connection string in AWS Secrets Manager.

C. Encrypt the connection string.

D. Reconfigure the application to programmatically retrieve the connection string.

140. You host an application that connects to a third-party service using an API key. You want to begin rotating the API key automatically on a regular basis. How can you do this securely and with minimal effort? (Choose two.)

A. Store the API key in AWS Secrets Manager.

B. Store the API key in Key Management Service (KMS).

C. Store the API key in a DynamoDB table.

D. Create a Lambda function to rotate the key.

141. Two days ago, you enabled GuardDuty on your account. Today while analyzing CloudWatch metrics you notice that an EC2 instance in your account is sending an unusually large volume of data. GuardDuty reports no findings. Which of the following could explain this?

A. GuardDuty findings are updated only twice a day.

B. It takes several days for GuardDuty to establish a baseline.

C. GuardDuty doesn't detect unusual traffic volume.

D. VPC flow logging isn't configured.

142. During a routine penetration test of Linux EC2 instances in a private subnet, you discover that a developer accidentally left a web service 8000. Which of the following would have alerted you to this fact?

A. Web Application Firewall

B. Macie

C. Inspector

D. GuardDuty

143. You want to receive a notification when a new Windows Server AMI is released. Which of the following SNS topics should you subscribe to?

A. arn:aws:sns:us-east-1:amazon:ec2-windows-ami-update

B. arn:aws-us-gov:sns:us-gov-west-1:aws-us-gov:ec2-windows-ami-update

C. arn:aws:sns:us-east-1:801119661308:ec2-windows-ami-private

D. arn:aws:sns:us-east-1:801119661308:ec2-windows-ami-update

144. Which of the following AWS CLI commands will yield the AMI ID of the latest Windows Server 2019 image in the us-east-1 (N. Virginia) region?

A. ```
aws ssm get-parameters --names /aws/service/ami-windows-latest/
Windows_Server-2016-English-Full-Base --region us-east-1
```

**B.** ```
aws ssm get-parameters --names /aws/service/ami-windows-latest/
Windows_Server-2019-English-Full-Base --region us-east-1
```

C. ```
aws ec2 describe-images --owners amazon --filters
"Name=name,Values=Windows_Server-2019-English-Full-Base* " --query
'sort_by(Images, &CreationDate)[].Name'
```

**D.** ```
aws ec2 describe-images --owners amazon --filters
"Name=name,Values=Windows_Server-2019-English-Full-Base* " --query
'sort_by(Images, &CreationDate)[].Name' --region us-east-1
```

145. Which of the following Amazon Inspector rules does *not* generate findings for Windows instances?

A. Unused listening TCP ports

B. Software without data execution prevention (DEP)

C. Non-secure client protocols

D. Non-secure server protocols

146. You need to determine how many times a Lambda function was triggered over the past month. The CloudWatch log group for the function has been deleted. How can you determine this information with minimal effort?

A. Create a metric filter for the function's log stream.

B. Restore the log group.

    C. View the Invocations metric for the functions in the Lambda CloudWatch namespace.

    D. Count the number of Invoke actions in the CloudTrail event logs.

147. Your organization is developing an application that will use a Simple Queue Service queue. You need to allow authorized users both with and without AWS accounts to add items to the queue. Which of the following approaches will achieve this with the least effort? (Choose three.)

    A. Create an IAM role.

    B. Create an SQS queue policy.

    C. Add the * principal to the queue policy.

    D. Add the role to the policy as a principal.

    E. Add the * principal to the role's trust policy.

148. How does CodeBuild isolate customer build environments?

    A. Separate compute instances

    B. Isolated Docker containers

    C. Access control lists

    D. Separate VPCs

149. You're using the Relational Database Service (RDS) to host a SQL database in a private subnet. The RDS instance connects to the Internet via a NAT gateway. You want to use CodeBuild to perform integration tests against data in this database. How can you connect to the RDS instance from the build environment? (Choose two.)

    A. Connect to the RDS instance's public endpoint.

    B. Connect to the RDS instance's private endpoint.

    C. Enable VPC access in your CodeBuild project.

    D. Configure port forwarding on the NAT gateway.

150. You want CodeBuild to pull a Docker image from your Elastic Container Registry (ECR) in the same account. Which of the following do you need to do to grant CodeBuild the necessary permissions?

    A. Add `codebuild.amazonaws.com` as a principal to the repository's resource-based policy.

    B. Add the ARN of the AWS account's root user to the repository's resource-based policy.

    C. Add the `ecr:BatchGetImage` action to a permissions policy applied to the user that will be running the build.

    D. Specify the SID `CodeBuildAccess` in the repository's policy.

151. You're currently storing a password as a SecureString parameter in AWS Simple Systems Manager (SSM). You reference the parameter named "password" from an application running on an EC2 instance. You want to automatically rotate this password regularly. How can you achieve this with minimal effort? (Choose two.)

   A. Manually rotate the password as needed.

   B. Store the password in AWS Secrets Manager and name it "password."

   C. Reference the secret using the SSM parameter name "/aws/reference/secretsmanager/password."

   D. Reference the secret using the name "password."

152. You stored a plaintext string named "secretstring" in AWS Systems Manager Parameter Store. When using the AWS CLI command `aws ssm get-parameters --names securestring` to retrieve it, you get back an encrypted value. How can you retrieve the unencrypted value of the string?

   A. Use the `aws kms decrypt` command.

   B. Obtain administrator access to the customer master key used to encrypt it.

   C. Obtain usage access to the customer master key used to encrypt it.

   D. Add the `--with-decryption` flag to the command.

153. Your organization currently uses Microsoft Active Directory (AD). You want to integrate your on-premises AD-aware applications with AWS but must remain compliant with Payment Card Industry Data Security Standard (PCI DSS) version 3.2. Which of the following AWS services helps to meet the requirement?

   A. LDAP

   B. AWS Managed Microsoft AD

   C. Simple AD

   D. AD Connector

154. Which of the following AWS Directory Service options support multi-factor authentication (MFA)? (Choose two.)

   A. AWS Directory Service for Microsoft Active Directory

   B. Simple AD

   C. AD Connector

   D. IAM

155. You need a Microsoft Active Directory–compatible service that supports group policies for 50 Windows instances. Which of the following solutions will meet your needs and require the least effort?

   A. AWS Directory Service for Microsoft AD

   B. Simple AD

   C. AD Connector

   D. Amazon Cloud Directory

156. You want to use Amazon Inspector to scan applications on your CentOS Linux and Windows EC2 instances for vulnerabilities. Which of the following applications will Inspector *not* scan? (Choose two.)

    A. Binary files copied directly to the instance

    B. Applications installed using yum

    C. Applications installed using Windows Installer

    D. Stand-alone executables compiled on the instance

157. Which of the following security services uses an agent installed on an EC2 or on-premises instance?

    A. Firewall Manager

    B. GuardDuty

    C. Inspector

    D. Macie

158. You're developing a Python web application that will run on AWS. Which AWS service will allow you to securely test and implement the application with minimal effort?

    A. EC2

    B. Lambda

    C. Elastic Beanstalk

    D. ECS

159. You need to apply a security patch to a large number of EC2 instances. What's the most efficient way to do this?

    A. Use AWS Systems Manager to apply the patch.

    B. Create a new AMI with the patch and apply it to the instances.

    C. Open a support case with AWS.

    D. Create a new AMI with the patch and update the Auto Scaling group to use the new AMI.

160. Where can you view the patching status of an RDS instance?

    A. The RDS Console

    B. SSM Patch Manager

    C. Artifact

    D. SSM Compliance Manager

161. You need to determine which instances were using a particular AMI exactly 99 days ago. Which of the following services can you use to get this information with the least effort?

    A. SSM Compliance Manager

    B. AWS Config

    C. CloudTrail logs

    D. CloudTrail events

162. You have a fleet of EC2 instances running the Apache web server. You routinely upgrade Apache as new security updates are released. You need to track which versions are installed on each instance over time. Which of the following should you use to achieve this with minimal effort? (Choose two.)

   A. AWS Config

   B. Systems Manager Automation

   C. CloudWatch Events

   D. Systems Manager Inventory

163. You want to receive a notification whenever anyone performs a port scan against your public EC2 instances. Which of the following services should you use to achieve this with the least effort? (Choose two.)

   A. GuardDuty

   B. Lambda

   C. CloudWatch Events

   D. Simple Email Service

164. You've used Inspector to perform network assessments against your running EC2 instances. Some of the findings show which processes are listening on accessible ports, but others don't. What do you need to do to ensure that the findings show listening processes on the remaining instances?

   A. Add an inbound security rule to allow the Inspector service to reach the instances.

   B. Stop the instances.

   C. Install the Inspector agent.

   D. Run an assessment using host assessments.

165. You're running a fleet of EC2 instances behind an application load balancer with an elastic IP address. You're allowing public IP access to TCP ports 80 and 443. Which of the following can alert you about distributed denial of service (DDoS) layer 7 attacks against the instance?

   A. Web Application Firewall (WAF)

   B. Shield Advanced

   C. Shield Standard

   D. Firewall Manager

166. You need to enlist the help of Amazon's DDoS Response Team (DRT) to mitigate potential attacks against your elastic load balancer. Which of the following tasks can the DRT perform on your behalf to achieve this?

   A. Identifying the source of the attack

   B. Creating WAF web access control lists in your account

   C. Stopping the attack at its source

   D. Proactively mitigating layer 7 attacks

167. Which of the following is most effective at absorbing a distributed denial of service (DDoS) attack?

    A. AWS AirBag

    B. CloudFront

    C. Elastic load balancing

    D. 10-gigabit EC2 network interfaces

168. You run a web application on a fleet of EC2 instances behind an elastic load balancer. You need to count the number of requests from China over a period of six months. Which of the following services can help you accomplish this with the least effort?

    A. GuardDuty

    B. Web Application Firewall (WAF)

    C. CloudWatch Metrics

    D. CloudFront

169. You need to monitor for suspicious access to files in your S3 buckets. Which of the following provides the most cost-effective solution with the least effort?

    A. Macie

    B. GuardDuty

    C. CloudWatch

    D. Lambda

Domain

6

Networking

✓ **Subdomain: 6.1 Apply AWS networking features**

✓ **Subdomain: 6.2 Implement connectivity services of AWS**

✓ **Subdomain: 6.3 Gather and interpret relevant information for network troubleshooting**

1. Where can you obtain the public IP address of a Linux EC2 instance?

   A. Ping the instance's private DNS name.

   B. The user data

   C. The instance metadata

   D. The `ifconfig` command

2. From within an EC2 instance, sending an HTTP GET request to which of the following URLs will return an instance's public IP address?

   A. `169.254.169.254/latest/meta-data/public-ipv4`

   B. `169.254.169.254/1.0/meta-data/local-ipv4`

   C. `169.254.169.254/latest/dynamic/public-ipv4`

   D. `169.254.169.254/latest/meta-data/local-ipv4`

3. Which of the following two components are required for configuring a VPN connection between a VPC and an on-premises network? (Choose two.)

   A. A default route to the virtual private gateway

   B. Virtual private gateway

   C. A default route to the Internet gateway

   D. Customer gateway

4. You're running a web service on EC2 instances in an Auto Scaling group. These instances are members of an application load balancer target group. How can you ensure an instance is replaced when the web service fails on it? (Choose two.)

   A. Configure the Auto Scaling group to use an EC2 health check.

   B. Configure a UDP health check to monitor the web service.

   C. Configure an ELB health check to monitor the web service.

   D. Configure the Auto Scaling group to use an ELB health check.

5. You're running a database-backed web application on six EC2 instances behind an application load balancer. The instances are evenly distributed across private subnets in three availability zones. CloudWatch shows that some instances are incurring significantly higher CPU utilization than others. Which of the following could be the reason?

   A. Clients are connecting directly to the public IP addresses of some instances.

   B. Session stickiness is enabled on the elastic load balancer.

   C. Health checks are occurring too rapidly.

   D. Cross-zone load balancing is disabled.

6. An EC2 instance in a private subnet needs to download security updates from the Internet. Which of the following resources can be used to achieve this? (Choose two.)

   A. NAT gateway

   B. NAT instance

   C. VPC peering

   D. VPC endpoint

7. You have several EC2 instances in a public subnet. All instances were launched using the same AMI. When you're trying to download operating system security updates for one of the instances, the download fails. Downloading the updates on the other instances works fine. Which of the following might resolve the issue?

   A. Add a default route to the subnet's route table.

   B. Create a NAT gateway.

   C. Assign an elastic IP address to the instance.

   D. Create an internet gateway.

8. Which of the following VPC resources allows outbound-only access to IPv6 resources on the Internet?

   A. Internet gateway

   B. Egress-only Internet gateway

   C. NAT gateway

   D. NAT instance

9. Which of the following Route 53 routing policies will ensure that all users near Ohio will always get routed to the us-east-2 (Ohio) AWS region?

   A. Geolocation

   B. Geoproximity

   C. Latency

   D. Region

10. You need to deploy a highly available web application across two AWS regions. Connections to the web application should be evenly distributed across all EC2 instances. Which of the following should you do to achieve this? (Choose two.)

    A. Launch an Auto Scaling group in each region and use the same group size for each.

    B. Configure cross-region load balancing.

    C. Configure a Route 53 weighted routing policy.

    D. Deploy the application using Lambda.

11. Which of the following Route 53 features ensures users get routed to the region with the best network performance?

    A. Geoproximity routing policy

    B. Latency routing policy

    C. Weighted routing policy

    D. Failover routing policy

12. You're running a web service on an EC2 instance. You want Route 53 to return the public IP address of the instance even if the web service on the instance is unhealthy. How can you achieve this? (Choose two.)

A. Create a simple basic resource record.

B. Create a simple alias resource record.

C. Create a simple basic resource record that uses a health check.

D. Create a multivalue answer resource record.

13. You've launched a NAT instance with a public IP address in a public subnet. In the same VPC, you created a private subnet and modified its default route table to include a default route that points to the NAT instance as a target. However, instances in the private subnet are unable to access the Internet. All security groups and NACLs are configured correctly. Which of the following should you try to fix the problem with the least effort?

A. Modify the default route to point to the NAT instance's private IP address as a destination.

B. Disable the source/destination check on the NAT instance.

C. Configure a NAT gateway instead.

D. Assign an elastic IP address to the NAT instance.

14. Which of the following IPv4 prefix lengths is allowed for a VPC CIDR block??

A. /8

B. /15

C. /28

D. /29

15. Which of the following is a valid IPv6 CIDR block for a VPC?

A. 2600:1f18:2551:8900/32

B. 2600:1f18:2551:8900/48

C. 2600:1f18:2551:8900/56

D. 2600:1f18:2551:8900/64

16. You're running a distributed application on EC2 instances in a VPC with a CIDR of 172.31.0.0/24. You're running out of private IP addresses and need to allocate more for additional instances. The instances must be able to communicate with each other using their private addresses. How can you allocate more IP addresses with the least amount of effort?

A. Change the VPC CIDR to 172.31.0.0/16.

B. Add a secondary CIDR of 172.31.1.0/24.

C. Add a secondary CIDR of 172.31.0.0/16.

D. Create a new VPC.

17. What is the limiting factor in the number of subnets you can have in a VPC?

   A. The number of availability zones

   B. The size of the VPC CIDR

   C. The number of VPCs

   D. The number of NACLs

18. You plan to run a fleet of EC2 instances in a VPC. You need to achieve the highest level of availability and the most efficient use of IP address space. Which of the following should you do?

   A. Create one subnet that spans three availability zones.

   B. Create three subnets, each in a different availability zone.

   C. Create three subnets in the same availability zone.

   D. Create two subnets in one availability zone and one subnet in a different availability zone.

19. Your organization is running servers on-premises using the IP address range 192.168.10.0/24. The servers have Internet access. Your organization is merging with another company that runs EC2 instances in a public subnet that uses the same IP address range. Which of the following will, with the least effort, enable the on-premises servers to communicate with the EC2 instances using standard HTTPS communication? (Choose two.)

   A. Implement a VPN.

   B. Assign a public or elastic IP address to each instance.

   C. Implement one-to-one NAT.

   D. Create a security group rule to allow inbound access on TCP port 443 from the on-premises servers.

20. Which of the following is true of an elastic network interface (ENI)?

   A. It must have only one primary private IP address.

   B. It can be associated with only one elastic IP address.

   C. It can have multiple private IP addresses from different subnets.

   D. It must be attached to an instance.

21. Which of the following prevents EC2 from automatically assigning a public IP address to an instance? (Choose two.)

   A. Assigning an elastic IP address to the instance and then unassigning it

   B. Assigning a secondary elastic network interface

   C. Launching the instance in a private subnet

   D. Removing the primary elastic network interface from the instance

22. You have some EC2 instances that access Internet resources over TCP port 443. The instances are able to access some of these resources but not others. You check the route table associated with the instances' subnets and see only the local route and a route with a destination of 0.0.0.0/0. Which of the following may resolve the problem? (Choose two.)

   A. Disable IPv6 in the VPC.

   B. Associate an egress-only Internet gateway with the VPC.

   C. Add an IPv6 default route.

   D. Associate an Internet gateway with the VPC.

23. In a VPC, which of the following is most analogous to connecting a router to a traditional network?

   A. Attaching an elastic network interface to an instance

   B. Associating a route table with a subnet

   C. Creating a default route

   D. Associating an elastic IP address with an instance

24. Your organization has proposed migrating an on-premises application to EC2. The application requires multicast and the servers it runs on must retain the same RFC 1918 IP addresses. Which of the following recommendations should you make regarding this proposed migration?

   A. The migration is feasible as proposed.

   B. The migration is feasible provided the subnet is between /16 and /28.

   C. The migration may not be possible because VPCs don't support RFC 1918 addresses.

   D. The migration isn't possible because VPCs don't support multicast.

25. You have two instances in different VPCs, instance A and instance B. Both instances have a public IP address. Each VPC contains only one subnet. VPC peering is not configured and there's no VPN. Instance A sends a packet to instance B. What does instance B see as the source IP address?

   A. Instance A's public IP address

   B. Instance A's private IP address

   C. The Internet gateway's public address

   D. The NAT gateway's public IP address

26. Which of the following are true of NACLs and security groups? (Choose two.)

   A. Security groups apply to a subnet.

   B. NACLs apply to a subnet.

   C. NACLs apply to an instance.

   D. Security groups apply to an elastic network interface.

27. Which of the following describes an elastic VPC resource that hides the public source IP address of an instance from hosts on the Internet?

    A. NAT gateway

    B. NAT instance

    C. Internet gateway

    D. Virtual private gateway

28. Which of the following is true regarding peering VPCs in the same region?

    A. The same two VPCs can have multiple peering connections with each other for redundancy.

    B. It doesn't support overlapping CIDR blocks.

    C. It supports transitive peering.

    D. It doesn't support IPv6.

29. Which of the following is a limitation of inter-region VPC peering?

    A. Both VPC CIDRs must reside in the same RFC 1918 address range.

    B. DNS resolution doesn't work.

    C. An MTU of less than 1500 isn't supported.

    D. IPv6 isn't supported.

30. You've created a peering connection between two VPCs in the same region. Which of the following do you need to do to enable bidirectional IP communication between the instances in these VPCs?

    A. Create the appropriate routes with the VPC peering connection as the target.

    B. Configure NAT.

    C. Assign public IP addresses to the instances.

    D. Enable DNS resolution.

31. Which of the following can change the public IP address of an EC2 instance?

    A. Removing the primary elastic network interface

    B. Removing the default route from the route table

    C. Rebooting the instance

    D. Changing the instance type

32. You're running an EC2 instance in a private subnet. The instance needs to resolve a resource record for a public domain that you have registered with a third-party domain name registrar. Which of the following will achieve this?

    A. Enable DNS hostnames in the VPC.

    B. Enable DNS support in the VPC.

    C. Transfer the domain name to Route 53.

    D. Assign an elastic IP address to the instance.

33. Which of the following speeds up transfers between S3 buckets and hosts on the Internet?

   A. CloudFront distribution

   B. S3 transfer acceleration

   C. Elastic load balancing

   D. S3 cross-region replication

34. Which of the following VPC resources will incur costs only if not associated with an instance?

   A. Elastic IP address

   B. Elastic network interface

   C. NAT gateway

   D. Elastic load balancer

35. You need to run a Lambda application that must communicate with EC2 instances in a private subnet. Which of the following features will enable this communication?

   A. Gateway VPC endpoint

   B. Interface VPC endpoint

   C. API gateway

   D. VPC peering

36. Which of the following is true of an interface VPC endpoint? (Choose two.)

   A. It supports TCP traffic.

   B. It supports IPv6 traffic.

   C. It supports UDP traffic.

   D. It exists in only one availability zone.

37. You've configured a VPC gateway endpoint for S3. Which of the following will allow you to restrict which EC2 instances can access S3 via the endpoint?

   A. Create a NACL rule and specify the S3 prefix list ID.

   B. Create a security group rule and specify the S3 prefix list ID.

   C. Use S3 bucket policies.

   D. Modify the instance role's permission policy.

38. Which of the following must you do to use IPv6 in a new VPC?

   A. Configure an egress-only Internet gateway.

   B. Assign a link-local IPv6 address to the VPC.

   C. Enable DNS hostnames.

   D. Configure an IPv4 CIDR.

39. Which VPC component controls traffic direction within a VPC?

   A. Internet gateway

   B. Security group

   C. Route table

   D. NACL

40. You need to create a subnet that will hold only 10 EC2 instances, each with a single elastic network interface. What's the smallest prefix length you can use?

   A. /8

   B. /16

   C. /28

   D. /29

41. How many IP addresses does AWS reserve in each VPC subnet?

   A. One

   B. Two

   C. Four

   D. Five

42. You've created the VPC subnet 10.0.0.0/24. Which of the following addresses is *not* available for assignment to an EC2 instance?

   A. 10.0.0.4

   B. 10.0.0.254

   C. 10.0.0.255

   D. 10.0.0.5

43. You've launched a Windows EC2 instance and configured its security group and the subnet's NACL to permit access from all other hosts in the subnet to the Remote Desktop Protocol (RDP) on TCP port 3389. However, when you're attempting to RDP to the server from a Linux host in the same subnet, the connection fails. You are able to RDP from the same host to other Windows servers. Which of the following could be the reason for the failure?

   A. RDP uses TCP port 2598.

   B. Linux hosts can't use RDP.

   C. The Windows firewall is blocking access on TCP port 3389.

   D. RDP uses UDP, not TCP.

44. You need to connect two VPCs to resources in a remote office via a site-to-site VPN. You need to ensure that resources in the VPCs can't communicate with each other. Which of the following can help you achieve this?

   A. VPC peering

   B. Transit gateway

   C. Virtual private gateway

   D. VPC endpoint

45. Which of the following is an advantage of using Direct Connect instead of a VPN connection?

    A. Reduced cost

    B. Data encryption

    C. Higher bandwidth

    D. Predictable latency

46. Servers in your datacenter are using a 10 Gbps Internet connection to connect to S3 using a public endpoint. Which of the following can improve the security of this configuration?

    A. Use HTTPS to connect to the S3 endpoint.

    B. Use Direct Connect.

    C. Use a VPN connection.

    D. Use a VPC endpoint.

47. Before you can use Direct Connect to connect a VPC to your datacenter, which of the following should you do to ensure proper connectivity? (Choose two.)

    A. Make sure the IP address ranges in the networks don't overlap.

    B. Use encryption.

    C. Configure the appropriate IAM policies.

    D. Configure routing.

48. Which of the following are options for connecting a site to AWS using Direct Connect? (Choose two.)

    A. Configure a VPN between the site and an AWS Direct Connect Location.

    B. Complete a cross-connect between your equipment and AWS at a Direct Connect location.

    C. Request AWS to install a Direct Connect connection to be installed at the site.

    D. Use a hosted connection from an AWS Direct Connect Partner.

49. Applications running in your datacenter currently connect to AWS services using their public endpoints. You plan to use Direct Connect to access these services but don't want to reconfigure the applications to use private AWS service endpoints. Which of the following types of virtual interfaces should you configure?

    A. Private virtual interface

    B. Public virtual interface

    C. Transit virtual interface

    D. Peer virtual interface

50. Which of the following BGP configuration tasks is required to use a Direct Connect public virtual interface?

    A. Advertise at least one public IP prefix.

    B. Advertise at least one private IP prefix.

    C. Specify a public autonomous system number (ASN).

    D. Enable jumbo frames.

51. You need a Direct Connect connection that supports up to 75 Mbps. Which of the following options is the most cost-effective?

   A. A hosted connection with a 50 Mbps port

   B. A hosted connection with an 80 Mbps port

   C. A hosted connection with a 100 Mbps port

   D. A dedicated connection with a 1 Gbps port

52. You're using almost the full bandwidth of your 1 Gbps hosted Direct Connect connection. Which of the following can you do to approximately double your Direct Connect bandwidth to AWS? (Choose two.)

   A. Upgrade the 1 Gbps connection to 2 Gbps.

   B. Create a new connection using a 2 Gbps connection and remove the 1 Gbps connection.

   C. Create a new connection using a 1 Gbps connection and add both connections to a link aggregation group (LAG).

   D. Create two new 50 Mbps connections and add them to a link aggregation group (LAG) along with the existing 1 Gbps connection.

53. What's the default maximum transmission unit (MTU) of a Direct Connect virtual interface?

   A. 1500 bytes

   B. 8500 bytes

   C. 9000 bytes

   D. 1472 bytes

54. How many VPN connections can you create to a single VPC?

   A. 1

   B. 5

   C. 10

   D. 25

55. Which of the following is true regarding an IPv6 BGP peering session over a Direct Connect virtual interface?

   A. You can specify your own IPv6 peer addresses.

   B. AWS assigns a /125 IPv6 CIDR to use.

   C. Direct Connect doesn't support IPv6 BGP peering.

   D. An IPv4 BGP peering session can't be used alongside an IPv6 BGP peering session.

56. How can you decrease the network overhead of a Direct Connect connection?

   A. Create a link aggregation group (LAG).

   B. Use jumbo frames on the virtual interfaces.

   C. Encrypt all data traversing the connection.

   D. Use a VPN tunnel.

57. How many routes are you allowed to advertise in a BGP session over a Direct Connect connection over a private virtual interface?

    A. 50

    B. 100

    C. 500

    D. 1000

58. What happens if you advertise more than 100 routes over a BGP session over a Direct Connect private virtual interface?

    A. The oldest routes will be discarded to bring the total number of routes to 100 or fewer.

    B. Additional routes over the first 100 won't be installed in the route table.

    C. The Direct Connect link will go down.

    D. The session will go down.

59. You're unable to create a BGP session over a Direct Connect connection. Which of the following could be the reason?

    A. BGP MD5 authentication mismatch

    B. Missing community tags

    C. Your router doesn't support multiprotocol BGP (MP-BGP).

    D. UDP port 179 is blocked.

60. How many prefixes are you allowed to advertise over a BGP session over a Direct Connect public virtual interface?

    A. 100

    B. 200

    C. 1000

    D. 2000

61. Which of the following can cause a BGP session to fail over a Direct Connect link?

    A. Not having any prefixes to advertise

    B. Incorrect autonomous system (AS) number

    C. Blocking TCP port 197

    D. Using the NO_EXPORT BGP community

62. From your datacenter, you have a Direct Connect connection to a VPC with six subnets. There are running EC2 instances in each subnet. AWS is advertising prefixes for all six subnets via BGP. You want to prevent only one of these prefixes from being installed in your datacenter router and without impacting existing EC2 instances. How can you accomplish this with the least effort?

    A. Remove the prefix from the VPC route table.

    B. Request AWS not advertise the prefix.

    C. Block the prefixes on your datacenter router.

    D. Delete the subnet.

63. You have a branch office connected to a VPC via a VPN. You also have a datacenter connected to the same VPC via Direct Connect. You need to pass traffic between the branch office and the datacenter. How can you do this with the least effort?

   A. Create a VPN connection between the branch office and datacenter.

   B. Configure VPN CloudHub to use the VPC for transit.

   C. Add a Direct Connect connection to the branch office.

   D. Add a private line between the datacenter and branch office.

64. You have a VPN connection and a Direct Connect connection between your datacenter and a VPC. BGP sessions on both connections have the exact same prefixes. Which connection will be preferred?

   A. Direct Connect

   B. VPN

   C. The connection advertising the prefix with the shortest AS PATH length

   D. The oldest connection

65. In your datacenter you have 200 prefixes that need to be reachable from a VPC via a Direct Connect virtual interface. How can you ensure all prefixes are reachable? (Choose two.)

   A. Advertise the default route.

   B. Use multiple BGP sessions to advertise all the prefixes.

   C. Summarize the prefixes into 100 or fewer prefixes.

   D. Advertise all 200 prefixes over a single BGP session.

66. Which of the following CIDR blocks can you use to establish a BGP session over a site-to-site VPN tunnel?

   A. 169.254.0.0/30

   B. 169.0.0.0/16

   C. 10.0.0.0/30

   D. 10.0.0.0/16

67. What are two differences between CloudHub and Direct Connect Gateway? (Choose two.)

   A. CloudHub connects on-premises networks and VPCs in any region.

   B. CloudHub connects on-premises networks and VPCs in only one region.

   C. Direct Connect Gateway connects on-premises networks and VPCs in any region.

   D. Direct Connect Gateway connects on-premises networks and VPCs in only one region.

68. Which of the following BGP communities propagates public prefixes to all AWS regions?

   A. 7224:9100

   B. 7224:9200

   C. 7224:9300

   D. 7224:8100

69. You're advertising the same prefix over two separate Direct Connect links. One prefix is advertised from your datacenter, and the other is advertised from your headquarters office. How can you ensure the datacenter route will take precedence for return traffic?

   A. Apply the community tag 7224:7100 to the prefix from the datacenter.

   B. Apply the community tag 7224:7300 to the prefix from the datacenter.

   C. Apply the community tag 7224:7300 to the prefix from the headquarters office.

   D. Use AS PATH prepending on the prefix from the datacenter.

70. You have two Direct Connect connections at your datacenter and want to load balance incoming traffic for all prefixes. Which of the following BGP attributes must be identical on all prefixes you advertise?

   A. Community tags

   B. Multi-exit discriminator (MED)

   C. Local preference

   D. Router ID

71. Which of the following is true regarding using a private AS number (ASN) on a Direct Connect public virtual interface?

   A. You must own the ASN.

   B. The ASN must be greater than 65535.

   C. It's not allowed; you must use a public ASN.

   D. AS path prepending won't work.

72. What are valid values for a VLAN? (Choose two.)

   A. 4000

   B. 6000

   C. 12000

   D. 1

73. You have an IPv4 BGP session established over a Direct Connect virtual interface. How can you advertise IPv6 prefixes over this connection with the least effort?

   A. Establish a second IPv4 BGP session.

   B. Establish an IPv6 BGP session.

   C. Advertise the IPv6 prefixes over the IPv4 BGP session.

   D. Create an IPv6 VPN tunnel over the Direct Connect link.

74. Which of the following is required to associate a transit gateway with a Direct Connect gateway?

   A. The ASNs of the transit gateway and the Direct Connect gateway must be different.

   B. The transit gateway and the Direct Connect gateway must be in the same VLAN.

   C. The ASNs of the transit gateway and the Direct Connect gateway must be the same.

   D. The transit gateway and the Direct Connect gateway must be in the same AWS account.

75. Which of the following CloudWatch metrics indicates the status of the egress fiber from the AWS side of a 10 Gbps Direct Connect connection?

    A. ConnectionState

    B. ConnectionLightLevelRx

    C. ConnectionLightLevelTx

    D. ConnectionPpsEgress

76. How many transit virtual interfaces can you create on a Direct Connect link aggregation group (LAG) composed of two 10 Gbps links?

    A. None

    B. One

    C. Two

    D. Four

77. What's the maximum number of Direct Connect dedicated connections you can have per link aggregation group?

    A. 2

    B. 4

    C. 8

    D. 16

78. You launch an instance into a subnet that has an IPv6 CIDR assigned. The application running on the instance requires a routable IPv6 address. The instance has one elastic network interface and doesn't have an IPv6 address assigned. What should you do to enable IPv6 connectivity for the application with the least effort?

    A. Assign a link-local IPv6 address to the instance.

    B. Attach an additional network interface to the instance and assign it a global unicast IPv6 address.

    C. Terminate the instance and launch a new one.

    D. Assign a global unicast IPv6 address to the instance.

79. You have an EC2 instance with a global unicast IPv6 address assigned. How can you ensure that hosts on the Internet are able to resolve the IPv6 address of the instance?

    A. No action is required; they can query the IPv6 record of the instance's DNS hostname.

    B. Create a publicly resolvable AAAA record that points to the instance's IPv6 address.

    C. Create a publicly resolvable A record that points to the instance's IPv6 address.

    D. Ensure that the instance's security group allows inbound access to UDP port 53.

80. The address fe80:db8:1234:1a00::1/64 is an example of which of the following?

    A. Elastic IP address

    B. IPv4 link-local address

    C. IPv6 link-local address

    D. IPv6 global unicast address

81. Which of the following addresses is released when an EC2 instance is stopped?

    A. Its primary private IP address

    B. Its public IPv4 address

    C. Its public IPv6 address

    D. Its elastic IP address

82. Your EC2 instance in the us-east-1 region is assigned the public IP address 203.0.113.25. Which of the following is its external DNS hostname?

    A. 203-0-113-25.compute-1.amazonaws.com

    B. 25.113.0.203.ec2.compute-1.amazonaws.com

    C. ec-203-0-113-25.compute-1.amazonaws.com

    D. ec2-203-0-113-25.compute-1.amazonaws.com

83. You created a default VPC and made no other changes to it. Which of the following is true of an EC2 instance launched into this default VPC? (Choose two.)

    A. Its primary private IP address has a /16 CIDR.

    B. It's in a public subnet.

    C. It has a public IP address.

    D. It has no outbound access.

84. Your EC2 instance in the us-east-1 region has a primary private IP address of 10.9.13.37/20 and a secondary private IP address of 10.8.13.37/20. Which of the following is the instance's private hostname?

    A. ip-10-9-13-37.ec2.internal

    B. ip-10-8-13-37.ec2.internal

    C. ip-10-9-13-37.ec2.compute-1.internal

    D. ip-10-8-13-37.ec2.us-east-1.internal

85. Which of the following VPC attributes determines whether an instance with a public IP address receives a public DNS hostname?

    A. enableDnsSupport

    B. enableDnsHostnames

    C. enableDnsResolution

    D. enableDns

86. Which of the following VPC attributes determines whether an instance can resolve the Amazon-provided private hostname of another instance in the same VPC?

    A. enableDnsHostnames

    B. enableDnsSupport

    C. enableDnsResolution

    D. enablePrivateDns

87. A subnet has the CIDR 2001:db8:1234:1a00::/64. Which of the following addresses can you *not* assign to an instance?

    A. 2001:db8:1234:1a00:ffff::

    B. 2001:db8:1234:1a00:1:1

    C. 2001:db8:1234:1a00::ffff

    D. 2001:db8:1234:1a00::

88. Using a virtual private gateway, you've created a site-to-site VPN connection between a VPC subnet and a datacenter. When creating routes to datacenter subnets, which of the following should you specify as the target?

    A. Virtual private gateway

    B. Customer gateway

    C. Internet gateway

    D. Transit gateway

89. When attempting to RDP into a Windows instance from the Internet, you get the error "Your credentials did not work." Which of the following could be the reason?

    A. TCP port 3389 is blocked.

    B. You're using the wrong SSH key.

    C. The password is incorrect.

    D. The instance doesn't have Internet access.

90. You have a custom-built Windows instance that's managed using Simple Systems Manager (SSM). You've attempted to connect to the instance via RDP from the Internet, but it doesn't respond. You've verified that both your NACL and the instance's security group allow RDP traffic. You can also use SSM to install official patches on the instance. Which of the following steps might resolve the issue with the least effort?

    A. Re-create the instance using an official AMI.

    B. Open up a PowerShell remoting session to the instance and enable RDP.

    C. Attach to the instance an instance role with RDP permissions.

    D. Run the `AWSSupport-TroubleshootRDP` SSM automation document to disable the Windows Firewall and enable RDP.

91. You're unable to RDP to a Windows EC2 instance after a reboot. Prior to this you were able to RDP into it via the Internet. Which of the following actions can help you determine the cause?

   A. Take an instance screen shot.

   B. View the system log.

   C. View the CloudTrail logs for the instance.

   D. View the AWS Config logs for the instance.

92. Which of the following changes to a Windows Server 2019 instance can result in a loss of all network connectivity for several hours after rebooting it?

   A. Changing the time zone

   B. Upgrading the PV driver

   C. The Windows Plug and Play Cleanup feature removing the EC2 network device

   D. Enabling TCP offloading

93. Which of the following IP addresses does AWS use for Windows activation?

   A. 169.254.169.250

   B. 192.168.169.250

   C. 169.168.169.254

   D. 169.254.0.254

94. An EC2 instance in your VPC is unable to connect to a Relational Database Service (RDS) instance hosting a database. Which of the following should you try to resolve the problem?

   A. Move the RDS instance into the same VPC as the EC2 instance but a different subnet.

   B. Reconfigure the EC2 instance's security group to allow access from the database instance.

   C. Move the RDS instance into the same VPC and subnet as the EC2 instance.

   D. Reconfigure the database instance's security group to allow access from the EC2 instance.

95. You're connected to an EC2 instance via SSH when you're abruptly disconnected. You attempt to reconnect to the instance's elastic IP address but are unsuccessful. Which of the following could explain this?

   A. A rule denying outbound TCP port 22 access was added to the instance's subnet's NACL.

   B. The outbound rules for the instance's security group were removed.

   C. All outbound rules for the instance's subnet's NACL were removed.

   D. A rule denying outbound TCP port 22 access was added to the instance's security group.

96. When attempting to SSH to an EC2 instance, you get the error that the user key is not recognized. You try a different SSH client and get a "permission denied" error. Which of the following could be the reason?

    A. Other users have read and write permissions to your private SSH key.

    B. There is a security group or NACL blocking SSH access to the instance.

    C. You entered the wrong passphrase for the private SSH key.

    D. The username you provided is incorrect.

97. When attempting to SSH to an EC2 instance from your workstation, you get the error "Permissions 0777 for '.ssh/private_key.pem' are too open." Which of the following actions can correct this error?

    A. Re-create the key using `ssh-keygen`.

    B. Delete the file `.ssh/private_key.pem`.

    C. Execute the command `chmod 0400 .ssh/private_key.pem`.

    D. Delete the public key from the `.ssh/authorized_keys` file.

98. You intermittently get disconnected from an SSH session to an EC2 instance. You're able to immediately reconnect. Which of the following may prevent the intermittent disconnection?

    A. Enable keepalives on your SSH client.

    B. Disable TCP keepalives on the server.

    C. Set the ClientAliveInterval on the server to 0.

    D. Run a continuous ping to the instance during the SSH session.

99. You need to be able to ping an EC2 instance's elastic IP address. Which of the following should you add to the inbound security group rules?

    A. ICMPv4 Echo Request

    B. ICMPv4 Echo Reply

    C. ICMPv6 All

    D. ICMPv4 Destination Unreachable

100. You attempt to ping an EC2 instance's public IPv4 address but get no response. Which of the following could be the reason?

    A. An inbound NACL rule denying UDP traffic

    B. An inbound NACL rule denying ICMPv4 Echo Replies

    C. An outbound NACL rule denying ICMPv4 Echo Requests

    D. An outbound NACL rule denying ICMPv4 Echo Replies

101. Which of the following can help an instance automatically recover from a loss of network connectivity caused by a problem with the underlying host?

    A. CloudWatch alarms

    B. CloudWatch Events

    C. Simple Notification Service

    D. Enhanced monitoring

102. What's the maximum number of instance recovery attempts allowed per day?

    A. Two

    B. Three

    C. Four

    D. No limit

103. Which of the following can tell you whether a security group or NACL has blocked traffic from a particular IP address?

    A. CloudTrail logs

    B. VPC Flow Logs

    C. CloudWatch basic metrics

    D. CloudWatch detailed metrics

104. You can configure VPC flow logging to limit the logging of traffic flows to which of the following? (Choose two.)

    A. Elastic load balancer

    B. VPC

    C. Placement group

    D. Host

105. Which of the following is *not* included in the 5-tuple of a VPC Flow Logs data?

    A. Source port

    B. Protocol

    C. Number of packets

    D. IPv4/IPv6 indicator

106. You've configured VPC flow logging for a VPC that has intermittent bursts of heavy traffic. The logs are stored in an S3 bucket. An hour later, you view the logs and notice that although there are several flow records containing a 5-tuple, some records appear without the 5-tuple and have "NODATA" at the end. What can you conclude from this?

    A. VPC flow logging is configured correctly.

    B. Some VPC traffic is not getting logged.

    C. There's too much traffic to log.

    D. Some traffic is getting blocked.

107. You want to use VPC flow logging to identify any traffic that's blocked by a security group. How can you accomplish this in the most cost-effective way?

    A. Enable VPC flow logging to log only rejected traffic to CloudWatch Logs.

    B. Enable VPC flow logging to log only rejected traffic to an S3 bucket.

    C. Enable VPC flow logging to log all traffic to an S3 bucket, and search the logs for the word *REJECT*.

    D. Enable VPC flow logging to log all traffic to CloudWatch Logs, and use a filter to view only rejected traffic.

108. When trying to add an alternative domain name to a CloudFront distribution, you get an "InvalidViewerCertificateException" error. Which of the following could be the reason?

  A. The certificate specifies an invalid cipher.

  B. The domain name is in all lowercase.

  C. The custom certificate you've provided isn't signed by a trusted certificate authority (CA).

  D. The attached certificate contains too many domain names.

109. You have a CloudFront distribution for the alternate domain name `www.example.com`. You try to add another alternate domain name for `www1.example.com` and receive an "InvalidViewerCertificateException" error. How can you enable the CloudFront distribution for both domains?

  A. Verify your ownership of the `www1.example.com` domain name.

  B. Supply a new certificate for the domain names `www.example.com` and `www1.example.com`.

  C. Use the default CloudFront certificate.

  D. Supply a new certificate for the domain name `www1.example.com`.

110. You're currently running a web application on a set of EC2 instances behind an elastic load balancer (ELB). You're storing static web assets for the application in an S3 bucket. Which of the following is the most scalable approach for serving these web assets using a CloudFront distribution?

  A. Create a streaming distribution.

  B. Add the ELB as an origin.

  C. Add the EC2 instances as origins.

  D. Add the S3 bucket as an origin.

111. You've placed video and media player files in an S3 bucket and created a streaming RTMP CloudFront distribution using the bucket as the origin. Users are unable to play the videos. How can you resolve this?

  A. Move the media player files into a different bucket.

  B. Serve the media player files from an HTTP CloudFront distribution.

  C. Ensure the bucket has public access.

  D. Enable HTTPS on the distribution.

112. You've created an RTMP distribution for streaming video. Most users are able to watch the videos, but users at one location aren't. Which of the following could be the problem?

  A. UDP port 1935 is blocked.

  B. The video files aren't served from an HTTP distribution.

  C. The media player files are served from the RTMP distribution.

  D. TCP port 1935 is blocked.

113. Some users are unable to access an RTMP streaming distribution due to TCP port 1935 being blocked. Only TCP ports 80 and 443 are allowed. Which of the following must occur in order for the users to access the distribution?

  A. Convert the RTMP distribution to HTTP.

  B. Switch to RTMPT.

  C. Convert the RTMP distribution to HTTPS.

  D. Add an inbound security group rule to permit access to TCP port 1935.

114. Which of the following is a valid URL for an RTMP distribution?

  A. `rtmp://s5c39gqb8ow64r.cloudfront.net`

  B. `rtmp://d111111abcdef8.cloudfront.net`

  C. `https://s5c39gqb8ow64r.cloudfront.net`

  D. `https://d111111abcdef8.cloudfront.net`

115. When does a CloudFront edge location first fetch a file from an origin?

  A. When the file is added to the origin

  B. When the distribution is created

  C. When the edge location receives a request for the file

  D. When the distribution enters a "deployed" state

116. You've created a CloudFront distribution using an alternate domain name `example.com`. In the Route 53 hosted zone for `example.com`, you've created a CNAME record for `example.com` that points to the distribution's domain name as an alias. You discover that you're being charged for queries of this record. How can you reduce your costs while continuing to use the `example.com` domain name for the distribution?

  A. Replace the CNAME record with an A record that points to the distribution as an alias target.

  B. Modify the CNAME record to point to the distribution as an alias target.

  C. Purchase a Route 53 zone reservation.

  D. Decrease the time-to-live (TTL) of the record.

117. You've created a CloudFront distribution with the alternate domain name `example.com` You've created an A record pointing to the distribution as an alias target. IPv4 users are able to access the distribution using the alternate domain name, but IPv6 users aren't. They can, however, access it using the distribution domain name. How can you resolve this?

  A. Convert the record to a non-alias record.

  B. Change the alternate name to `www.example.com` and update the A record accordingly.

  C. Change the A record to a CNAME record.

  D. Create an AAAA record.

118. Which of the following is not a valid alternate domain name for a CloudFront distribution?

  A. *.example.com

  B. example.example.com

  C. *.www.example.com

  D. www.*.example.com

119. You're storing an object named `production/index.html` in a bucket named myawsbucket. You want to make this object accessible via a CloudFront distribution using just the alternate domain name `example.com/index.html`. Which of the following steps is required to accomplish this?

  A. Restrict access to the bucket.

  B. Set the origin path to `/production`.

  C. Set the origin path to `/myawsbucket/production`.

  D. Create a CNAME record for `example.com`.

120. Which of the following is a network protocol that CloudFront supports?

  A. RSA

  B. WebSocket

  C. UDP

  D. RTSP

121. How can you enable Internet users to access a CloudFront distribution without allowing public access to its origin S3 bucket?

  A. Use an origin access identity.

  B. Create a bucket policy that grants read permissions to the * principal.

  C. Create a bucket ACL to grant the CloudFront service access to the bucket.

  D. Put a password on the bucket.

122. You're hosting audio files and a custom player on a set of EC2 instances behind an elastic load balancer (ELB) in a public subnet. You want to use a CloudFront distribution to host this content while preventing users from accessing the audio files or player from the EC2 instances directly. How can you accomplish this with the least effort? (Choose two.)

  A. Create a custom distribution with the EC2 instances as custom origins.

  B. Move the audio files to a non-public S3 bucket and create a streaming distribution with the bucket as the origin.

  C. Move the audio player to an non-public S3 bucket and create a distribution with the bucket as the origin.

  D. Place the instances in a private subnet.

123. Which of the following can be a custom CloudFront origin??

    A. None of these

    B. A non-public S3 bucket

    C. A private web server on a company intranet

    D. A public web server open to the Internet

124. You've created a target group that you plan to use with a network load balancer (NLB). The target group contains several EC2 instances, all in the same subnet, and all of the instances are configured to listen for HTTPS traffic on TCP port 443. One of the EC2 instance targets isn't entering the InService state. You check and find that the instance is failing its health check. All targets are configured with the same health check settings. From other instances in the same subnet you're able to access TCP port 443 on the problem instance. Which of the following could be the reason the instance is failing its health check?

    A. The instance's TLS certificate isn't valid.

    B. The instance's security group isn't allowing traffic from the NLB.

    C. The subnet NACL isn't allowing traffic from the NLB.

    D. The instance is stopped.

125. You've created a network load balancer (NLB) and have added instances to a target group. Some of the instances are in the same VPC as the NLB, while others are in a peered VPC. Requests aren't getting routed to instances in the peered VPC. Why?

    A. The instances are getting overwhelmed with health checks.

    B. The target group doesn't reference the instances by instance ID.

    C. The target group doesn't reference the instances by IP address.

    D. NLB doesn't support VPC peering.

126. Which of the following IP addresses can you *not* specify in a network load balancer target group?

    A. 10.0.0.15

    B. 100.64.0.7

    C. 100.127.7.7

    D. 65.156.1.101

127. Which of the following elastic load balancers supports the Lambda target type?

    A. Network load balancer

    B. Application load balancer

    C. Classic load balancer

    D. Lambda load balancer

128. You are running a web application on a set of EC2 instances. The application requires that each incoming TCP connection has the source IP address of the client. Which type of load balancing should you use?

    A. Network load balancer

    B. Application load balancer

    C. Classic load balancer

    D. Route 53 weighted resource records

129. When browsing to the public URL of an application load balancer, users receive a "Bad Gateway" error. The target group contains only EC2 instances. What could this indicate?

    A. The users are unable to connect to the application load balancer.

    B. A web application firewall (WAF) rule blocked the request.

    C. The target instance closed the connection from the load balancer.

    D. The target instance didn't accept the connection from the load balancer.

130. When browsing to the public URL of an application load balancer, users receive a "Gateway Timeout" error. The target group contains only EC2 instances. What could this indicate?

    A. The users are unable to connect to the application load balancer.

    B. The target instance didn't accept the connection from the load balancer.

    C. The target instance closed the connection from the load balancer.

    D. A web application firewall (WAF) rule blocked the request.

131. Which of the following CloudFront metrics tracks the number of server errors generated by an application load balancer?

    A. `HTTPCode_ELB_2XX_Count`

    B. `HTTPCode_ELB_4XX_Count`

    C. `HTTPCode_ELB_5XX_Count`

    D. None of these

132. Where can an application load balancer store logs containing client IP address, latencies, and server responses?

    A. Web application firewall

    B. S3 bucket

    C. CloudWatch Logs

    D. CloudTrail logs

Domain

7

Automation and Optimization

✓ **Subdomain: 7.1 Use AWS services and features to manage and assess resource utilization**

✓ **Subdomain: 7.2 Employ cost-optimization strategies for efficient resource utilization**

✓ **Subdomain: 7.3 Automate manual or repeatable process to minimize management overhead**

1. Which of the following does a CloudWatch metric always contain?

    A. Timestamp

    B. Dimension

    C. Unit of measure

    D. Namespace

2. How frequently does EC2 collect CPU utilization metrics?

    A. Every minute

    B. Every 90 seconds

    C. Every 5 minutes

    D. Every 10 minutes

3. Which monitoring type sends metrics to CloudWatch every minute?

    A. Basic

    B. Detailed

    C. Regular

    D. High-resolution

4. You send custom metrics to CloudWatch every 30 seconds. How should you store these metrics in CloudWatch to ensure no metric values are overwritten?

    A. Average the metric values over a minute and send the average every minute

    B. As regular-resolution metrics

    C. As high-resolution metrics

    D. Timestamp each metric 1 minute in the past

5. Which of the following is *not* a statistic in CloudWatch Metrics?

    A. Sum

    B. Minimum

    C. Percentage

    D. Sample Count

6. How long does CloudWatch retain metric data points stored at 1-hour resolution?

    A. 1 month

    B. 63 days

    C. 6 months

    D. 15 months

7. Which of the following CloudWatch statistics would be most appropriate for graphing the number of web requests in a 24-hour period?

    A. Maximum

    B. Average

    C. Sum

    D. Sample count

8. Which of the following distinguishes two CloudWatch metrics that are in the same namespace and have the same name?

    A. Timestamp

    B. Data point

    C. Dimension

    D. Region

9. You update a CloudWatch metric with a timestamp of 10:00:30 and a value of 98. You then update the same metric with a timestamp of 10:00:59 and a timestamp of 97. Assuming the metric is a regular-resolution metric, what will CloudWatch do?

    A. Record the first value and ignore the second value.

    B. Record the second value and overwrite the first value.

    C. Record both values.

    D. Store the average of the two values.

10. You need to graph the individual values stored in a CloudWatch metric. The metric is stored at 1-minute resolution. Which statistic and period should you use?

    A. The Sample Count statistic with a 1-minute period

    B. The Average statistic with a 5-minute period

    C. The Sum statistic with a 5-minute period

    D. The Sum statistic with a 1-minute period

11. A week ago, you created a CloudWatch alarm to monitor the `CPUUtilization` metric on an EC2 instance. Yesterday, the alarm briefly entered an `INSUFFICIENT_DATA` state and then went back to an `OK` state. What is a possible reason for this?

    A. The alarm was paused.

    B. The instance was terminated.

    C. The CPU utilization went above the alarm threshold.

    D. The instance was stopped and restarted.

12. Which of the following services should you monitor to ensure you don't exceed your allocated capacity?

    A. Lambda

    B. EBS

    C. S3

    D. EFS

13. Which of the following can automatically scale EC2 instances in or out in response to a metric?

   A. Auto Scaling launch configuration

   B. Auto Scaling group

   C. EC2 launch template

   D. Elastic load balancer

14. You're running a dynamic web application on two EC2 instances in the same region. You're load balancing traffic to the application using Route 53 weighted resource records. The web application uses HTTPS to provide encryption in transit. The CPU utilization on these instances intermittently spikes to nearly 100% and users report a slowdown during this time. Which of the following will offer the most performance improvement? (Choose two.)

   A. Implement an Auto Scaling group.

   B. Implement a network load balancer.

   C. Implement an application load balancer.

   D. Use Route 53 latency records instead of weighted records.

15. You're storing several large files in an S3 bucket and making them available for public download. The files are in the Standard storage class. Over time, transfer and storage costs for the bucket has increased, resulting in an ever-growing AWS bill. Which of the following can help you reduce these costs without impacting availability or durability?

   A. Move the files to the Standard-Infrequent Access (IA) storage class.

   B. Enable versioning.

   C. Move the files to Glacier.

   D. Delete unneeded files from the bucket.

16. Which of the following can you use to proactively alert you to possible excess resource utilization in your AWS account?

   A. CloudTrail

   B. AWS Budgets

   C. CloudWatch Events

   D. Cost Explorer

   E. AWS Config

17. You need to implement a MySQL database in AWS. It must be backed up every 5 minutes, but recovery in the case of a database instance failure must *not* be automatic. Which of the following Relational Database Service (RDS) options should you choose?

   A. Automated snapshots

   B. Multi-AZ

   C. Amazon Aurora

   D. Read replica

18. You're running a relational database on an EC2 instance backed by an EBS gp2 volume. Recently, as the frequency of writes to the database has increased, database performance has suffered. CPU and memory utilization remain at less than 50%, even during peak usage. Which of the following should you look at to determine where the bottleneck is?

   A. Volume queue length

   B. Network utilization

   C. The number of EBS snapshots being stored

   D. Provisioned IOPS

19. Users in your organization have been uploading files to an S3 bucket for temporary storage and driving up the organization's AWS bill. You deleted the S3 bucket but want to know as soon as anyone attempts to create another one. Which of the following services will assist you in this? (Choose two.)

   A. S3 server logs

   B. CloudTrail

   C. CloudWatch Events

   D. AWS Config

20. You've been using a custom automation solution to take EBS snapshots every 6 hours. Every month someone manually goes in and cleans up snapshots older than 30 days. You want to automate this process using a solution blessed by AWS. Which of the following fits the bill?

   A. Lambda

   B. S3 lifecycle configuration rules

   C. EBS data lifecycle manager

   D. AWS Systems Manager

21. Which of the following Relational Database Service (RDS) instance classes offers dedicated bandwidth for storage volumes?

   A. Burst-capable

   B. Memory-optimized

   C. Standard

   D. Network-optimized

22. If you enable automatic snapshots, how many days will RDS retain them by default?

   A. 1

   B. 7

   C. 28

   D. 35

23. How many days will RDS retain manual snapshots by default?

   A. 7 days

   B. 28 days

   C. 35 days

   D. Indefinitely

24. You've configured CloudTrail to log all management events in all regions. How long will these logs be retained by default?

   A. Indefinitely

   B. 14 days

   C. 15 days

   D. 60 days

   E. 90 days

25. You're storing CloudTrail logs and application logs in the same CloudWatch log group. The retention period for the log group is set to 1 year. Going forward, how can you ensure that the CloudTrail logs are retained for at least 2 years while the application logs continue to be retained for only 1 year? (Choose two.)

   A. Move the application log stream to a different log group.

   B. Change the log group retention period to 2 years.

   C. Change the log stream retention period to 2 years for the CloudTrail logs.

   D. Export the CloudTrail logs to an S3 bucket.

26. You want to create an alarm to monitor the `VolumeReadOps` metric for an EBS volume. The metric is stored with a 5-minute resolution. You need the alarm to trigger as soon as the metric crosses a threshold. What period should you use?

   A. 1 minute

   B. 5 minutes

   C. 10 minutes

   D. 15 minutes

27. You want to configure a CloudWatch alarm for a metric that updates every minute. You want the alarm to trigger if it crosses and remains crossing a threshold for 5 minutes. How should you configure this alarm? (Choose two.)

   A. Set the period to 1 minute.

   B. Set the period to 5 minutes.

   C. Set the datapoints to alarm to 1 out of 5.

   D. Set the datapoints to alarm to 5 out of 5.

28. Four hours ago, you configured a CloudWatch alarm to monitor CPU utilization on an EC2 instance, but today the alarm is in an INSUFFICIENT_DATA state. Which of the following could explain this? (Choose two.)

   A. The instance was restarted.

   B. The instance is stopped.

   C. The CPU utilization hasn't crossed the alarm threshold.

   D. The alarm period hasn't elapsed yet.

29. You want to be alerted if the average CPU utilization of an instance exceeds 90% *or* if the instance is stopped for more than 5 minutes. Which of the following will achieve this with minimal effort? (Choose two.)

   A. Create a single alarm to monitor the instance's `StatusCheckFailed_Instances` and `CPUUtilization` metrics.

   B. Configure the alarm to treat missing data as breaching.

   C. Create a single alarm to monitor the `CPUUtilization` metric.

   D. Create two alarms: one alarm to monitor CPU utilization and another to monitor the instance status.

30. You need to track the size of files in an S3 bucket over time. Which of the following can you use to get this information with minimal effort?

   A. AWS Config

   B. CloudTrail

   C. S3

   D. CloudWatch

31. What's the easiest way to assess your account's service limits for EBS IOPS?

   A. The EBS service Console

   B. CloudWatch

   C. A request sent to AWS support

   D. The EC2 service Console

32. You're running an application on an EC2 instance. The application is licensed for two CPU cores. What do you need to do to determine whether you're within your licensing agreement?

   A. Disable hyperthreading.

   B. View the number of vCPUs and make sure it's not more than two.

   C. Reconfigure the instance as a dedicated instance.

   D. Move the instance to a dedicated host.

33. You have an account limit of 10,000 customer master KMS keys. How many files can you store using SSE-KMS encryption before having to request a limit increase?

A. 1,000

B. 10,000

C. 100,000

D. Unlimited

34. You've created a VPC subnet with a CIDR of 10.0.0.0/24. How many IP addresses do you have available for use?

A. 255

B. 254

C. 251

D. 240

35. You're configuring a DynamoDB table for an application. Which of the following will ensure the application gets the most up-to-date data when reading from the table?

A. Enable strongly consistent writes.

B. Enable strongly consistent reads.

C. Enable eventually consistent reads.

D. Enable eventually consistent writes.

E. Use provisioned throughput.

36. One DynamoDB read capacity unit (RCU) will allow you to read, per second, one item up to what size? (Choose two.)

A. Anything between 1 and 8 KB using a strongly or eventually consistent read

B. 2 KB using a strongly consistent read

C. 4 KB using a strongly consistent read

D. 8 KB using an eventually consistent read

37. How many writes per second does 100 DynamoDB write capacity units (WCUs) give you for items each up to 1 KB in size?

A. 1

B. 10

C. 40

D. 100

38. Approximately how many in-flight messages can you have in a standard SQS queue?

A. 1000

B. 20,000

C. 120,000

D. 1,200,000

39. Approximately how many in-flight messages can you have in a FIFO SQS queue?

    A. 1000

    B. 20,000

    C. 120,000

    D. 1,200,000

40. Which of the following storage options provides the lowest storage rates per GB?

    A. EBS gp2

    B. Glacier

    C. S3 Standard

    D. S3 Standard-Infrequent Access

41. Which of the following offers the lowest priced transfer up to 1 GB per month?

    A. They are all the same.

    B. S3 Standard

    C. S3 One Zone-Infrequent Access

    D. S3 Standard-Infrequent Access

42. Which is best for seeing how your AWS bill has changed over time?

    A. Cost and Usage Reports

    B. Cost Explorer

    C. Budgets

    D. Trusted Advisor

43. Which of the following costs money to access via the API but is free using its web-based user interface?

    A. Cost and Usage Reports

    B. Budgets

    C. Cost Explorer

    D. Reserved Instance Reports

44. What's the maximum number of AWS Budgets custom budgets you can create for free?

    A. None

    B. One

    C. Two

    D. Four

45. You're running a set of applications in a single AWS region. You want to expand these applications to an additional region but need to determine how much it will cost. Which of the following can help you?

   A. Total Cost of Ownership (TCO) calculator

   B. Simple Monthly Calculator

   C. AWS Budgets

   D. Cost Explorer

46. Which of the following are *not* appropriate for running a long-running process? (Choose two.)

   A. Reserved instance

   B. On-demand instance

   C. Spot Instance

   D. Lambda

47. The number of on-demand EC2 instances you can run simultaneously in a region is limited by what?

   A. The memory limit

   B. The number of network interfaces

   C. The running on-demand EC2 instances limit

   D. The instance family's vCPU limit

48. A t2.small instance uses 1 vCPU. Your account has a per-region vCPU limit of 2400 vCPU for all standard instances. How many on-demand instances can you run simultaneously in a region?

   A. 24

   B. 25

   C. 120

   D. 1200

   E. 2400

49. You're running a SQL-backed Linux web application on several EC2 instances. Which of the following will allow you to run the application with minimal changes and at minimal cost?

   A. Lambda

   B. Auto Scaling

   C. ECS

   D. DynamoDB

50. You're running an application on a fleet of EC2 instances. As the application usage has grown, each instance is nearing its memory capacity. Which of the following can you do to minimize your operational costs while ensuring each instance doesn't run out of memory?

   A. Use a dedicated host.

   B. Use dedicated instances.

   C. Purchase non-convertible reserved instances.

   D. Purchase convertible reserved instances.

51. Which of the following is *not* a payment option for a reserved instance?

   A. All upfront

   B. Partial upfront

   C. On demand

   D. No upfront

52. You're using almost the full bandwidth of your 1 Gbps Internet connection. You're using this connection to access AWS resources. Which of the following Direct Connect options will give you at least 1 Gbps of bandwidth to AWS at the lowest cost?

   A. VPN

   B. Dedicated connection

   C. Hosted VIF

   D. Hosted connection

53. Which of the following can you *not* track using AWS Budgets?

   A. EC2 CPU utilization

   B. Reserved instance coverage

   C. EC2 running hours

   D. Unused elastic IP addresses

54. You've created cost allocation tags, but they don't show up in the Billing and Cost Management Console. Which of the following could explain why?

   A. You're not using AWS Organizations.

   B. Cost allocation tags are not retroactive.

   C. Cost allocation tags take up to 24 hours to show up in the Billing and Cost Management Console.

   D. You haven't activated the AWS-generated cost allocation tags.

55. What's the most cost-effective way to move 500 TB of data from your datacenter to S3?

   A. Get a Direct Connect connection and copy the data to S3.

   B. Use multiple AWS Snowball appliances.

   C. Use multiple AWS Snowball Edge appliances.

   D. Use a single AWS Snowball appliance.

56. Some files in an S3 bucket are usually accessed once every six months but occasionally are accessed more frequently. Other files in the bucket are accessed daily. How can you minimize S3 storage costs while keeping these infrequently accessed files available for immediate access?

    A. Move the files to the S3 Intelligent-Tiering storage class.

    B. Move the files to the Standard-Infrequent Access storage class.

    C. Create a lifecycle policy to move files older than six months to the Standard-Infrequent Access storage class.

    D. Enable versioning on the bucket.

57. You're running a web application on four EC2 instances in two availability zones. Every year during the Christmas season, your application experiences triple the amount of traffic. Which of the following is the most cost-effective approach to dealing with this seasonal spike?

    A. Purchase instance reservations.

    B. Use dynamic Auto Scaling.

    C. Use scheduled Auto Scaling.

    D. Use a step Auto Scaling policy.

58. Which of the following is the top cost-saving benefit of using ECS instead of EC2?

    A. Simplified configuration

    B. Faster launch times

    C. Better memory utilization

    D. Better CPU utilization

59. Which of the following are the most cost-effective uses of an instance reservation? (Choose two.)

    A. A Windows application that must run continuously Monday through Friday

    B. A Lambda function that launches an instance daily for batch processing

    C. An instance that processes batch jobs on files stored in S3

    D. ECS containers running a highly available Ruby application

60. Which of the following are valid Spot InstanceInstance durations? (Choose two.)

    A. 1 hour

    B. 4 hours

    C. 8 hours

    D. 24 hours

61. Your Ruby application needs to run a daily batch job that takes approximately 4 hours. Which of the following is the lowest cost option?

    A. Instance reservation

    B. Scheduled Spot Instance request

C. Persistent Spot Instance request

D. One-time Spot Instance request

62. You have two VPCs in different regions, and each VPC has three subnets. You want to connect your two datacenters to each of these subnets. The datacenters are not connected to each other. How many Direct Connect connections do you need?

A. One

B. Two

C. Three

D. Six

63. You have a branch office connected to a VPC via a VPN. You also have a datacenter connected to the same VPC via Direct Connect. You need to pass traffic between the branch office and the data center. How can you do this at the lowest cost?

A. Configure a transit gateway.

B. Configure VPN CloudHub to use the VPC for transit.

C. Add a Direct Connect connection to the branch office.

D. Add a private line between the datacenter and branch office.

64. Which of the following results in a Spot Instance terminating?

A. Increasing the target capacity

B. The spot request is cancelled.

C. The instance's workload completes.

D. The spot price rises above your maximum price.

65. Which of the following is the best way to minimize your costs when using Spot Instances?

A. Use on-demand instances alongside Spot Instances.

B. Reduce total target capacity.

C. Set an overall target cost per hour.

D. Stop instances instead of terminating them when interrupted.

66. How are you billed for DynamoDB usage in provisioned capacity mode?

A. Kilobytes read and written

B. Tables created

C. Read and write capacity units provisioned

D. Items read and written

67. How are you billed for DynamoDB usage in on-demand capacity mode?

A. Kilobytes read and written

B. Tables created

C. Read and write capacity units provisioned

D. Read and write request units used

68. You have a DynamoDB table in the us-east-1 region. You plan to use the global tables feature to replicate this table to US West 1 for high availability. How will this impact your cost?

 A. It will be reduced because you'll receive discounted pricing.

 B. It will stay the same.

 C. It will increase by approximately 50%.

 D. It will approximately double.

69. Which of the following S3 operations costs nothing?

 A. DELETE

 B. LIST

 C. GET

 D. Lifecycle transition requests into a non-Glacier storage tier

70. Which of the following cost nothing for inbound data transfers to AWS? (Choose two.)

 A. Direct Connect

 B. Elastic load balancer

 C. NAT gateway

 D. RDS

71. What's the cheapest option for storing one week of VPC flow logs?

 A. S3

 B. CloudWatch Metrics

 C. CloudTrail logs

 D. CloudWatch Events

72. What's the most cost-effective way to enable searching the last 180 days of API calls on a single account? (Choose two.)

 A. S3 Select

 B. Streaming CloudTrail logs to CloudWatch Logs

 C. Delivering CloudTrail logs to S3

 D. CloudTrail event history

 E. CloudWatch Logs Insights

73. Which of the following is the cheapest?

 A. Application load balancer

 B. NAT gateway

 C. RDS instance

 D. Nginx web proxy running on a t3.large on-demand instance

74. You need to log every GET request against an S3 bucket in the us-west-1 region. What's the most cost-effective way to do this?

    A. Create a CloudTrail to log global service events.

    B. Create a CloudTrail to log S3 data events.

    C. Create a CloudTrail to log S3 management events.

    D. Enable S3 server logging.

75. Which of the following is a factor in the cost of AWS resources?

    A. Availability zone

    B. Region

    C. Internet connection speed

    D. Linux distribution

76. You've registered the domain name example.com with a non-AWS registrar. Your lease on the domain is 10 years. Which of the following is the most cost-effective option for using this domain name to host a web application hosted behind an AWS application load balancer?

    A. Create a Route 53 public hosted zone.

    B. Transfer the domain name to Route 53.

    C. Create a non-alias resource record.

    D. Create a Route 53 private hosted zone.

77. How much data transfer out does CloudFront offer in the free tier?

    A. 1 GB

    B. 5 GB

    C. 10 GB

    D. 50 GB

78. What is the cost of using a dedicated IP address per SSL/TLS certificate at a CloudFront edge location?

    A. Free

    B. $60 per month

    C. $600 per month

    D. $600 per year

79. Which of the following is true regarding the cost-effectiveness of using CloudFormation?

    A. CloudFormation costs extra to use versus creating resources manually.

    B. Resources can be provisioned as needed and deleted quickly.

    C. CloudFormation uses Lambda, and you must pay these execution costs.

    D. Resources created with CloudFormation cost less.

80. EC2 Auto Scaling dynamic scaling policies are an example of which of the following approaches?

   A. Prediction-based

   B. Time-based

   C. Demand-based

   D. Buffer-based

81. Which of the following is free?

   A. A public IP address attached to a stopped instance

   B. An elastic IP address attached to a stopped instance

   C. A public IP address attached to a running instance

   D. A Route 53 public hosted zone attached to a running instance

82. On a regular basis, you manually update an application running on a fleet of EC2 instances. You're considering automating the update process so that developers can trigger automatic updates by simply pushing application updates to an S3 bucket. Which of the following services is most cost-effective for this task? (Choose two.)

   A. CodeCommit

   B. CodeBuild

   C. CodePipeline

   D. CodeDeploy

83. Which of the following is the most cost-effective and automated option for performing a rolling application upgrade on EC2 instances in an Auto Scaling group?

   A. CodeStar

   B. CloudFormation

   C. CodeDeploy

   D. AWS Systems Manager

84. Which of the following can you use to dynamically populate a CloudFormation parameter with a specific AMI ID?

   A. Systems Manager

   B. Simple Notification Service

   C. Lambda

   D. S3

85. You have thousands of EC2 instances spread across multiple regions. These instances do not persistently store data on their EBS volumes. No less than every three months, you have to ensure these instances have the latest operating system patches and application updates. Which of the following is the most cost-effective approach to handling these regular updates?

   A. Use CodeDeploy to update the instances.

   B. Use AWS Systems Manager to update the instances.

C. Create a new AMI with the changes baked in, and use it in all regions.

D. For each region, create a new AMI with the changes baked in.

86. Which of the following is the cheapest option for sending 90,000 notification emails per month?

A. Simple Email Service

B. Simple Notification Service

C. Simple Queue Service

D. CloudWatch Alarms

87. You have an EC2 instance running Amazon Linux in a private subnet. What's the most cost-effective way to temporarily connect it to the Internet to download operating system updates? (Choose two.)

A. Create a NAT gateway.

B. Create an Internet gateway and default route.

C. Assign the instance an elastic IP address.

D. Use AWS Patch Manager.

88. Your company needs to host a static website for employees to use. The website will consist of images, videos, and JavaScript. Which of the following is the most cost-effective way to host this application on AWS?

A. CloudFront

B. EC2

C. S3

D. DynamoDB

89. Which of the following elastic services allows multiple consumers to read the same message from a single producer?

A. Simple Queue Service

B. Amazon MQ

C. Kinesis

D. SNS

90. Which of the following is true regarding Amazon Certificate Manager (ACM)?

A. Certificates are never copied across regions.

B. It can automatically install certificates on EC2 instances.

C. You can export public certificates generated by ACM.

D. It renews certificates automatically.

91. You run a video hosting website that stores videos in S3. All resources are in the us-west-1 region. What's the most cost-effective way to minimize buffering time for mobile users in Japan?

    A. Use CloudFront.

    B. Replicate the videos to buckets in the Tokyo region.

    C. Use Route 53 latency records.

    D. Use AWS Mobile Hub.

92. You're running a web service on EC2 instances behind an elastic load balancer. These instances are part of an EC2 Auto Scaling group that monitors the ELB status. Users access the web service elastic load balancer listener using the domain name example.com, for which you have a public Route 53 hosted zone. If the web service on an instance fails, you want the instance taken out of load balancing in under 10 seconds. How can you accomplish this?

    A. Configure the Auto Scaling group to use instance health checks.

    B. Configure the example.com resource record to evaluate the target's health less than every 10 seconds.

    C. Create a Route 53 health check that checks the ELB health less than every 10 seconds.

    D. Configure the target group's health check and set the interval to less than 10 seconds.

93. You own a block of public IP addresses. Which of the following services can you assign them to using Bring Your Own IP (BYOIP)?

    A. Network load balancer

    B. Lambda

    C. S3

    D. RDS

94. You're developing a custom monitoring application that will access the AWS Health API. Which of the following is required to achieve this at the lowest cost?

    A. Root API credentials

    B. API gateway

    C. A Business support plan

    D. A Developer support plan

95. Which of the following is the cheapest S3 encryption option?

    A. SSE-KMS customer-managed CMK

    B. SSE-KMS AWS-managed CMK

    C. Client-side encryption using KMS

    D. SSE-ACL

96. Your development team uses a set of EC2 instances. Each developer has their own instance that they have customized. The instances don't need to be available after 6:00 p.m. or on the weekends. How can you maximally reduce the cost of these instances without ongoing manual intervention?

    A. Use CloudWatch Events to stop and start the instances on a schedule.

    B. Purchase instance reservations for the instances.

    C. Use Scheduled Auto Scaling actions to set the group size to 0 at 6:00 p.m.

    D. Use CloudWatch Events to terminate and re-create the instances on a schedule.

97. Which of the following services is the most cost-effective for querying 1 TB of data stored in a PostgreSQL database?

    A. Redshift

    B. Redshift Spectrum

    C. RDS

    D. DynamoDB

98. What's the most cost-effective option for synchronous database replication with RDS?

    A. Multi-AZ

    B. Read replica

    C. Automated snapshots

    D. S3 replication

99. What's the most cost-effective option for asynchronous database replication with RDS?

    A. Multi-AZ

    B. Read replica

    C. Automated snapshots

    D. S3 replication

100. What's the most cost-effective solution for backing up an on-premises application running on a Windows Server 2016 VM?

    A. Use AWS VM import/export.

    B. Perform a block copy of the server to a Snowball appliance.

    C. Perform a block copy of the server to a Snowball Edge appliance.

    D. Use Storage Gateway.

101. What happens if your maximum Spot price for an instance consistently exceeds the on-demand price?

    A. Your maximum Spot price will be automatically reduced to the on-demand price.

    B. The instance will run indefinitely.

    C. The instance will terminate or hibernate.

    D. This isn't allowed; Your Spot price can't exceed the on-demand price.

102. How can you use Spot Instances in an Auto Scaling group?

   A. You can't.

   B. Request Spot Instances in the launch template.

   C. Request Spot Instances in the Auto Scaling group configuration.

   D. Create the Spot Instances first and add them to the group.

103. You're running a fleet of Amazon Linux EC2 instances in an Auto Scaling group. A new Amazon Linux AMI has been released with the latest security updates. What's the most cost-effective and easiest way to update your instances?

   A. Create a new launch configuration that uses the new AMI.

   B. Update the launch configuration with a script that installs any available security updates.

   C. Use AWS Systems Manager Patch Manager.

   D. Update the launch template to use the new AMI.

104. What's the most cost-effective and secure way of granting an application on an EC2 instance access to a DynamoDB table? (Choose two.)

   A. Grant a role access to the table.

   B. Hardcode AWS credentials into the application.

   C. Use AWS Secrets Manager.

   D. Associate an instance profile role with the instance.

105. You're running an RDS instance that is running low on memory, resulting in slow read queries for your application. What's the most cost-effective and quickest way to resolve this?

   A. Reboot the instance.

   B. Use multi-AZ.

   C. Upgrade the instance type.

   D. Create a read replica.

106. You plan to migrate an on-premises MySQL database to AWS. You expect this database to double in size every six months. Which of the following is the most cost-effective option that requires the least ongoing effort?

   A. RDS using the MySQL engine

   B. Amazon Aurora

   C. RDS using the MariaDB engine

   D. An EC2 instance running MySQL

107. You need to identify any traffic that's allowed by a VPC security group. How can you accomplish this in the most cost-effective way?

   A. Enable VPC flow logging to log only allowed traffic to CloudWatch Logs.

   B. Enable VPC flow logging to log all traffic to an S3 bucket and search the logs for the word *NODATA*.

C. Enable VPC flow logging to log all traffic to an S3 bucket, and search the logs for the word *ACCEPT*.

D. Enable VPC flow logging to log all allowed traffic to an S3 bucket.

108. You have an EC2 instance running a web server in a private subnet, an S3 bucket, and a CloudFront distribution. You need to make a 2 GB file available for download. Which of the following is the cheapest and quickest option?

A. Store the file on an EFS volume.

B. Upload the file to an S3 bucket and make the file public.

C. Upload the file to the instance and make it available for download.

D. Make the file available via the CloudFront distribution.

109. Which of the following is the least expensive option for migrating files on an on-premises NFS file server to AWS S3?

A. Snowball

B. Snowball Edge

C. Storage Gateway—Volume Gateway

D. Storage Gateway—File Gateway

110. You have an on-premises server that connects to an iSCSI LUN for storage. You want to continuously back up this data to AWS. Which of the following should you use?

A. Snowball

B. Snowball Edge

C. Storage Gateway—Volume Gateway

D. Storage Gateway—File Gateway

111. What's the costliest Glacier retrieval type?

A. Bulk

B. Standard

C. Expedited

D. Provisioned

112. Which of the following does *not* include a capacity reservation?

A. Dedicated instances

B. Dedicated hosts

C. Standard reserved instances

D. Convertible reserved instances

113. What's the minimum yearly required utilization for a scheduled instance?

A. 416 hours

B. 600 hours

C. 1200 hours

D. 2400 hours

Domain

8

Practice Test

1. Which of the following is not a valid ECS metric?

   A. MemoryUtilization

   B. GPUReservation

   C. ClusterService

   D. CPUReservation

2. Which of the following may cause an EC2 instance to fail its status check? (Choose two.)

   A. Boot sector corruption

   B. Overloaded network interface

   C. Application memory leak

   D. Disk full

3. Which AWS CLI command can show you the system status of an EC2 instance?

   A. `aws cloudwatch describe-instance-status`

   B. `aws ec2 describe-instance-status`

   C. `aws ec2 describe-system-status`

   D. `aws cloudwatch get-instance-status`

4. A junior administrator uses the AWS CLI for routine tasks. He's trying to use the AWS CLI to view the status of EC2 instances. Every time he tries, he receives an error indicating he doesn't have access. How can you resolve this?

   A. Grant the admin permissions in the CloudWatchReadOnlyAccess AWS managed IAM policy.

   B. Grant the admin permissions in the AmazonEC2ReadOnly AWS managed IAM policy.

   C. Create a new API key for the admin.

   D. Tell the admin to use the AWS management Console.

5. Which of the following operating systems can the CloudWatch agent *not* run on?

   A. BSD

   B. Windows Server 2008

   C. RHEL

   D. SUSE Linux

6. You want to find out which users are authenticating to a Windows server running on-premises. Which of the following can help you gather this information?

   A. CloudWatch Logs agent

   B. EC2

   C. CloudWatch Events

   D. AWS Directory Service

7. What does the CloudWatch Logs agent use to encrypt log data in transit?

A. PGP

B. KMS

C. HTTPS

D. SSL

8. What does the CloudWatch Logs use to encrypt log data at rest?

A. KMS

B. PGP

C. Client encryption

D. CloudHSM

9. Which of the following shows you all AWS service issues?

A. Simple Notification Service

B. Service Health Dashboard

C. CloudWatch

D. Personal Health Dashboard

10. Which of the following AWS services analyzes VPC traffic for security threats?

A. Inspector

B. GuardDuty

C. CloudTrail

D. VPC Flow Logs

11. Which of the following lets you securely run arbitrary commands on a Red Hat EC2 instance in a private subnet without using your own SSH client?

A. Telnet

B. EC2 Instance Connect

C. RDP

D. EC2 Console Output

12. Which of the following services uses SQL?

A. EMR

B. RedShift

C. CloudWatch Log Insights

D. Minerva

13. Which EC2 Auto Scaling option requires the least effort to implement?

A. Dynamic scaling policies

B. Scheduled scaling

C. Predictive scaling

D. Lifecycle scaling

14. You're running a dynamic web application on two EC2 instances in different regions. You're load balancing traffic to the application using Route 53 latency resource records. The CPU utilization on these instances intermittently spikes to nearly 100% and users report a slowdown during this time. Which of the following will offer the most performance improvement?

   A. Implement Auto Scaling groups.

   B. Move the instances into the same region.

   C. Implement an application load balancer.

   D. Use Route 53 weighted records instead of latency records.

15. Which of the following is true of a launch template?

   A. It's versioned.

   B. It can be used with ECS.

   C. It can't be edited.

   D. You can tag specific versions of a launch template.

   E. It requires an AMI ID.

16. Which of the following is true of a launch configuration? (Choose two.)

   A. It's not versioned.

   B. It can be used with ECS.

   C. It can't be edited.

   D. It requires an AMI ID.

17. You need to implement a highly available MySQL database in AWS. It must be synchronously backed up. Which of the following Relational Database Service (RDS) options should you choose?

   A. Automated snapshots

   B. Multi-AZ

   C. Amazon Aurora

   D. Read replica

18. Which of the following services allows for decoupling application components by reliably passing messages between applications?

   A. Lambda

   B. SQS

   C. Email

   D. SNS

19. By default, how long does a sent message remain in an SQS queue?

    A. It's deleted immediately.

    B. 1 day

    C. 4 days

    D. 14 days

    E. 30 days

20. What's the longest a sent message can stay in an SQS queue?

    A. 1 minute

    B. 1 day

    C. 4 days

    D. 14 days

    E. 30 days

21. Which of the following can be used to temporarily store a 1 MB binary file? (Choose two.)

    A. S3

    B. DynamoDB

    C. SQS

    D. Lambda

    E. SNS

22. Which of the following should you *not* use to store session state?

    A. DynamoDB

    B. Redis

    C. Elasticache

    D. Memecached

    E. SQS

23. You have two different AWS accounts. In one account you have an instance in the availability zone us-east-1a, while in the other account you have an instance in the AZ us-east-1b. Which of the following is true of this configuration?

    A. This is a violation of the AWS terms of service.

    B. The instances are in different physical locations.

    C. The instances may be in the same physical location.

    D. The instances may be in different regions.

24. Using one domain name, you want to direct traffic to a different instance based on the URL path. Which of the following should you use? (Choose two.)

    A. Network load balancer

    B. Application load balancer

    C. Host-based routing

    D. Path-based routing

25. A friend who uses AWS for her personal website is reporting that the US-West-1c availability zone is having an EC2 outage. Your company has EC2 instances in the US-West-1c zone but isn't experiencing any problems. How should you respond to your friend's report?

    A. Take no action.

    B. Migrate your instances to a different zone.

    C. Create an Auto Scaling group.

    D. Open a proactive support ticket with AWS.

26. You want to grant a user in another AWS account access to a file in an S3 bucket. Which of the following should you do?

    A. Use an IAM policy.

    B. Disable SSE-S3 encryption.

    C. Make the file public.

    D. Use a resource-based policy.

27. You have an EC2 instance running an Apache web server on TCP port 444. A public-facing application load balancer is configured to listen for HTTPS traffic and proxy it to the instance. But when you browse to the load balancer's endpoint, you get a "gateway timeout" error. Which of the following should do to resolve this? (Choose two.)

    A. On the security group attached to the instance, add an inbound rule for HTTPS.

    B. On the security group attached to the instance, add an inbound rule for TCP port 444.

    C. On the security group attached to the application load balancer, add an outbound rule for TCP port 444.

    D. On the security group attached to the application load balancer, add an outbound rule for HTTPS.

28. Which of the following is designed to store long-term credentials?

    A. IAM

    B. STS

    C. Secrets Manager

    D. KMS

29. You have an IAM role to grant specific permissions to DynamoDB. This role is attached to an instance profile. You need to also grant the role permissions to an S3 bucket. Which of the following can you do to accomplish this? (Choose two.)

    A. Create a bucket policy to grant the role access.

    B. Add the permissions to the instance profile.

    C. Create a new IAM role with just the S3 permissions and add it to the instance profile.

    D. Add the permissions to the IAM role.

30. The KMS custom key store depends on which of the following?

    A. IAM

    B. CloudHSM

    C. VPC

    D. CloudTrail

31. Which of the following can you export?

    A. KMS-generated CMK

    B. Private TLS certificates from ACM

    C. Marketplace AMIs

    D. SSE-S3 key

32. You've created a custom Windows AMI and used it to successfully launch several EC2 instances, but none of the instances show up in AWS Simple Systems Manager inventory. Which of the following could be the reason? (Choose two.)

    A. The instances are in a private subnet.

    B. The SSM agent never ran.

    C. The instances are in a public subnet.

    D. The instances' security group has no outbound rules.

    E. The instances aren't running.

33. You need to provide a client's IAM principal with access to an S3 bucket. The client has given you a 64-character string. What else do you need to grant them access?

    A. ARN

    B. Account number

    C. IAM username

    D. The IAM principal's access key ID

34. A colleague wants to create a VPC subnet with a CIDR of 10.0.0.0/28. What should you tell them?

    A. AWS doesn't allow this CIDR.

    B. It will give them 11 usable addresses.

    C. It will give them 10 usable addresses.

    D. It will give them 16 usable addresses.

    E. This CIDR will leave room for only one subnet.

35. You've attempted to use your root access key to enumerate some AWS resources using the AWS CLI, but you're getting an error. Which of the following could be the reason?

    A. The access key is expired.

    B. Root access keys are blocked by default.

    C. The time on your workstation is wrong.

    D. The root user doesn't have the proper permissions.

36. For the next 24 hours you want to monitor a VPC for unusually large volumes of traffic Which of the following should you do?

    A. Enable GuardDuty.

    B. Enable VPC flow logging.

    C. Enable Inspector.

    D. Create a CloudWatch alarm to monitor VPC traffic.

37. You're running a web service on an EC2 instance. You want Route 53 to return the private IP address of the instance. How can you achieve this?

    A. Use a private hosted zone.

    B. Create a simple resource record.

    C. Create an alias record.

    D. This isn't possible.

38. You're attempting to set up a VPC peering connection between two VPCs, VPC A and VPC B. In VPC A you've created the peering connection and configured the route table, NACLs, and security groups to allow access to an ENI in VPC B. Which of the following must you do to get a working VPC peering connection? (Choose two.)

    A. Create a new peering connection on the VPC B side.

    B. Accept the peering connection on the VPC B side.

    C. Create a transit gateway in VPC A.

    D. Configure the route table, security groups, and NACLs in VPC B.

    E. Create a transit gateway in VPC B.

39. A dual-stack Windows application requires IPv4 and IPv6. Which of the following is required to implement this application in a VPC?

    A. Allocate an IPv6 CIDR for the VPC.

    B. Place the instance in a public subnet.

    C. Create an IPv6 gateway.

    D. IPv6 isn't supported for Windows instances.

40. Which of the following does Direct Connect provide?

   A. Reduced jitter

   B. Packet capture

   C. Encryption

   D. Authentication

41. Which of the following elastic load balancing features can result in an uneven distribution of traffic to instances?

   A. Session stickiness

   B. Cross-zone load balancing

   C. SSL offload

   D. Path-based routing

42. You have an EC2 instance with an elastic IP address associated with it. IPv6 is enabled in the instance's public subnet. How can you ensure that hosts on the Internet are able to reach the instance via IPv6?

   A. Disable IPv4 on the instance.

   B. Assign a global unicast IPv6 address to the instance.

   C. Allocate and associate an elastic IPv6 address to the instance.

   D. Create an egress-only Internet gateway.

43. Which of the following VPC attributes determines whether the Amazon DNS server is enabled?

   A. enableDnsSupport

   B. enableDnsHostnames

   C. enableDnsResolution

   D. enableDns

44. You suspect unauthorized SSH access to an EC2 instance. How can you immediately shut down all SSH access to the instance without affecting other instances in the same subnet?

   A. Shut down the instance.

   B. Modify the instance's security group to remove the rule allowing SSH access.

   C. Create an inbound NACL rule to deny SSH access to the instance's private IP address.

   D. Create an inbound NACL rule to deny SSH access to the instance's public IP address.

45. Which of the following does the URL `https://d123456abcdef7.cloudfront.net` indicate?

    A. An elastic load balancer

    B. A CloudFlare distribution

    C. An HTTP distribution

    D. An RTMP distribution

46. Which of the following cannot be a CloudFront origin?

    A. A public S3 bucket configured for static website hosting

    B. An elastic load balancer

    C. A public web server

    D. A Lambda function

47. You have an EC2 instance with a private and public IP address. You want to add this instance as a target to a network load balancer target group in the same VPC. How can you do this?

    A. Add the instance's private IP address to the target group.

    B. Add the instance's public IP address to the target group.

    C. Create a VPN connection.

    D. Create an elastic IP address for the instance.

48. When browsing to the public URL of an application load balancer, users receive a "503 Service Unavailable" error. The target group contains only EC2 instances. What could this indicate?

    A. The target instance didn't accept the connection from the load balancer.

    B. The target instance closed the connection from the load balancer.

    C. There are no healthy instances.

    D. The users are unable to connect to the application load balancer.

49. You want to use CloudWatch to find the average CPU utilization for an instance over a 30-minute period. The metric is updated every 5 minutes. Which statistic and period should you use?

    A. The Average statistic with a 5-minute period

    B. The Sample Count statistic with a 6-minute period

    C. The p50 statistic with a 30-minute period

    D. The Average statistic with a 30-minute period

    E. The Average statistic with a 6-minute period

50. You're running a relational database on an EC2 instance backed by an EBS io1 volume. As the frequency of writes to the database has increased, database performance has declined. Which of the following configuration parameters should you adjust to improve performance?

   A. Reduce the frequency of snapshots.

   B. Decrease the volume queue length.

   C. Increase the number of provisioned IOPS.

   D. Increase the disk size.

51. Which of the following protocols does EFS use?

   A. CIFS

   B. SMB

   C. NetBIOS

   D. NFS

   E. FSx

52. On which type of gateway does AWS Storage Gateway allow you to use iSCSI?

   A. Volume Gateway

   B. File Gateway

   C. Tape Gateway

   D. Block Gateway

53. On which type of gateway does AWS Storage Gateway allow you to use NFS?

   A. Volume Gateway

   B. File Gateway

   C. Tape Gateway

   D. Block Gateway

54. Which of the following is required to enable MFA Delete?

   A. An EBS volume

   B. S3 object versioning

   C. A bucket policy

   D. A hardware token

55. You want to create a custom AMI based on an AMI from the AWS Marketplace. How can you do this? (Choose two.)

   A. Download the AMI.

   B. Launch an instance from the AMI.

   C. Copy the AMI.

   D. Take a snapshot of the instance.

   E. Take a snapshot of the AMI.

56. Which of the following can launch the SBE EC2 instance types from an AMI?

    A. Fargate

    B. Snowball Edge

    C. ECS

    D. There is no such thing as the SBE instance type.

57. An SSE-C encrypted object named `file.txt` exists in an S3 bucket on which versioning is enabled. What will happen if you try to delete this object?

    A. S3 will create a delete marker.

    B. S3 will create a delete marker only if you provide the encryption key.

    C. S3 will delete the object.

    D. S3 will delete the object only if you provide the encryption key.

    E. S3 will neither delete the object nor create a delete market.

58. What happens when you delete a delete marker from a versioned S3 object?

    A. This isn't possible.

    B. It disables versioning.

    C. The object is deleted.

    D. The object reappears.

59. Which Glacier retrieval option lets you access data in less than 5 minutes?

    A. Defrost

    B. Expedited

    C. Icepick

    D. Emergency

    E. Bulk

60. Where does AWS Storage Gateway permanently store data?

    A. NFS vaults

    B. EBS

    C. Local volumes

    D. S3 buckets

Appendix

Answers to Practice Tests

Domain 1: Monitoring and Reporting

1. C. The correct command to view the metrics available in the Amazon EC2 instance namespace is aws cloudwatch list-metrics --namespace AWS/EC2. The others are not using the appropriate commands/syntax.

2. B. You can look up available Amazon CloudWatch metrics in the CloudWatch Console, which is available inside of the AWS Management Console. Once you are in the CloudWatch Console, simply click Metrics and then you can search for the desired metric. You can't look up Amazon CloudWatch metrics in the Amazon EC2 Console, the Amazon CloudTrail Console or the Amazon Trusted Advisor Console.

3. D. You can access Amazon CloudWatch via the Amazon CloudWatch Console, the AWS CLI, the Amazon CloudWatch API, and the AWS SDK (this was not listed as an option in this question but is a valid method to access Amazon CloudWatch).

4. C. Amazon EC2 Auto Scaling can be set up to utilize Amazon CloudWatch alarms to trigger when an autoscaling event needs to occur. AWS Lambda scales automatically as needed, and Amazon S3 and Amazon VPC are not related to compute load.

5. A, B, D. ALARM, OK, and INSUFFICIENT_DATA are valid alarm states for AWS CloudWatch. READY, OFFLINE, and WARNING were made up for this question.

6. A. You will be able to do as you have been asked since a single region can have up to 5000 Amazon CloudWatch alarms.

7. B. INSUFFICIENT_DATA occurs for a few reasons. In this case, an *existing* alarm was showing this alarm state on an established server. The best explanation as to why this is occurring is that there is not enough data available for the metric to determine whether it should be in OK or ALARM, so the data is most likely missing. It is highly unlikely that CloudWatch is experiencing an outage, especially since this is a single server having the issue. As this is a server that is established and has been monitored for a while, it is unlikely that the alarm has just been started. If your server is offline, you will most likely be getting calls stating that an application or service is unavailable. Since this is not the case, the server is probably online.

8. C. INSUFFICIENT_DATA occurs for a few reasons. In this case, a new alarm was showing this alarm state on an established server. The best explanation as to why this is occurring is that there is not enough data available for the metric to determine whether it should be in OK or ALARM because the alarm has just started. It is highly unlikely that CloudWatch is experiencing an outage, especially since this is a single server having the issue. If your server is offline, you will most likely be getting calls stating that an application or service is unavailable. Since this is not the case, the server is probably online.

9. A. An SNS topic can send text (SMS) messages when an Amazon CloudWatch alarm is triggered. Your bosses would need to subscribe to the SNS topic, and then they will be able to receive text messages when the Amazon CloudWatch alarm is triggered. While you could write a custom Lambda function to send an email, emails are not real-time

notification. Since the Lambda function would need to be written and maintained, it would have higher administrative overhead than the SNS topic would. An SQS queue is wrong in this case as these queues are designed to handle communications between applications, services and microservices. SQS queues don't sent SMS text messages. The answer to questions on AWS exams will never be third-party solutions.

10. D. You can get to your evaluation interval (the 5-minute time period) by multiplying the number of data points by the number of units in the time period. Since you want Amazon CloudWatch to trigger an alarm after four failed evaluations in a 5-minute period, you would set data points to alarm at 4, and the evaluation period would need to be 1 minute.

11. B. Amazon CloudWatch keeps 1-minute data points for 15 days, 5-minute data points for 63 days, and 1 hour data points for 455 days. You can't "create" an archive for data points, though you can archive them with an API call using *GetMetricStatistics*. You can't set CloudWatch to never delete data points.

12. A. Namespaces are used to group together Amazon CloudWatch metrics that are used for a similar source. For instance, AWS/EC2 is the namespace for Amazon EC2 metrics in Amazon CloudWatch.

13. C. Metrics for Amazon EC2 are located in the AWS/EC2 namespace. AWS/ELB contains the metrics for classic load balancers, AWS/EBS contains the metrics for Amazon EBS, and AWS/Auto Scaling contains the metrics for autoscaling. The names of the namespaces are usually straightforward depending on the service for which you want to locate metrics.

14. B. Metrics for an Application Load Balancer are located in the AWS/ApplicationELB namespace. AWS/ELB contains the metrics for classic load balancers, AWS/EBS contains the metrics for Amazon EBS, and AWS/Auto Scaling contains the metrics for autoscaling. The names of the namespaces are usually straightforward depending on the service for which you want to locate metrics.

15. D. You need to search for the statistic with a dimension in the same format that it was published. To retrieve statistics for a server metric that was created with the dimension listed in the question, you would need to specify the dimension in the same format: Server=Production,Site=Location1. Server=Production would not work by itself, and Server=Prod would not work as it is not a valid dimension either. Last, Server=Production,Site=Location is not valid because of the value after Site. It does not match the published dimension.

16. C. Memory utilization, including memory used and memory available, requires that an agent be installed on the EC2 instance for Amazon CloudWatch to gather statistics from it. Disk performance, network utilization and CPU utilization work with no agent installed.

17. B, E. EC2 instances have two types of status checks in Amazon CloudWatch, system status checks and instance status checks. System status checks monitor the hardware that the instance is using, whereas instance status checks monitor the network configuration and the software on your individual EC2 instances. The other types of checks were made up for this question.

18. A. There are many reasons an instance status check might fail. The most common issues include exhausted memory, a filesystem that has become corrupted, an incompatible kernel version, incorrect networking configurations, and possibly incorrect startup configurations.

19. C. There are many reasons an instance status check might fail. The most common issues include exhausted memory, a filesystem that has become corrupted, an incompatible kernel version, incorrect networking configurations, and possibly incorrect startup configurations.

20. D. There are many reasons an instance status check might fail. The most common issues include exhausted memory, a filesystem that has become corrupted, an incompatible kernel version, incorrect networking configurations, and possibly incorrect startup configurations.

21. D. The command to check the status of your Amazon EC2 instances is `aws ec2 describe-instance-status`. The others were made up for this question and are not actual commands.

22. A. The managed policy CloudWatchReadOnlyAccess will give users the ability to view the metrics in CloudWatch without needing to gain access to the other AWS services. AmazonEC2ReadOnly would give them read-only permissions to EC2 but would not give them the permissions they need for Amazon CloudFront to work properly. The other two options, CloudWatchMetricsAccess and MetricsReadOnlyAccess, don't actually exist.

23. B. Basic monitoring provides metrics every 5 minutes, whereas detailed monitoring provides metrics every minute. The other two options are not valid monitoring types.

24. D. Basic monitoring provides metrics every 5 minutes, whereas detailed monitoring provides metrics every minute. The other two options are not valid monitoring types.

25. C. With Amazon CloudWatch Logs you can monitor logs from systems that are running in your on-premises datacenter or that are running in your AWS environment. Amazon CloudWatch Events is what sends the metrics to Amazon CloudWatch. Amazon S3 and Amazon EBS are both storage solutions but in this case would not be the correct response.

26. D. Supported Linux versions are Amazon Linux, Ubuntu, CentOS, Red Hat Enterprise Linux, and Debian. Solaris is not on the supported list. This is one of those things that you will just have to remember for the exam. As a side note, the Amazon CloudWatch Logs agent does in fact require Python. You can run version 2.6 and up.

27. B. You can use Red Hat Package Manager to install awslogs updates by using the `sudo yum update -y` command. This command can be scheduled in a cron job so that it is done automatically on a scheduled basis. Using wget to copy the package still results in a manual process, which is what you are trying to avoid in this question. Copying the package via FTP still results in a manual process. While you could script the installation of the package, the creation and the maintenance of the script result in higher administrative overhead.

28. C. When the Amazon CloudWatch Agent for Linux is originally installed by a Python script, then is later updated with RPM, configuration issues may result. RPM has no technical limitations that would result in the configuration issue mentioned. The update package in question would not require a restart for the agent to start sending logs to Amazon CloudWatch. A Debian package will generally not install on a Red Hat Linux–based system.

29. D. The Amazon CloudWatch Logs agent for Windows can be used to send IIS logs to CloudWatch.

30. B. The Amazon CloudWatch Logs agent for Windows can be used to send system logs to CloudWatch.

31. A. The EC2Config service is no longer supported in Windows Server 2016. Instead, you must use the Systems Manager (SSM) Agent. Since logs are getting to Amazon CloudWatch, you can rule out an issue with the log agent. The log agent does not rely on any specific update...the EC2Config service is not supported on Windows Server 2016 regardless of patch level. Amazon CloudWatch has no visibility into the internal workings of the server, including OS- and application-level logs without the log agent. If the log agent was not installed, you would not be getting logs sent to Amazon CloudWatch at all.

32. C. Log data is encrypted in transit and at rest within Amazon CloudWatch. This requires no special configuration on the part of a system administrator.

33. A. Detailed billing was made available to AWS customers back in December 2016. Detailed billing gives customers the ability to create reports to review usage in the AWS account, or the cost associated with individual log groups. There's no such thing as basic billing.

34. B. Each log group in Amazon CloudWatch can utilize up to 50 tags.

35. C. The best solution for your accounting department would be to use tags to identify the department that resources should be billed to. Tags will allow them to filter views in Amazon Cost Explorer. While your accounting department could certainly track usage manually, it is not the best method. You could prefix the names of most things with a department code, but that is a very manual process and not as easy to filter on.

36. D. AWS CloudTrail allows you to audit all API access including access from the AWS Management Console, AWS API, and the AWS CLI. While AWS IAM gives you the ability to add users and specify how they will authenticate and be authorized to use services, it does not provide auditing. AWS Trusted Advisor provides recommendations based on security, cost savings, etc., but does not provide auditing. Amazon CloudWatch is used to monitor systems and logs but does not audit access either.

37. A. By default, the trails created by AWS CloudTrail are stored in an S3 bucket that was specified when the trails were created. EBS is used to create drives for EC2 instances, EFS provides a filesystem that systems can map drives to, and Glacier is used for long-term storage archival options.

38. B. Amazon CloudWatch monitors performance and availability metrics, and AWS CloudTrail feeds API activity into Amazon CloudWatch Logs. By sending the API activity into Amazon CloudWatch, you are able to configure alarms on events of interest. CloudTrail does not send alerts—it only logs API activity. To get alerts from your trails, you must send the trail data to Amazon CloudWatch Logs. While Amazon CloudWatch can be used for billing alerts, AWS CloudTrail does not have anything to do with billing. It logs API activity.

39. C. In Amazon CloudWatch, basic monitoring updates using 5-minute periods, where detailed monitoring updates using 1-minute periods. The other two options were made up for this question.

40. A. In Amazon CloudWatch, basic monitoring updates using 5-minute periods, where detailed monitoring updates using 1-minute periods. The other two options were made up for this question.

41. A. `aws ec2 monitor-instances --instance-ids <instance-id>` will enable detailed monitoring for the EC2 instance specified by the instance-id provided in the command. The other commands don't exist.

42. C. `aws ec2 unmonitor-instances --instance-ids <instance-id>` will disable detailed monitoring for the EC2 instance specified by the instance-id provided in the command. The other commands don't exist.

43. D. Using the Sum statistic adds together all of the metrics and is very useful when trying to determine the total amount for any metric. In this example, you might use Sum on the DiskReadOps metric to get the information your boss requested. Average would not give you a total; instead it provides the average of all the metrics. Minimum and Maximum are used to find the highest and lowest metrics, so they would also not meet the criteria.

44. A. Admittedly this question was a bit easier…if you want to know the average of metrics, then you use an Average statistic. Minimum and Maximum are used to find the highest and lowest metrics so they would not meet the criteria. Sum is used to find the total of a given metric, not the average.

45. B. Using the Maximum statistic will give you the highest metric that has been measured. Minimum would give you the lowest metric measured. Sum is used to find the total of a given metric, and Average is used to find the average metric.

46. C. Minimum will yield the lowest numbered metric. Maximum would return the highest number, Sum would return the total amount of the metrics that were measured, and Average would return an average of all the metrics that were measured.

47. A. SampleCount can give you the total number of metrics that are being used in a statistical calculation. This can be helpful if you are trying to determine sample size. Sum gives you the total value of all the metrics added together but not the number of metrics. Sample and Number are not statistics that you can use.

48. A, D. In order to aggregate statistics across multiple Amazon EC2 instances, you must first enable detailed monitoring; then in Amazon CloudWatch, you can select the Amazon EC2 namespace, and select Across All Instances. Basic monitoring is enabled by default, but you need detailed monitoring to be able to do what the question asks. The Amazon CloudWatch namespace will not have Amazon EC2–related metrics. Standard monitoring is not a real thing; it was invented for this question.

49. B, C, E. You can choose to filter statistics by a specific Amazon EC2 instance, an Auto Scaling group, or by the AMI in use. You can't filter statistics by an AWS CloudTrail trail or by the elastic/application load balancer in use.

50. A. When the desired action is to reboot the Amazon EC2 instance that is having difficulty (failing its health checks for example), you can set the alarm action to trigger a reboot when a particular alarm is activated. Stopping and terminating don't reboot an Amazon EC2 instance. Recovering the instance does cause a reboot, but it will also migrate the Amazon EC2 instance to another physical host.

51. D. When you want an Amazon EC2 instance to recover itself, meaning that it migrates itself to another host, you select the alarm action of Recover the Instance. Reboot, stop and terminate are not used to recover an Amazon EC2 instance.

52. A. In this case, the best solution is to use Amazon CloudWatch to watch for low CPU utilization and set the alarm action to stop the instance. This will ensure that when the Amazon EC2 is not in use it will be turned off.

53. C. Terminating the Amazon EC2 instance effectively destroys it. It is a useful alarm action when you have some Amazon EC2 instances running a job. Once the job is complete, when you set the alarm action to terminate, the Amazon EC2 instances are destroyed afterward, which prevents you from paying for instances that are not in use. If you need to use an Amazon EC2 instance later, it is better to stop it than to terminate it. If an Amazon EC2 instance needs to run 24x7, then you should not use terminate on it.

54. D. You can view prior Amazon CloudWatch alarms in the History tab that is available in the Amazon CloudWatch Console. There is no History tab in the AWS Management Console. There is no Alarms tab in the AWS Management Console or the Amazon EC2 Management Console.

55. B. AWS Billing and Cost Management allows you to view your usage and create budgets. Trust Advisor can help determine methods to save money—think cost optimization—but it does not let you view usage in relation to billing. While AWS Billing and Cost Management exists in the AWS Management Console, you don't get usage information from the AWS Management Console; you get it from AWS Billing and Cost Management.

56. D. AWS CloudTrail logs every action taken in the AWS Billing and Cost Management Console. It can tell you if the change was made as the root user or an IAM user. Amazon CloudWatch does not track who made changes to what.

57. A. AWS Budgets includes the ability to set up an AWS Free Tier alert out of the box that will tell you if you are getting close to exceeding the limits of AWS Free Tier or if you are likely to exceed it based on forecasting of your usage. AWS CloudTrail does not make alarms on its own. Amazon CloudWatch does not have an out-of-the-box report for AWS Free Tier, though you could set one up manually.

58. C. To enable billing alerts, you must be logged in as the root user for the AWS account. You don't need a TAM; you can set up the billing alert once you are logged in as the root account.

59. C, D. When a health check is run on an Amazon EC2 instance, you can get types of statuses. OK means that all of the health checks have passed. If any of the health checks fail, then the status displayed is Impaired.

60. D. As the status checks themselves are a part of the Amazon EC2 instances, you can't disable them. You can, however, disable the CloudWatch alarms that utilize the status checks to trigger.

61. A,C. If you need to view the status checks for your organization's Amazon EC2 instances, you can look at them in either the Amazon EC2 Console or the Command Line. Status checks are not available through either Amazon CloudWatch or AWS CloudTrail.

62. A. You can create alarms based on status checks in the Amazon EC2 Console. This type of alarm is not created in Amazon CloudWatch. AWS CloudTrail is not used to create alarms, and the AWS Management Console does not give you the ability to create alarms, though it does allow you to get to the Amazon EC2 Console.

63. C. Amazon CloudWatch statistics are retained for 15 months. This gives you historical information on the availability and performance of your various systems.

64. B. You would use AWS CloudTrail to monitor all of the API calls performed against Amazon EC2 and Amazon EBS, including activities performed in the AWS Management Console. Amazon CloudWatch is not used to monitor API calls. The Amazon API Gateway is used as an API management service but would not be an appropriate response in this case. AWS Lambda allows you to execute code but does not monitor API calls.

65. D. AWS CloudTrail stores its trails in S3 buckets. Amazon EBS is used to provide storage drives on Amazon EC2 instances. Amazon EFS provides file-server-like experiences, but it is not used for storing AWS CloudTrail trails. Amazon EC2 instances are not used to store trails from AWS CloudTrail.

66. A. You should explain to your boss that you can validate AWS services using the Service Health Dashboard. The Service Health Dashboard allows you to select a continent and view the health of the various services. Amazon CloudWatch and AWS CloudTrail do not monitor all of the AWS services; they monitor the resources within your account.

67. C. The Personal Health Dashboard displays similar information to the Service Health Dashboard. The biggest difference is that you don't need to select a continent for the Personal Health Dashboard as you log in and it gives you the information based on where your assets are deployed. Neither Amazon CloudWatch nor AWS CloudTrail will give you the kind of information you are looking for.

68. A. Amazon Route 53 is Amazon's DNS service. If the DNS service is degraded and customers are not able to resolve name records to IP addresses, then your website will be down. Additionally, if you are using Amazon Route 53 for internal DNS, you have systems that are not able to communicate internally. Amazon Route 53 does not provide content caching services; that is the job of Amazon CloudFront. As Amazon Route 53 is an Amazon service, it will show up in both the Service Health Dashboard and the Personal Health Dashboard.

69. C. You can't grant access in Amazon CloudWatch for specific resources with AWS IAM. You must give permissions to view Amazon EC2 metrics as a whole; for example, you can't specify an instance or even a load balancer individually. The other options would not work and may give the end user more permissions than they need to do their job.

70. B. Using Amazon CloudWatch Logs allows you to collect all of your event logs in one location and filter on parts of those logs. From there, you can set an alarm in Amazon CloudWatch to trigger Amazon SNS, which will send a notification to anyone who is subscribed to the Amazon SNS topic. AWS CloudTrail does not collect event logs, nor does it allow filtering on logs. Amazon EC2 logs to Amazon CloudWatch, so Amazon EC2 Logs is not real. Amazon SNS is used to send the notification, but it does not collect and parse logs.

71. D. Amazon CloudWatch Logs can allow you to implement real-time monitoring. That paired with highly durable storage that has a low cost makes this the best solution. The answer on AWS exams will never be a third-party product, so that's generally an easy way to weed out a wrong answer if you're stuck. AWS CloudTrail is not used to monitor availability or performance; it monitors API calls. Amazon SNS is not used to monitor availability and performance, though it does pair well with Amazon CloudWatch to send notifications when an alarm is triggered.

72. C. Amazon CloudWatch Logs is the clear winner here. Using the Amazon CloudWatch Logs agent, you can rotate logs off of systems to preserve drive space and store those logs in low-cost storage within AWS. Amazon SNS does not store logs; it sends notifications based on topics. AWS CloudTrail does not store logs; it monitors API calls and then stores the data into trails on S3. Amazon EBS is used to add storage to servers and would not be the appropriate response in this case as you would need to attach it to an Amazon EC2 instance, which would raise the cost.

73. A. You can use access keys to authenticate the Amazon CloudWatch Logs agent instead of a username and password. As the access key is still tied to a username, you may want to check with your security team that it meets their criteria. While access keys are created in AWS IAM, AWS IAM is not a granular enough response to satisfy this question. While you can link your Active Directory environment to AWS, this is still not getting away from the need for service accounts. While Windows systems support mSA and gMSA, those may not work on older Windows Server systems and will not work on Linux systems.

74. C. You can use IAM roles to authenticate the Amazon CloudWatch Logs agent instead of a username and password. There is no username or password to manage with this approach, and it is the best solution to solve the need for the Amazon CloudWatch Logs agent while also meeting your security team's criteria. While IAM roles are created in AWS IAM, AWS IAM is not a granular enough response to satisfy this question. While you can link your Active Directory environment to AWS, this is still not getting away from the need for service accounts. While Windows systems support MSA and gMSA, those may not work on older Windows Server systems and will not work on Linux systems.

75. D. Amazon CloudWatch Logs Insights gives you the ability to take the data you have in Amazon CloudWatch and make it more actionable. It aids in the analysis of data and gives the ability to visualize the data more thoroughly. The Amazon CloudWatch Logs agent collects data from inside of the operating system but does not provide the greater analytics and visualization that they are requesting. AWS CloudTrail is not used for analytics; it collects any API-related events. Amazon Redshift is a data warehousing solution, and while it can aid with analytics, it is not a good fit for what the Operations Center has requested.

76. B. While you can't manually delete metrics, they are removed based on a schedule: 1-minute metrics are available for 15 days, 5-minute metrics are available for 63 days, and 1-hour metrics are available for 15 months.

77. C. You can accomplish this by creating a custom metric with a high resolution. High-resolution custom metrics can get data per second and can be retrieved in intervals of 1, 5, 10, 15, 30, or 60 seconds. Standard resolution is not correct as it gathers data every minute. Fast and detailed resolutions don't exist. For questions regarding custom metrics, just remember that you can have high or standard resolutions.

78. D. Amazon CloudWatch only allows you to use high-resolution metrics when you are using custom metrics.

79. C. To set a custom metric to use high resolution, you set the StorageResolution parameter to 1 through the PutMetricRequest API. StorageResolution is an optional field; if it is not specified, then standard resolution will be used by default.

80. C. High-resolution metrics don't cost any more or any less than standard-resolution metrics. You can do 1-, 5-, 10-, 15-, 30-, and 60-second intervals with high resolution.

81. A. The Amazon CloudWatch Logs agent default sending time is every 5 seconds; however, this is configurable. So the best solution would be to adjust this timer. The setting change is made to the Amazon CloudWatch Logs agent, not to Amazon CloudWatch itself. AWS CloudTrail is not used for pulling logs; instead it logs API activity.

82. C. Metric filters allow you to define what information a metric will count. In this case, you might create a metric filter that looks for the word *error* or search IIS logs for server-side errors such as the 500 series of HTTP response codes. The other filters listed are not real; they were made up for this question.

83. D. Amazon Kinesis allows you to connect your log stream and process the logs using the regex that you wanted to search on. Amazon CloudWatch Metric Filters do not support regex. Neither Amazon CloudWatch nor the AWS Management Console give you the ability to search by regex.

84. A. Amazon CloudWatch allows you to create high-resolution alarms that work with high-resolution custom metrics. These allow you to alert at 10- or 30-second intervals. Standard Amazon CloudWatch alarms do not allow you to alarm under a minute. There is no such thing as a detailed Amazon CloudWatch alarm.

85. B. Since none of your systems are having issues, you can safely adjust the threshold so that it is no longer breached. This will allow the Amazon CloudWatch alarm to clear and be OK. Deleting and re-creating the alarm won't help if the thresholds are set the same. While rebooting the instances may help temporarily, it is not a long-term solution. Installing the Amazon CloudWatch Logs agent will not help clear the alarm as Amazon CloudWatch is already receiving data for the alarm in question.

86. D. Amazon CloudWatch Dashboards will allow your Operations Center people to create their own custom dashboards. Amazon CloudWatch Logs does not give you the ability to create dashboards, and neither does AWS CloudTrail. You could potentially get some business analytics software on an Amazon EC2 to do what you are needing, but it would not be the best solution.

87. B. You can create a dashboard in Amazon CloudWatch Dashboards and monitor all of your systems and resources across all of the regions you are using. Both Amazon CloudWatch Logs and Amazon CloudWatch Logs Agent collect data, but they do not provide dashboards.

88. C. AWS CloudTrail is enabled by default on your account. The default setup will log 90 days' worth of API calls, though it is limited to logging management events only when the activity includes create, modify, or delete.

89. B. By default, AWS CloudTrail only logs management events that had a create, modify, or delete activity. To ensure that you are logging all events as your security team has requested, you will need to create a new trail and set it to gather all events, including management, data, and read-only activities.

90. C. Since all activity in the AWS Management Console calls APIs, all activity within the AWS Management Console is recorded by AWS CloudTrail. AWS Trusted Advisor makes recommendations based on best practices but does not log API calls. Both Amazon CloudWatch and Amazon CloudWatch Logs ingest logs. While Amazon CloudWatch creates alarms off of AWS CloudTrail data, it does not record API activity.

91. C, D. There are two methods you can use to ensure that AWS CloudTrail uses all regions, including new regions that are added. You can select Yes to apply to all of the regions while you are in the trail configuration page, or you set the IsMultiRegionTrail to True if you are using the AWS CLI/SDKs. You can't select Global from the region drop-down list, though it does appear if you go into a service with account-wide reach like IAM. While you can add the existing region manually, the ask is to ensure that future regions are added to the trail automatically.

92. A. As you can create up to five AWS CloudTrail trails in an AWS region, you can certainly create the two that your boss is asking for. Additionally, you can create one for management activity and one for data activity.

93. C. AWS CloudTrail log files are encrypted by default using S3 Server-Side Encryption (SSE). The only thing you would need to do is set up who should have access. This can be done via S3 bucket policies or with IAM.

94. B. By enabling MFA Delete, you guarantee that items in the S3 bucket can't be accidentally deleted as an MFA token must be used as a second factor of authentication before you are allowed to delete anything. While restricting access to the S3 bucket is certainly a best practice, it won't necessarily prevent people from accidentally deleting log files. Enabling versioning may be helpful, but it will not prevent accidental deletion. Lifecycle policies don't archive deleted objects; they can expire them and then transition them to long-term storage like Amazon Glacier.

95. D. The best way to meet the requirements of your legal team is to create a lifecycle rule in S3 that will automatically delete log files that are older than 90 days. You would not make this change in AWS CloudTrail or Amazon CloudWatch.

96. B. When an API event occurs, AWS CloudTrail will send that event into the log files within 15 minutes. There is no way to speed up the delivery of the event.

97. A. The most likely cause of the missing log files is that there was no API activity during that time frame. If AWS CloudTrail was misconfigured, then you would not see log files in the Amazon S3 bucket at all. If you don't have permissions to view the log files, you wouldn't know that some are missing from a specific time frame. If AWS CloudTrail doesn't have access to write to the Amazon S3 bucket, you would have no log files at all.

98. C. AWS CloudTrail offers the ability to enable log file integrity validation. This creates a hash value for the log file, which you can validate through the AWS CLI. Enabling encryption in Amazon S3 is a best practice, but it does not validate that the files have not been modified. An AWS Lambda function could be made to do this; however, it would require a fair amount of overhead. Manually hashing the files would work but would result in a lot of administrative overhead.

99. C. AWS Config allows you to evaluate configuration changes that are made against desired configuration to see if there is a conflict. If a conflict is identified, you can have AWS send a message via Amazon SNS to the security team and they can follow up. While Amazon CloudWatch provides monitoring, it does not monitor for baseline configurations. AWS CloudTrail is used for monitoring API calls, not desired configuration. AWS Lambda is used to run functions when something triggers the function.

100. C. To meet your legal department's request, you should enable AWS Config, and then create an SNS topic. Subscribe them to the topic and they will get notifications anytime a configuration change is made to their system. Amazon CloudWatch and AWS CloudTrail would not be used for notifying users about configuration changes, though SNS certainly would be. It is tempting to think of SMS as a text message, but in AWS terms, that belongs to another product. Using Amazon SNS will allow you to send text messages and emails.

101. D. The best solution to this would be to use AWS Config to view the configuration history of the resource that suffered the outage and use AWS CloudTrail to see who made the change. Amazon CloudWatch would not be a good solution for this case. You may get information once the outage occurred, but Amazon CloudWatch is not monitoring for configuration changes. While you could use AWS CloudTrail to look for the events that led up to the outage, you will have a lot of noise that you will need to sort through to find the relevant records. AWS Config can certainly send messages anytime a configuration change is made, but this could end up being noisy. If it wasn't set up prior to this event occurring, you won't have any emails related to the incident.

102. A. You can create rules in AWS Config that look for things like unsecured port numbers, etc. You can then create a report based on the outcome of those rules. AWS CloudTrail would not be a good solution as you would have to know exactly what to look for. Amazon CloudWatch does not monitor for compliance; it monitors for availability and performance metrics.

103. C. AWS Config can measure for configuration drift and alert you to changes; however, it can't prevent changes, nor can it change settings back. There is no Enforce option when you set up AWS Config. AWS Config doesn't automatically revert settings; it can only alert that a change has occurred that has taken the system out of compliance with the desired configuration.

104. B. AWS Config has the ability to work using multi-account multi-region data aggregation. To view the data in AWS Organizations, you will need to create the aggregator in AWS Organizations. While you can create an aggregator in one of the regions you are using, the question asked if you can create it in AWS Organizations.

105. A. AWS Config has the ability to work using multi-account multi-region data aggregation. Since you want to combine the results of AWS Config from several regions into the region that has the majority of your resources, you should create the aggregator in the region where you want to combine results. You would not create the aggregator in AWS Organizations as you want to view the combined data in one of your regions, not from your AWS Organizations console.

106. C. AWS Config is not enabled by default. You need to enable it once per region for any region you want to have monitored.

107. C. Since changes made in AWS Config are API calls, AWS CloudTrail will log all changes that are made to AWS Config. Amazon CloudWatch would not monitor API calls; it monitors performance and availability metrics. AWS IAM does not monitor API calls.

108. B. With AWS Config, you are limited to 150 rules. If you need more than 150 rules, then you need to contact AWS to increase the number of rules allowed on your account. Once the increase has been completed, you will be able to create the necessary rules.

109. B. You can set periodic rules to run every 1, 3, 6, 12, or 24 hours. So your response should be to set up the rule to run every 6 hours.

110. D. You will need to authorize the aggregator account in AWS Config so that it can be used to gather data from AWS Config and return it to the aggregator in the other account that you created. AWS Config will not be able to gather information from your other AWS accounts until it has been authorized. Creating a role does not authorize the aggregator account to do what it needs to do. Adding a new AWS IAM account into each AWS account does not provide authorization.

111. C. AWS Config sends notification when the status on an object changes. Since the resource was already reported as noncompliant, you will not get another notification until it is compliant. It would be highly unlikely that AWS Config is experiencing an outage. If AWS Config was misconfigured, you would not have received the first notification at all.

112. D. When you add a security group to an Amazon EC2 instance, AWS Config records changes for the Amazon EC2 instance, the security group, primary resources, and related resources.

113. A. You can tell your Operations Center team that AWS Config can record OS patches, application installations, network configurations, and really any change that is made to the systems.

114. B. The master account is the one used to create the organization as well as invite or remove other AWS accounts. The root account is the most privileged user in an AWS account but not in AWS Organizations. An IAM user would not be able to create an organization or add/remove AWS accounts. A shared access key is used to log in through the CLI, not into the AWS Management Console where you set up AWS Organizations.

115. C. The AWS Billing and Cost Management Dashboard will allow them to monitor what the current spend is now and even sort by service. AWS Budgets is good for setting alerts when you exceed a specified amount. The AWS Management Console does not contain the current spend…though it does provide a shortcut to get to the AWS Billing and Cost Management Dashboard. AWS Trusted Advisor gives you recommendations in several areas but does not track your spend.

116. D. Cost Explorer allows you to get a forecast of your likely usage and cost for the next three months based on current and previous usage. AWS Organizations will not give you the forecasting you are looking for. AWS Trusted Advisor makes recommendations based on the Well Architected Framework, but it does not provide cost/usage forecasting. AWS Budgets allows you to define alarms that will let you know if you exceed a set amount.

117. B. AWS Organizations allows your accounting department to view billing and cost information for all of the AWS accounts in your organization. While AWS Trusted Advisor can give recommendations regarding cost savings and cost optimization, it does not provide a central area to view billing and usage. The AWS Management Console gives you shortcuts to set up AWS Organizations but does not offer the central view of billing that AWS Organizations does. AWS Budgets is used to set a budget so that you can get alerts if it looks like you will go over budget.

118. D. AWS Cost Explorer monitors the current amount due on your AWS account. AWS Management Console provides a shortcut to AWS Cost Explorer but does not provide the information you are looking for. AWS Trusted Advisor can make recommendations to optimize cost, but it does not give you the current or forecasted amounts due. AWS Budgets allows you to set a desired spend amount and notifications if you are in danger of exceeding the desired spend amount.

119. A. AWS Cost Explorer monitors the current amount due on your AWS account. AWS Management Console provides a shortcut to AWS Cost Explorer, but it does not provide the information you are looking for. AWS Trusted Advisor can make recommendations to optimize cost, but it does not give you the current or forecasted amounts due. AWS Budgets allows you to set a desired spend amount and notifications if you are in danger of exceeding the desired spend amount.

120. B. In the Reservation Recommendations screen of AWS Cost Explorer, you will get a message stating there are no purchase recommendations if your instances haven't been running long enough. All instance types/sizes can be converted to reserved instances. If the accounting department didn't have appropriate permissions, they would get an Access Denied error.

121. D. AWS Trusted Advisor provides recommendations on cost savings, performance, and security, but does not provide alarms for going over budget. AWS Budgets provides the capability to set billing alarms and notifications based on those alarms.

122. B, E. With the free support plan, you get access to seven basic checks, which AWS refers to as core checks. If you need access to all of the checks available in AWS Trusted Advisor, then you will need to upgrade your support plan to Business or Enterprise level. The Developer support plan only includes the seven basic checks just like the Basic support plan. Teams-level support was made up for this question.

123. A. This one comes down to memorization...AWS Trusted Advisor checks for cost optimization, security, service limits, fault tolerance, and performance.

124. C. This one comes down to memorization...AWS Trusted Advisor checks for cost optimization, security, service limits, fault tolerance, and performance.

125. D. This one comes down to memorization...AWS Trusted Advisor checks for cost optimization, security, service limits, fault tolerance, and performance.

126. B. This one comes down to memorization...AWS Trusted Advisor checks for cost optimization, security, service limits, fault tolerance, and performance.

127. C. This one comes down to memorization...AWS Trusted Advisor checks for cost optimization, security, service limits, fault tolerance, and performance.

128. A. To keep a resource from being reported in AWS Trusted Advisor, you can add an exclusion for reporting the resource at the resource level. You can't do exclusions at the check level. Exclusions for AWS Trusted Advisor are not made in Amazon CloudWatch.

129. D. You have to wait for 5 minutes to refresh a check from the last time it was checked. It has probably not been 5 minutes since the last refresh, so you will need to wait.

130. B. AWS Trusted Advisor provides checks on service limits. From AWS Trusted Advisor, you can see which service limits you are approaching and which ones you have met. Amazon CloudWatch, AWS CloudTrail, and AWS Config would not provide the service limit information you require.

131. C, D. You have two options here. You can either deprovision old resources and reclaim some of your elastic IP addresses, or if that isn't an option, you can contact AWS and ask for a service limit increase. You can't increase service limits on your own from the AWS Management Console, CLI, or SDK.

132. A. AWS Trusted Advisor uses on-demand rates to calculate savings with reserved instances. This makes sense when you take into account the constant price fluctuation with the spot instance market. AWS Trusted Advisor analyzes a month of activity, so spot instances will show up at the end of the month.

133. C. Amazon Inspector allows you to run security assessments against your resources in AWS. AWS WAF protects web applications, AWS Systems Manager provides patching and baselining services, and Amazon GuardDuty looks for malicious traffic on your network.

134. A, D. While you can capture open network ports with the agentless scan from Amazon Inspector, you need to install the agent if you want to know which processes are running on the open ports. Amazon GuardDuty analyzes network traffic for malicious activity, and AWS WAF protects web applications.

135. A. To provide your security team with the report they are wanting, you will need to create or choose an assessment template and ensure that it contains the CIS rules package you are wanting to test your systems against. AWS Config and AWS Systems Manager don't provide a report like this.

136. C. Amazon Inspector is not the cause of the performance issue as the agentless configuration does not cause performance issues. According to AWS, there is a minimal hit to performance if the agent is installed. Amazon Inspector not scanning might have seemed like a good fit; this is where you need to remember that the agent install can cause a small impact to performance. That wouldn't necessarily require an active scan to be occurring.

137. A. Only the rules provided by AWS are allowed to be used for assessment runs, so you can't create rules packages.

138. B. Amazon Inspector can only find applications installed by the operating system's package manager. It can't find applications installed by automation software like Chef, Puppet. or Ansible.

139. C. The findings report is a high-level report containing an executive summary of the findings from the scan. A full report is a detailed report that is perfect for IT and InfoSec teams. Executive reports and basic reports don't actually exist.

140. A. A full report is a detailed report that is perfect for IT and InfoSec teams. The findings report is a high-level report containing an executive summary of the findings from the scan. Executive reports and basic reports don't actually exist.

141. A. Amazon GuardDuty allows you to monitor for threats by analyzing AWS CloudTrail events, VC Flow Logs, and DNS logs. Amazon Inspector allows you to do security assessments against your infrastructure.

142. C. Amazon GuardDuty allows you to monitor for threats by analyzing AWS CloudTrail events, VPC Flow Logs, and DNS logs. Amazon CloudWatch allows you to monitor logs from all of your AWS resources, Amazon Inspector allows you to do security assessments against your infrastructure, and Amazon Macie classifies data in S3 and applies behavioral analysis.

143. D. Amazon Macie classifies data in S3 and catalogs the normal behaviors from users who are accessing that data. Amazon GuardDuty allows you to monitor for threats by analyzing AWS CloudTrail events, VPC Flow Logs, and DNS logs. Amazon CloudWatch allows you to monitor logs from all of your AWS resources, and Amazon Inspector allows you to do security assessments against your infrastructure.

144. D. Amazon GuardDuty monitors for reconnaissance activity and account and instance compromise. It does not monitor for events like a DDoS attack.

145. B, C. Amazon GuardDuty sends detailed security alerts to Amazon CloudWatch Events. Alerts that make it to Amazon CloudWatch Events can be used to send a notification through Amazon SNS. Amazon GuardDuty security alerts are sent to Amazon CloudWatch Events, not Amazon CloudWatch Logs. Amazon SQS is a queue system used for message delivery, not appropriate in this case. Amazon Inspector is used to conduct security assessments.

146. A. Amazon GuardDuty keeps findings in the Amazon GuardDuty Console for 90 days. After 90 days, they are deleted.

147. B. Amazon Macie not only finds and classifies data, it also monitors the data for anomalous access. Amazon Inspector is used to perform security assessments. Third-party products will never be the answer on an AWS exam.

148. A. The AWS Well-Architected Tool allows you to check your workloads against the five pillars of the Well-Architected Framework. Amazon CloudWatch is a monitoring solution, AWS CloudTrail monitors API calls, and Amazon Inspector is a security assessment tool.

149. B, C. AWS License Manager, when paired with AWS Systems Manager, can inventory your software both on-prem and in AWS. Once your software is managed by AWS License Manager, you can apply licensing rules to it. Amazon Inspector is used for security assessments. AWS Config monitors configuration drift, and Amazon CloudWatch monitors logs and events across AWS.

150. B. The most efficient method to manage licenses will be to add all of the AWS accounts in your organization to AWS Organizations. Then you can centrally manage all licensing with AWS License Manager. While you could have your IAM account added to each AWS account, this is certainly not the most efficient route to take. Individual account owners reporting usage is definitely not efficient.

151. D. Amazon CloudWatch is well-suited for infrastructure monitoring and troubleshooting since it collects both availability and performance metrics. It can also collect HTTP responses on web servers, so it can monitor for issues like bad response codes.

152. B. Since Amazon CloudWatch is able to monitor availability and performance metrics, it provides a great use case for those who need to benefit from resource optimization.

153. C. Amazon CloudWatch is able to provide monitoring for applications. For web applications, it can monitor for HTTP response codes, and for installed applications, you can use the Amazon CloudWatch agent to retrieve events from applications.

154. D. Amazon CloudWatch allows you to collect, analyze, and visualize your logs. This allows you to customize dashboards for relevant information so that you can better monitor for issues and for performance.

155. A. Amazon CloudWatch Logs Insights is a managed service that allows you to query large sets of logs. You can even use regex to extract data from event fields. Amazon Kinesis performs real-time processing of streaming data but is not intended to be used for monitoring with logs. Amazon Athena is a query service designed to work with S3, and Amazon RedShift is a data warehousing solution.

156. C. Amazon CloudWatch Logs Insights allows you to run interactive queries against your logs and create visualizations that include dashboards in Amazon CloudWatch. Amazon CloudWatch, Amazon CloudWatch Logs, and Amazon CloudWatch Events do not give you that capability by themselves.

157. E. In October 2018, AWS introduced the ability to use StatsD and collectd to collect custom metrics to be consumed by Amazon CloudWatch.

158. C. Amazon CloudWatch snapshot graphs allow you to display charts on a web page or a third-party tool. This functionality is not provided by Amazon CloudWatch Logs, the Amazon CloudWatch Logs agent, or Amazon CloudWatch APIs.

159. B. As AWS CloudTrail monitors all API access, it is able to provide a history of all actions taken on your account, so it is useful in aiding compliance efforts. AWS CloudTrail does not provide firewalling, API management, or log monitoring.

160. C. AWS CloudTrail can be used to detect data exfiltration by collecting activity data from your S3 buckets. Amazon CloudWatch is the tool that monitors logs and detects application issues and HTTP response codes.

161. D. AWS CloudTrail is a great fit for security analysis as its data can be fed into a SIEM to look at end user behavior. AWS Systems Manager is used for installing software and patches and monitoring for installed software.

162.   A. AWS CloudTrail allows you to review the most recent changes in your AWS environment, which provides greater visibility into actions that may cause operational issues. AWS Systems Manager is responsible for installing security updates, and Amazon CloudWatch handles monitoring logs and HTTP response codes.

163.   A. Invoke API allows you to see when and who executed an AWS Lambda function. Management events are also used in AWS CloudTrail to monitor AWS Lambda creation, modification, and delete events, but management events don't include the who and the when. AWS Lambda sends logs to Amazon CloudWatch and AWS CloudTrail depending on what the AWS Lambda function is doing. There is no log data event type.

164.   C. The solution with the least amount of administrative effort would be to save the AWS CloudTrail trails to S3 and create a lifecycle policy that will automatically delete trails older than one year.

165.   D. AWS Systems Manager provides a dashboard that allows you to view your resources in resource groups. Since you can group together all the resources supporting an application, for example, you can get a really good picture on any issues that would affect the uptime or usability of an application. Amazon CloudWatch monitors logs, AWS CloudTrail monitors API calls, and Amazon Inspector monitors vulnerabilities in your environment.

166.   B. AWS Systems Manager makes it simple to automate common administrative jobs with its various components like Run Command, Patch Manager, and State Manager. The Amazon API Gateway provides API management, federated access can be set up in AWS IAM, and Amazon CloudWatch provides log monitoring.

167.   B. AWS Systems Manager improves visibility and control of your assets using resource groups and integrations with AWS Config that allow you to view changes to your resources. Amazon Inspector provides security assessments and can be used to tighten down network accessibility on servers. API management is accomplished with the Amazon API Gateway.

168.   A. AWS Systems Manager provides the management capability via the SSM agent to manage both on-prem and AWS resources from a single console. Visibility into logs is provided by Amazon CloudWatch, security assessments are provided by Amazon Inspector, and AWS CloudTrail provides visibility into API calls.

169.   C. AWS Systems Manager gives you the ability to maintain security and compliance by providing a central management console to manage patching and configurations (through a tie-in with AWS Config). Managing API calls is provided by the Amazon API Gateway, security assessments are performed with Amazon Inspector, and logs are monitored through Amazon CloudWatch.

170.   D. The Run Command provides a way to automate common administrative tasks without the need for remote access provided by opening up SSH or RDP or by using bastion hosts. Session Manager provides console access without the need to open up the common administrative ports for SSH, as an example.

171. A. Session Manager within AWS Systems Manager allows remote console sessions via an interactive web browser with no need to open inbound ports or use bastion hosts to access your systems. Configuration management and tracking are provided by the AWS Systems Manager State Manage and AWS Config. API management is provided by the Amazon API Gateway.

172. D. AWS Systems Manager Patch Manager provides patch management and reporting for both Linux and Windows systems on-prem and in the cloud.

173. C. State Manager provides configuration management for both on-prem and AWS resources so long as the AWS Systems Manager SSM agent is installed. It does not control backups.

174. A. The Parameter Store provides a centralized storage repository for license keys, database strings, secrets, and other configuration data. It is able to interact with AWS KMS, AWS IAM, and AWS Lambda, but it is not limited to working with these services.

175. B. With Amazon Athena, you can query data across a multitude of AWS services, including AWS CloudTrail, Amazon CloudFront, Elastic Load Balancer, Amazon Virtual Private Cloud, Amazon CloudFormation, AWS Glue Data Catalog, Amazon QuickSight, and IAM. Amazon CloudWatch is used for monitoring logs, and AWS CloudTrail is used for monitoring API calls.

176. C. Amazon Athena gives you the capability to analyze the data contained within your S3 buckets and run queries against that data. Amazon CloudFront is a caching and content delivery service that can use S3 as an origin server. Amazon RDS is a relational database system, and AWS Lambda is a serverless solution that allows you to run code that is triggered by a schedule or an event.

177. A, B. Amazon Athena integrates seamlessly with Amazon QuickSight. Amazon Athena allows you to analyze the data in S3, while Amazon QuickSight allows you to more easily visualize your data. AWS CloudTrail is used to monitor API calls; AWS Lambda is a serverless solution for running code on a schedule or by a trigger. Amazon Inspector is a security assessment tool.

178. B. The AWS Glue Data Catalog is purpose-built to store persistent metadata for Amazon S3. Amazon Athena is used to query data in S3, Amazon RDS is a relational database service, and Amazon Elasticache is an in-memory data store used to improve performance.

179. D. Amazon QuickSight has two editions, Standard and Enterprise. The Enterprise Edition will support Active Directory groups from AWS Directory Service. The Standard edition allows you to invite IAM users, or users directly with an email address. Developer and basic are not valid edition names for Amazon QuickSight.

180. A. Amazon QuickSight is billed on a pay-per-session rate. You pay only for what you use.

181. C. Amazon Athena is a serverless solution that is capable of scaling from few to many users running queries. It is not free; you pay per query at a rate of $5 per terabyte scanned by the query.

182. A. Amazon Athena supports the use of standard SQL and can use quite a few data formats, including JSON and CSV, though these are certainly not the only data formats it accepts. Supporting proprietary SQL would not be a benefit. Amazon Athena uses Amazon S3 as its data store, not Amazon EBS.

183. D. Amazon Athena is billed per query at a rate of $5 per terabyte scanned by the query.

184. B. Amazon Athena is able to execute queries quickly because it uses parallel query execution, meaning that more than one query can run at any given time. It does not use SQS to queue queries, nor does it use Elasticache or DynamoDB.

185. D. One of the most common use cases for AWS Config is continuous monitoring of configuration changes. Security assessments are handled by Amazon Inspector, AWS CloudTrail monitors API calls, and Amazon CloudWatch monitors logs.

186. A. AWS Config is very useful when troubleshooting issues related to configuration changes. AWS IAM will allow you to perform modeling of permissions, and AWS CloudTrail will let you look at API calls to see if they were rejected due to inappropriate permissions. Amazon CloudWatch can be used to help troubleshoot issues with storage space and processor usage.

187. B. You can use AWS Config to audit configurations for compliance with organizational baselines. This simplifies both security and compliance initiatives. Vulnerabilities fall under security assessments, which would be Amazon Inspector. Best practices are typically reported by AWS Trusted Advisor (according to the Well-Architected Framework). AMI IDs are not checked by AWS Config, so you need to ensure that you are using the correct AMI ID for the region that you are in.

188. C. You can use AWS Config as an enterprise configuration management tool. It allows you to view the compliance status for configurations across multiple AWS accounts. It does not provide compliance status based on API calls, logs, or password policies.

189. A. AWS Config can help you mature your change management program as you can track what changes were made by whom, and if they cause an outage, you can see if the change was actually an approved change. Security assessments are performed by Amazon Inspector. Logs are monitored by Amazon CloudWatch, and APIs are monitored by AWS CloudTrail.

190. B. Amazon Inspector allows you to inspect applications from the beginning of development to an application that's in production to minimize vulnerabilities as much as possible. Amazon GuardDuty monitors and identifies exploit traffic on the network. AWS Trusted Advisor gives you best practices according to the Well-Architected Framework. AWS Config helps you to identify configuration changes in your environment.

191. D. Amazon Inspector can be used to assess your AWS environment against security best practices. Configuration changes are monitored by AWS Config; API calls are monitored by AWS CloudTrail, though not for security-specific incidents. Finally, while Amazon Inspector can tell you if there might be an inbound misconfiguration, it is not designed to tell you if there is an outbound configuration issue with a NACL.

192. C. In DevSecOps, you move security assessments to the left so that they occur earlier in the process. Since Amazon Inspector is API driven, you can have it perform a security assessment whenever a new release is checked into source control. Amazon GuardDuty identifies malicious traffic on the network. AWS CloudTrail is used to monitor API calls, and AWS Config is used to identify configuration changes.

193. A. Since the results of the assessments done by Amazon Inspector can be made visible to your security team, you are better able to validate that you are following security best practices. Validating patch levels and installing patches is done by Patch Manager, a component of AWS Systems Manager. Validating that the user access is appropriate is something that should be done via your IAM team. Validating configurations against organizational baselines is done with AWS Config.

194. B. With Amazon Inspector, you can better support your developers who use Agile methodology. Agile stresses small frequent releases, and Amazon Inspector can scan each of these incremental releases for issues before they make it to production. Fixes can be produced quickly and released. Waterfall is an old methodology that relies on less frequent and larger releases, and it makes fixing new security issues more difficult. AWS CloudTrail is used to monitor API calls, though you would have to define what an insecure request is. Configuration changes are monitored by AWS Config.

195. C. With Amazon Inspector, you can define which standards your applications must adhere to. For example, if you are writing an application for processing credit cards, you can set Amazon Inspector to perform an assessment for PCI-DSS compliance. Patching is done by Patch Manager, a component of AWS Systems Manager. Network intrusions can be found by Amazon GuardDuty, and Trusted Advisor is used to compare your environment to Well-Architected Framework best practices.

196. C. Amazon GuardDuty identifies network threats and even suspicious account activity. AWS Trusted Advisor compares your existing environment to best practices laid out in the Well-Architected Framework. Security assessments are performed by Amazon Inspector. Patch levels are maintained by Patch Manager, a component of AWS Systems Manager.

197. A. Amazon GuardDuty not only identifies threats on your network, it can automatically respond to those threats as well. Identifying stale user accounts or users/groups with excessive permissions is something that should be done by your IAM team, utilizing AWS IAM. Automated security assessments are performed by Amazon Inspector.

198. D. Amazon GuardDuty can support multiple AWS accounts, giving visibility across your enterprise. Patching is handled by Patch Manager, a component of AWS Systems Manager. Encryption keys are managed by AWS Key Management Service (KMS).

199. C. Amazon GuardDuty will give your security department the visibility they want into the identified threats in your AWS environment. Amazon Inspector is used for security assessments, AWS Trusted Advisor is used to compare against best practices laid out in the Well-Architected Framework, and Amazon QuickSight is used to create visualizations of the data in your AWS environment but is not focused on visualization of network threats.

200.   A. Amazon GuardDuty can monitor for suspicious user activity in addition to network threats. AWS IAM and AWS Directory Service are used to control user access but do not monitor for suspicious access. AWS Organizations is used to enforce policies across an organization and to provide visibility into logging across the organization.

201.   B. Amazon RedShift provides the fastest performance when you need to run a large report that includes complex queries.

202.   A. Amazon Elastic Map Reduce (EMR) is best suited to replace a data lake using Hadoop on-premises. You can define the requirements of the workload that you are wanting to run to support whatever analysis you want to perform.

203.   C. Amazon Athena is designed to run ad hoc queries against data contained in Amazon S3.

204.   D. Amazon Athena is the most cost-effective option to use to query a large dataset in Amazon S3. Amazon RDS is a relational database, Amazon CloudWatch is used to monitor logs, not analyze datasets, and AWS Lambda works off of triggers. Since you get charged each time AWS Lambda is run, it would not be a cost-effective option for this use case.

205.   B. Amazon Macie can provide visibility into the management functions that are used to work with storage locations in AWS. At the time of this writing, that is limited to Amazon S3, but it will be expanded in the future. Security assessments are performed by Amazon Inspector, ad hoc queries against S3 are performed by Amazon Athena, and the management of encryption keys for storage is performed by AWS KMS.

206.   C. Amazon Macie integrates with Amazon CloudWatch Events, which allows you to build custom alerts off of events identified by Amazon Macie and to perform automatic remediation if desired. API usage is monitored by AWS CloudTrail, and versioning is provided within S3 and can be managed from the S3 Dashboard. Lifecycle events in S3 are managed from within S3.

Domain 2: High Availability

1.   B. By using Amazon CloudWatch to trigger an autoscale event, you can provision new servers before performance is impacted. You can create another Amazon CloudWatch trigger to scale down when CPU usage drops again. You would not use AWS CloudTrail to trigger an autoscaling event; it is used to log API calls. You know that performance is impacted when the CPU is at 95% utilization, so you would want to scale before it reaches that point. Your boss wants a cost-efficient solution…by having scale-up happen at 80% and scale-down happen at 75%, it is likely that you will have constant scaling events, which will become expensive and will not help performance.

2. C. When you want to set up an EC2 Auto Scaling group, you must first create a launch configuration to define how the Amazon EC2 instances being launched by autoscaling should be configured. While an ELB does aid in high availability, you are not required to make one to create an Auto Scaling group. Launch configurations can be created by copying an existing EC2 instance, but you only need an AMI to create the launch configuration. Setting up monitoring in Amazon CloudWatch is a great idea if you want to use Amazon CloudWatch to kick off autoscaling events but is not required to create an Auto Scaling group.

3. D. The set of instructions sent by Amazon CloudWatch to the Auto Scaling group is referred to as a policy. The policy defines what the Auto Scaling group should do with the alarm it receives from Amazon CloudWatch. An Amazon Machine Image (AMI) can be used by the Auto Scaling group to create an Amazon EC2 instance when needed. The "config file" option was created for this question. The launch configuration is needed by the Auto Scaling group to define how it should launch new instances.

4. A. Scaling events can be triggered by schedule. The schedule is not created in Amazon CloudWatch, and you don't need an alarm from Amazon CloudWatch to scale.

5. C. Predictive scaling is a feature of AWS Auto Scaling that can look back at previous activity and use that to schedule the needed scaling changes based on both daily and weekly patterns. There is no such thing as analytics scaling or behavioral scaling in this context.

6. A. Predictive scaling needs at least two weeks of data before it can generate a scaling schedule based on your normal activity. Predictive scaling does support EC2 instances; in fact, EC2 instances are the only supported type at the time of this writing.

7. D. Amazon Relational Database Service (RDS) as a general rule is not one of the services that can take advantage of Auto Scaling groups. Amazon ECS, DynamoDB, and Aurora replicas within Amazon Aurora can take advantage of Auto Scaling groups using either Auto Scaling groups or the Auto Scaling API.

8. B. If minimum capacity is set to 0 and there is no load, then it is entirely possible for you to have 0 instances. If you leave desired capacity blank, then the minimum capacity is used. If maximum capacity is set to 1, then your Auto Scaling group can have up to one EC2 instance. If autoscaling wasn't available in your region, you wouldn't have been able to set up your ASG in the first place.

9. C, E. The Pending state is used when an EC2 instance is starting up, and InService is used when an EC2 instance is ready to service requests. Active, online, and starting are not valid states.

10. D. If an Amazon EC2 instance fails health checks, the Auto Scaling group will terminate it and launch a new instance to take its place. If the EC2 instance is getting hit by too many requests, that is a prime opportunity for autoscaling to scale out, not to terminate. If the threshold set in AWS Budgets is met or exceeded, instances are not terminated. You will simply get an alert if you have it set to send one.

11. **A.** The launch configuration defines the AMI ID to use, the instance type, the keypair for connecting to the instances, security groups, and storage that the EC2 instances will need. A launch template is similar to a launch configuration, but it is versioned. The other options were made up for this question.

12. **D.** Creating a launch configuration using the EC2 instance as a template is the simplest way to create a matching launch configuration. Manually creating a launch configuration would work but requires more administrative effort and the question asked for the least amount of administrative effort. You can attach the EC2 instance to the Auto Scaling group, but if the Auto Scaling group was created manually and the launch configuration was created manually, this is more administrative work than using the EC2 instance as a template. Attaching the EC2 instance to a security group is a best practice but is not the correct answer to this question.

13. **B, D.** First, you will use the EC2 instance to create another launch configuration, and then you will change the Auto Scaling group to use the new launch configuration. Making changes to the EC2 instance that was used as a template will not make the changes to the launch configuration.

14. **B.** Since you need to avoid downtime, your best option is to manually terminate the old instances so they are relaunched using the new launch configuration. This allows you to control how many instances are offline and avoid downtime. If you set the desired capacity to zero, you may cause an outage, so this would not be a great solution if the most important factor is to avoid an outage. You can't set the launch configuration per instance. Since you need to refresh your instances now, waiting for them to age out is not a good solution.

15. **A.** Launch templates use versioning to track changes. You can't enable versioning on launch configurations directly. Manually numbering launch configurations is not easily scalable and would be error prone.

16. **D.** To get true high availability, you will want to set the database to be multi-AZ. Taking frequent snapshots is great if your main goal is to have recent backups but will not make the database highly available. Read replicas are meant to boost performance. While they can be promoted to be the primary database, they are not designed for high availability as the synchronization is asynchronous.

17. **C.** The most likely cause of the failover is that the primary availability zone became unavailable. If your database becomes corrupt, it will impact your customers but will not cause a failover event in the AZ. RDS is a managed service, but disk space is not. If your database becomes too big and runs out of space, it will impact your customers but will not cause a failover event to the other availability zone. Running out of memory would impact customers but would not cause a failover.

18. **A.** Your database may have failed over because network connectivity to the primary AZ was interrupted. If network connectivity is slow but remained online, then a failover wouldn't have occurred. You don't really have control of the IP address of your RDS instance, and the IP changing would not cause it to fail over. Your database becoming unresponsive is bad…but would not initiate a failover event.

19. D. If the host your RDS instance was running on suffered a hardware failure, it would fail over to the other AZ. The other reasons—database becoming corrupt, RDS instance running out of space or memory—would be customer impacting but would not cause a failover to another AZ.

20. C. If the storage your RDS instance was running on suffered a failure, then that would cause a failover to the other availability zone. Your RDS instance running out of space or memory would not initiate a failover, and encrypting your storage would certainly not cause a failover event.

21. C. A region is a geographic area that is not bound by country boundaries.

22. A. An availability zone consists of one or more isolated datacenters connected with low-latency links.

23. D. Ensure that your EC2 instances are in separate availability zones to make your application highly available and still able to use the same AMI. If you place your EC2 instances into different regions, you will need to use different AMIs per region. It doesn't matter if the EC2 instances are running on Windows or Linux in this case.

24. A. By using loose coupling, you can take advantage of managed services that are naturally highly available like SWF, SQS, SNS, ELB, and Route 53. This will enable you to make your application more highly available than relying on servers alone. Adding more memory or CPU might improve your application's performance but not its availability. Creating more frequent backups will assist in lowering your recovery time; however, it will not make your application more highly available.

25. C. Simple Queue Service (SQS) guarantees delivery of a message at least once. Simple Notification Service (SNS) will send messages but doesn't guarantee at-least-once delivery. Simple Workflow Service (SWF) is made to run jobs that have multiple steps, not to queue or deliver messages. Email doesn't guarantee at-least-once delivery, nor is it designed to facilitate communication between applications.

26. A. Amazon Simple Queue Service (SQS) is best described as a highly available message queueing service that offers FIFO at-least-once delivery.

27. B. Simple Queue Service (SQS) will queue up the messages that need to be sent until the destination system is back up and able to process messages again. SNS, SQS, and S3 are not queuing solutions.

28. D. Your best solution in this case will be Simple Queue Service (SQS). As messages come in for the backend system, they are queued, and the backend systems can pull messages from the queue when they are ready to process them. SWF, SNS, and S3 will not provide a mechanism like this that will help the backend systems cope with the amount of traffic coming through.

29. B. Messages sent to an SQS queue can be kept for up to 14 days, so you can meet their requirements.

30. D. Messages can be kept for up to 14 days, so you can't meet their requirements.

31. B. The best option is to configure an Auto Scaling group for the backend servers. Have them scale out when the SQS queues start getting busy, then have them scale in when the SQS queues are idle. An elastic load balancer could be handy for communications to the backend systems, but it will not automate the termination and spinning up of instances. Neither Route 53 nor a placement group will help with the spinning up and terminating of instances either.

32. C. The most likely cause is that AWS deleted it as it had been inactive for over 30 consecutive days. They have the right to delete it without any notification. SQS queues don't expire, although the messages within them can. A glitch like this is highly unlikely as the SQS is a highly available service. If you had the wrong region selected, you likely wouldn't have been able to start your application.

33. A. Standard queues do try to preserve the order of the messages, but they don't guarantee the order of messages. If the order of the messages is important for your application to function properly, then you should define the queue as a FIFO queue rather than a standard queue. LIFO, FILO, and LILO are not options for SQS queues.

34. B, E. Short polling and long polling are the two methods used with Amazon SQS. Short polling consists of a sample done across all your queues regardless of whether they are empty or not, where long polling doesn't send a response until there is a message in the queue. Small, tall, and fast polling don't really exist.

35. C. The visibility timeout is used by SQS to prevent multiple systems from processing the same message. It places a lock on the message while it is being processed and then deletes the message once it has been processed. The other options were made up for this question.

36. D. A dead letter queue is created to deal with messages that have failed to process successfully after a threshold of attempts has been reached. There is no such thing as a normal queue. Standard queues attempt to process messages in the order they are received, and FIFO queues do process messages in the order they are received.

37. A. You can only share an SQS queue within the same region. If you have access to SQS and can set up queues normally, then sharing a queue would not be an issue. It is highly unlikely that SQS is unavailable in one of the regions you are attempting to use. There is no limit on the number of SQS queues you can create in your account.

38. C. Amazon Simple Notification Service (SNS) can push messages to those who have subscribed to a topic. In this case, availability alerts from Amazon CloudWatch could be sent through an SNS topic. SQS manages messages for applications but does not send notifications to cell phone numbers via SMS text. S3 is object storage and does not send notifications. Amazon Simple Texting Service is not a real product.

39. B. There are five different ways to subscribe to an SNS topic. They are AWS Lambda, Amazon Simple Queue Service (SQS), HTTP and HTTPS, email, and SMS text.

40. C. There are five different ways to subscribe to an SNS topic. They are AWS Lambda, Amazon Simple Queue Service (SQS), HTTP and HTTPS, email, and SMS text.

41. A. There are five different ways to subscribe to an SNS topic. They are AWS Lambda, Amazon Simple Queue Service (SQS), HTTP and HTTPS, email, and SMS text.

42. D. There are five different ways to subscribe to an SNS topic. They are AWS Lambda, Amazon Simple Queue Service (SQS), HTTP and HTTPS, email, and SMS text.

43. D. There are five different ways to subscribe to an SNS topic. They are AWS Lambda, Amazon Simple Queue Service (SQS), HTTP and HTTPS, email, and SMS text.

44. D. A NAT gateway is a highly available service and when deployed in each availability zone can create a highly available architecture. AWS Direct Connect provides a connection to another network but doesn't meet the goals stated in the question. Security groups would not work since they would allow Internet accessibility for downloads. A NAT instance is not inherently highly available as it is a specialized Amazon EC2 instance.

45. B. An Elastic Load Balancer will stop sending traffic to an unhealthy Amazon EC2 instance. Auto Scaling groups are a way to ensure that you can self-heal should an issue occur, but they do not stop routing traffic to affected instances. A launch configuration isn't a service; it is how you configure an Auto Scaling group. Amazon CloudWatch can be used to alarm on unhealthy instances but doesn't actually perform remediation directly.

46. A. When you make the application stateless (i.e., using Amazon DynamoDB or Amazon Elasticache to track session state), your customers will not be impacted if your elastic load balancer stops routing traffic to an unhealthy instance. Enabling sticky sessions ensures that a customer stays with the instance they were connected with. This would not improve customer experience. While Route 53 does provide health checks, it would not solve the issue of the customer sessions being dropped when an instance became unhealthy. Rebooting an unhealthy instance may make it healthy again but will still impact customer experience.

47. A, C. DynamoDB and Elasticache are perfect solutions for tracking user state. Amazon RDS would not be a good solution for tracking session state, and Redshift is a data warehousing solution.

48. D. S3 will be able to meet your needs. You can enable cross-region replication on any bucket that you want to have replicate to another region for high availability.

49. B. Since the virtual private gateway is already highly available and supports two VPN endpoints, it makes sense to create another customer gateway and to enable dynamic routing.

50. C. Since Amazon SQS can handle a maximum message size of 256 KB, it would not be a good solution in this case.

51. D. Since Amazon SQS can handle a maximum message size of 256 KB, it would be a good solution in this case.

52. B. Amazon SNS can handle messages up to 256 KB in size.

53. B. By using latency-based routing on Route 53, you can ensure that your customers will be connected to the lowest-latency datacenter. Elastic Load Balancing won't route based on latency. Geolocation routing will match your users with the datacenter closest to them; however, that may not be the datacenter offering the lowest latency. Failover routing doesn't examine latency; it only offers health checks. When the primary system fails a health check, Route 53 routes traffic to the secondary system.

54. C. Geolocation routing will match your users with the datacenter closest to them. Elastic load balancer won't route based on location. Latency-based routing allows you to ensure that your customers will be connected to the lowest-latency datacenter. Failover routing doesn't examine location; it only offers health checks. When the primary system fails a health check, Route 53 routes traffic to the secondary system.

55. D. Failover routing with Route 53 offers health checks. When the primary system fails a health check, Route 53 routes traffic to the secondary system. Elastic load balancer can do health checks; however, it is not the best choice given the desire to have a primary and a secondary system. Latency-based routing allows you to ensure that your customers will be connected to the lowest-latency datacenter but is not concerned with having a primary and a secondary system. Geolocation routing will match your users with the datacenter closest to them but is not concerned with having a primary and a secondary system.

56. D. An alias record can be used to point to an elastic load balancer rather than using an IP address or a domain name. A records and CNAME records are concerned with IP addresses and domain names, and SRV records tell systems where services are available.

57. C, D. You can choose from either Memcached or Redis for the engine when setting up Elasticache. NoSQL is a type of database, not an engine, and RDS is a relational database service offered by AWS.

58. C. Amazon Elasticache is a highly available service and can self-heal. When it detects a node that has failed, it will automatically replace that node. Amazon RDS is Amazon's managed relational database offering. Redshift is a data warehousing solution, and PostgreSQL is a relational database. Of these options, only Elasticache will work well for managing session state.

59. A. AWS Lambda is highly available and is the most cost-effective solution as you only get charged when the code is executed. While building another EC2 instance could make it highly available, it is not the most cost-effective option. Elastic Beanstalk is highly available; however, you are still paying for an additional Amazon EC2 instance, which is not the most cost-effective option. An elastic load balancer could potentially make this more highly available, but you would still need to build another Amazon EC2 instance.

60. C. You can't use the same function because AWS Lambda is based on region. You can, however, copy the function to the other region.

61. B. You can set the timeout value to something reasonable for your code to execute, such as, for instance, 5 minutes (300 seconds). This way the function will be terminated after 5 minutes. There is no such thing as a lockout value. Creating a CloudWatch monitor wouldn't solve the issue at hand. Manually stopping the function would work, but it is not very efficient, and chances are the function would run for longer than necessary.

62. A, D. The best way to build in high availability to your network is to ensure that there are at least two subnets for each tier and choose different availability zones for each subnet.

63. D. An Internet gateway when attached to a subnet allows inbound/outbound traffic and is a highly available service. A VPN gateway wouldn't allow for direct traffic to and from the Internet. A NAT gateway or NAT instance would allow outbound traffic but not inbound traffic.

64. B. The best solution is to create a NAT gateway in two availability zones as the NAT gateway is naturally highly available. If you use a NAT instance, you are still introducing a point of failure because the instance is not natively highly available. You would not use a customer gateway or virtual private gateway for this as they do not provide a direct connection out to the Internet.

65. C. AWS CloudTrail provides an audit trail for every API call. This includes the deletion of the elastic load balancer as well as who deleted it. SSM, Amazon CloudWatch, and VPC flow logs won't give you the information you are looking for.

66. A. Choose to rebuild with an application load balancer and enable deletion protection. Deletion protection is not available on classic load balancers. Access control through IAM is important, though the ability to delete load balancers should be pretty restricted already. MFA Delete is a function available in S3 but not elastic load balancers.

67. B. Application Load Balancers can support content-based routing, which routes based on the content in the request. Classic Load Balancers and Network Load Balancers do not have this capability.

68. C. Host-based routing will allow you to route traffic based in the domain name in the request. Content-based routing routes traffic based on the content of the request. Path-based routing will route traffic based on the URL path that is in the HTTP header.

69. B. Path-based routing will route traffic based on the URL path that is in the HTTP header. Host-based routing will allow you to route traffic based in the domain name in the request. Content-based routing routes traffic based on the content of the request.

70. C. Of the options here, the only one that supports HTTP/2 is the application load balancer.

71. B. Amazon CloudFront is the service that caches content so that it is more readily available to customers. With S3 as the origin server, your site is highly available all the way through. AWS CloudTrail and Amazon CloudWatch have nothing to do with caching; they audit API calls and monitor your environment respectively.

72. A. The Amazon API Gateway is a highly available service that is capable of throttling incoming API requests. Neither Lambda, CodePipeline, nor CodeDeploy is designed to throttle incoming requests.

73. B, C. You can monitor for error rates with Amazon CloudWatch or the Amazon API Gateway Console. AWS CloudTrail is tempting since we think of it in terms of APIs; however, we are monitoring for error rates not auditing who called what.

74. C. The network load balancer operates at layer 4 of the OSI model.

75. D. Network load balancers in AWS don't support Server Name Indication (SNI).

Domain 3: Deployment and Provisioning

1. **B.** Auto Scaling groups will increase or decrease your instances and can be based on demand. AWS CloudFormation is not tied to demand and can be used to create whole environments, not just instances. The user data field can be used in conjunction with Auto Scaling groups to configure your EC2 instances but isn't actually the process by which you scale. Amazon CloudWatch can trigger scaling events but is not what actually scales your instances either.

2. **C.** The user data field can be used in conjunction with Auto Scaling groups to configure your EC2 instances. Auto Scaling groups will increase or decrease your instances and can be based on demand, but they don't handle the configuration as far as the internals of the EC2 instances. AWS CloudFormation is not tied to demand and can be used to create whole environments, not just instances, though you can use user data in a CloudFormation template. Amazon CloudWatch can trigger scaling events but does not configure instances.

3. **A.** AWS CloudFormation is the best solution for this requirement. You can create a CloudFormation template that can deploy the web servers along with all of their dependencies, exactly the same every time. Auto Scaling groups are not used for deploying resources; rather, they are used to scale to meet demand. The user data field can be used to configure EC2 instances when they are provisioned but does not do anything as far as dependencies outside of the instance. Amazon CloudWatch is a monitoring tool and does not perform deployments.

4. **A, C.** CloudFormation templates can be written in JSON or YAML.

5. **B.** One of the most common use cases for a template parameter in CloudFormation is to specify the instance type and size at the time of creation. Passwords should not be stored in plaintext in configuration files and/or templates. IAM roles will most likely be static, so there is no reason to parameterize them.

6. **D.** If CloudFormation is unable to successfully create your stack, it will roll back everything that it did create. This may happen because you were out of elastic IP addresses so it could not issue one. Since the template has worked in the past and there have been no changes, the AMI should still be correct. The template has not been changed and has worked previously, so it is unlikely that the syntax is incorrect. Since you have been able to use the AMI in the past, it is unlikely that your permissions are incorrect.

7. **B.** WaitCondition can be used to block other resources from being created until the resources they depend on are operational. DelayCondition and SyncCondition don't exist.

8. **C.** You can have 200 stacks in any account. To go over 200, you must request a higher limit for your account with AWS. While the template certainly could have problems, the most likely issue is that you have reached the account limit of 200 stacks. While permissions could certainly be an issue, the account limit for stacks has been reached, so nobody can create stacks at the moment.

9. D. While you are limited in number of stacks, there is no limitation in the number of templates.

10. B. A stack is an instance of a template. You can create multiple stacks from a single template.

11. A. EC2 instances created by CloudFormation are just like regular EC2 instances. You can increase the disk space as you normally would. The CloudFormation API could be used to adjust the template but is not an appropriate choice to adjust the EC2 instance already in existence. You do not need to redeploy the stack from the updated template. There is no issue with using disks…S3 storage could be used but doesn't really address the question.

12. B. To automatically update the EC2 instances in the stack, you can use a change set to model the change and then execute it. EC2 instances created by CloudFormation are just like regular EC2 instances; you can increase the disk space as you normally would, but this is a manual process. You do not need to redeploy the stack from the updated template. There is no issue with using disks…S3 storage could be used but doesn't really address the question.

13. D. In CloudFormation templates, the only required section is the Resources section.

14. B. In CloudFormation templates, the only required section is the Resources section.

15. C. Since you are a new system administrator, the most likely cause is that you don't have permissions to create the underlying resources, and your permissions will need to be fixed to continue. Your administrative credentials would be set in IAM, which is a global service, so being in the wrong region would not cause a permissions issue. The root account should never be used for day-to-day activities.

16. D. CloudFormation Designer gives you a drag-and-drop environment where you can work on your templates and save and/or create stacks from them. While you could certainly use Visio or Omnigraffle to visualize how the template will work, it is not integrated with CloudFormation or the build of the template. Additionally, the answer on an AWS exam will never be a non-AWS product.

17. A. CloudFormation templates are used to define the resources that you need and what their settings will be. Stacks are instances of a template, not the other way around.

18. B. A CloudFormation stack is a logical grouping of resources that can be managed together as a single entity. The resources in a stack may or may not have the same metadata, and they certainly don't have to exist on the same subnet.

19. D. The correct command in the CLI to create a stack would be
`aws cloudformation create-stack`.

20. A. AWS Elastic Beanstalk is the ideal solution for this use case. Environments can be provisioned and deprovisioned, and no interaction with the resources running the code is needed. AWS Lambda isn't meant for running web applications; it's more suited to functions that are triggered by something like an event or a scheduled time. Amazon CloudFormation requires a lot of focus on the resources in the environment, which is not considered desirable in this use case.

21. D. Elastic Beanstalk supports multiple languages, including Go, Java, .NET, Node.js, PHP, Python, and Ruby. It also supports Docker web applications.

22. C. By default, you can't log in to an EC2 instance created with Elastic Beanstalk. To troubleshoot the EC2 instances, you will need to enable login access in the Elastic Beanstalk Console. Checking CloudWatch logs will most likely not give you any useful information on your application if the issue is software related. Redeploying the application would also not likely help, especially if there is a software dependency not being met.

23. C. The best option is to enable managed platform updates in the Elastic Beanstalk Console. Once they are enabled, you can choose what type of updates you want and when you want updates to occur. Manually updating instances would work but would require a lot of administrative overhead. Enterprise patching systems are great for OS and applications, but they aren't always so great about platform dependencies or language updates.

24. B. Managed platform updates only update minor versions, not major versions. To update a major version, you must manually initiate the update. Managed platform updates can be used to update the operating system, applications, platforms, and languages that you need. There is no approval process needed in Elastic Beanstalk to update. Instead, you simply need to manually initiate the update if it is a major version behind.

25. A. Maintenance windows for managed platform updates in Elastic Beanstalk are 2-hour time periods that occur every week.

26. D. Elastic Beanstalk is free; you just pay for the resources created.

27. C. AWS recommends that you clone the primary environment. This gives you an exact copy to work on without any concerns of something being missed as you might have with a backup or setup scripts.

28. A. All at once is the fastest deployment policy since all of the systems are updated at once, but it does require downtime. Rolling allows you to keep your application up while deploying an update, though it can only support a lower capacity. Rolling with additional batch allows your application to stay up during the update, though it incurs additional cost due to the EC2 instances that need to be spun up. Immutable is also a zero-downtime deployment policy. It is very fast and offers the fastest failback of all the options; it is also the most expensive.

29. D. Immutable is a zero-downtime deployment policy. It is very fast and offers the fastest failback of all the options, but it is also the most expensive. All at once is the fastest deployment policy since all of the systems are updated at once; however, it does require downtime. Rolling allows you to keep your application up while deploying an update, though it can only support a lower capacity. Rolling with additional batch allows your application to stay up during the update, though it incurs additional cost due to the EC2 instances that need to be spun up.

30. B. Rolling allows you to keep your application up while deploying an update, though it can only support a lower capacity. It is the least expensive option with no downtime. Immutable is a zero-downtime deployment policy. It is very fast and offers the fastest failback of all the options, but it is also the most expensive. All at once is the fastest deployment policy since all of the systems are updated at once, but it does require downtime. Rolling with additional batch allows your application to stay up during the update, though it incurs additional cost due to the EC2 instances that need to be spun up.

31. C. Rolling with additional batch allows your application to stay up during the update, though it incurs additional cost due to the EC2 instances that need to be spun up. Rolling allows you to keep your application up while deploying an update though it can only support a lower capacity. It is the least expensive option with no downtime. Immutable is a zero-downtime deployment policy. It is very fast and offers the fastest failback of all the options, it is also the most expensive. All at once is the fastest deployment policy since all of the systems are updated at once, but it does require downtime.

32. B. A rolling deployment policy can be set to ensure that 50% of the systems remain up and able to process traffic. As you are not creating new instances with this deployment type, it is the least expensive option to utilize that does not incur downtime.

33. D. The immutable deployment policy offers the fastest failback capability of all the deployment policy types. Since the supervisor has said that this capability is the highest priority, the immutable policy is the best answer.

34. C. By using rolling with additional batch, you ensure that you are operating at full capacity, which will not impact performance as the supervisor requested. Rolling with additional batch is a less expensive option than immutable as you are only spinning up instances to cover the systems that are being taken offline as opposed to all of the instances as you would do if immutable was being used.

35. B. Since the application will not suffer at 50% capacity later in the evening and your supervisor wants to keep costs down, rolling is the best option. Since no new instances are provisioned, this keeps the cost down, and you can specify that only 50% of the instances are getting updated at any point in time.

36. A. Since this is a development environment and it is considered acceptable to have downtime, all at once is the best deployment policy. It is the fastest method, and the cost is kept down since no new instances are spun up.

37. B. Once you have selected the rolling with additional batch deployment policy, you would enter in 50% for the batch size in the percentage field. Batch size with Fixed would work if you wanted to specify a number of instances as opposed to a percentage of your fleet. The other options in this question are not options that exist in the console.

38. C. Once you have selected the rolling with additional batch deployment policy, you would select Batch size and Fixed, then enter in the number of instances that can be taken down at any given point in time. Batch size with Percentage works when you want to specify a percentage of your fleet that may be updated at the same time. The other two options don't actually exist.

39. D. The most likely explanation is that "Ignore health check" is selected in Deployment preferences. This prevents the deployment from being marked failed if the health check doesn't pass within the configured command timeout window. It is highly unlikely that Elastic Beanstalk service is degraded. The command timeout being set too long would delay the overall failure but would not prevent rollback once an instance was marked unhealthy. It is unlikely the health checks are incorrect.

40. B. If a health check URL is not configured, then instances are marked as healthy as soon as they accept a TCP connection. The services the application relies on may not be up and responding by then. It is unlikely that instances are being marked healthy incorrectly. If the application has issues, it wouldn't start working after a slightly longer time frame; this appears to be an issue of dependencies not being met.

41. B, C, F. The three variables created are AWS_EB_PLATFORM_ARN, AWS_EB_PLATFORM_NAME, and AWS_EB_PLATFORM_VERSION. The others are not automatically created by Elastic Beanstalk and don't actually exist.

42. A. The command that is being used requires the Elastic Beanstalk CLI to be installed. The command is typed correctly and is a valid command, but without the EB CLI, it will not work. You can configure Elastic Beanstalk with the AWS CLI, but the commands are different and start with AWS rather than EB.

43. C. Amazon RDS is a managed SQL service provided by Amazon. It allows you to focus on your databases rather than the servers they are running on and supports multiple database engines, including Microsoft SQL Server and Oracle SQL. While you could certainly run Microsoft SQL Server and Oracle SQL in EC2 instances, this does not meet your supervisor's requirement of not having to manage the underlying servers.

44. D. MongoDB is not supported in RDS. However, it does support multiple database engines, including Amazon Aurora, MySQL, MariaDB, Oracle, Microsoft SQL Server, and PostgreSQL.

45. C. Amazon DynamoDB is a managed NoSQL service and is the best answer to this question. Amazon RDS is a relational database, not a NoSQL database. Amazon Elasticache is a memory caching service. While you could certainly move your NoSQL database to an EC2 instance, the preference for a managed service was mentioned, and if you install your NoSQL database on an EC2 instance, you are not getting a managed service.

46. C. ACID stands for Atomicity, Consistency, Isolation, and Durability. The components in ACID help to ensure database transactions complete properly.

47. A. Atomicity is used to refer to the integrity of a database transaction.

48. C. Isolation describes the ability to process multiple transactions without any transaction interfering with another transaction.

49. D. Durability ensures that data is only saved once a transaction is complete.

50. B. Consistency ensures that data can only be written if it follows validation rules.

51. B. In a NoSQL implementation, databases are referred to as stores, and there are four types of stores: document, graph, key/value, and wide column. The other options are real database terms but are not applicable to what the question is asking.

52. A. Document stores pair a key identifier with a document. That document may be an actual document, a key/value pair, or even a key/value array.

53. D. Wide column stores are a type of NoSQL store that is optimized for querying large scale datasets.

54. B. Graph stores in NoSQL are designed to hold data that you want to represent with graphs.

55. C. Key/value stores are used to store data using a key and a value. Keys are typically names, and values are the data associated with the names. For example, you might set a system as Env:Prod. Env is the key, and Prod is the value.

56. B. Each AWS account can have a total of 40 database instances. To be able to go over the 40, which is a soft limit, you would need to contact AWS and request that the limit be raised.

57. C. T, M, and R are all valid instance types for Amazon RDS. While there are free tier instances available in Amazon RDS, they are not referred to as F for free tier. That was made up for this question.

58. B. Amazon Aurora creates a cluster volume that spans across three availability zones.

59. D. This is part of the shared responsibility model. The customer is responsible for the VPC security groups, database authentication, and IAM. Since Amazon Aurora is a part of Amazon RDS, which is a managed service, AWS manages antivirus on your behalf.

60. A. When using Amazon RDS, you can't increase storage for Microsoft SQL Server. You can, however, increase it for MariaDB, MySQL, and PostgreSQL.

61. C. The best answer would be to scale up your storage. Provisioned IOPS is one of the fastest storage types, so it would make no sense to scale down to magnetic (slowest) or General Purpose SSD.

62. D. Read replicas use asynchronous replication. Whenever there is a change to the data source, the change is replicated to the read replicas. However, if your main data source went down before it had a chance to replicate the changes, that explains why there is missing data.

63. B. If you are using MySQL in Amazon RDS, then you may only have five read replicas at any time. While permissions could be an issue, it is more likely that the max number of read replicas being reached is the issue. In this case, five read replicas is not a soft limit, so you can't request a limit increase. Read replicas are used for performance; multi-AZ is used for high availability. The two have different use cases, so multi-AZ is not the answer to this question. AWS exams do like to focus on the difference between the two.

64. A. If you are using Amazon Aurora in Amazon RDS, then you can have up to 15 Aurora read replicas and 5 MySQL read replicas. In this case, 15 read replicas is not a soft limit so you can't request a limit increase. Read replicas are used for performance; multi-AZ is used for high availability. The two have different use cases, so multi-AZ is not the answer to this question. AWS exams do like to focus on the difference between the two.

65. C. In general, it is a bad idea to disable automatic backups. One of the few exceptions is when you are loading a large amount of data. To re-enable the automatic updates going forward, simply change the value of the backup retention parameter to anything other than zero. Automated backups are on by default, so it is not likely they have never worked. Automated backups would not be disabled due to the system being overloaded or due to a system error.

66. C. You can protect your databases in Amazon RDS using VPC security groups, EC2 security groups, and DB security groups. Table security groups aren't real. If you need to restrict access to specific tables, an IAM user/role would be a better fit.

67. A. Since encryption must be enabled at creation time, you would need to create a new encrypted database and then migrate your data to it. You can't simply enable encryption on your existing databases. Read replicas must be encrypted with the same key as the main data source. You can't have an encrypted read replica with an unencrypted data source.

68. C. Amazon RDS Enhanced Monitoring gives you real-time monitoring data for both database instances and database clusters. Amazon CloudWatch allows you to monitor events, usually in 1- and 5-minute intervals. AWS CloudTrail is used to monitor API calls, and Amazon RDS events are used in concert with Amazon SNS to send notifications when there are system issues or changes.

69. D. Amazon RDS events will utilize SNS to send notifications when changes are made to database instances, clusters, snapshots, and security groups. Amazon CloudWatch allows you to monitor events, usually in 1- and 5-minute intervals, and AWS CloudTrail is used to monitor API calls. Amazon RDS Enhanced Monitoring gives you real-time monitoring data for both database instances and database clusters but does not handle communications.

70. D, E. When using Amazon Elasticache, you have the choice of either Memcached or Redis. The other options are memory caching options, but they are not used within AWS.

71. B. The Elastic Container Service (ECS) is a managed service that is purpose built to run a cluster of Docker containers. Elastic Kubernetes Service (EKS) is a managed Kubernetes cluster service. While you could make this work with either Windows or LinuxEC2 instances, the best managed service solution is ECS.

72. B. When using Amazon ECS, you can use container registries inside of AWS and outside of AWS. So you could use your existing container registry in Docker Hub, and in fact Docker Hub is used by default.

73. C. The best solution is to use the Amazon EC2 Container Registry (ECR) to store the images that you previously stored on Docker Hub. This allows you to create a private repository and allows you to still use Docker commands.

74. D. Since the question seems to be asking about one instance, the User data field would be the simplest way to customize the instance. Logging in and manually making changes or logging in and running a script will require more effort than the User data field. Using SSM to push a script is certainly doable, but there is setup work involved to get it to work properly.

75. A. The User data field is limited to 16 KB. If you need to run something larger than that, you can link a large script from within the User data field. This keeps the size of the field under 16 KB but allows you to call a larger script if you need it.

76. A. Data on instance storage does not persist after an instance is stopped or terminated; however, it works very well as a temporary drive or as a caching drive.

77. D. S3 is a block storage service within AWS and is a clear choice when you need a storage service that will work especially well with APIs.

78. C. EFS can be set up to work much like a normal file share would and removes the need to maintain a separate file server to support network file shares.

79. B. When you need to add storage to a server that requires high IOPS, you are going to want Provisioned IOPS SSD, which is a type of Elastic Block Storage (EBS).

80. C, E. The AWS Service Health Dashboard gives you a window into the health of various AWS services. You can look to see if Amazon Route 53 is degraded in your regions as well as subscribe to the RSS feed for a service. The AWS Personal Health Dashboard lists issues that may impact services that you use, including what time the issues started. Amazon Inspector is used to conduct security assessments. Amazon CloudWatch is used to monitor the resources within your environment. AWS Trusted Advisor makes recommendations based on best practice in accordance with the five pillars identified in the AWS Well-Architected Framework.

81. A. Amazon CloudWatch with basic monitoring collects metrics every 5 minutes and would fulfill your requirement. Detailed monitoring would collect metrics every 1 minute. AWS CloudTrail is used to monitor APIs and does not have basic and/or detail monitoring levels as Amazon CloudWatch does.

82. D. AWS Systems Manager utilized agents to manage systems in AWS and in an on-premises datacenter. Patch Manager, a component of AWS Systems Manager, can be used to patch both Windows and Linux systems. Amazon GuardDuty functions like an intrusion detection system, Amazon Inspector does automated security assessments, and AWS Trusted Advisor makes recommendations based on best practices.

83. C. Spot instances are great, low-cost options for running jobs that are tolerant of being stopped at any point in time. On-demand are cost effective as you pay by the hour, but they are more expensive than spot instances. Reserved instances offer significant cost savings but are better suited for long-running workloads. Dedicated instances are the most expensive of the group and are instances that run on hardware dedicated to a specific customer.

84. A. On-demand are cost effective as you pay by the hour and they can be shut down at any time. You are only billed for the time that they are active. Spot instances are great, low-cost options for running jobs that are tolerant of being stopped at any point in time. Reserved instances offer significant cost savings but are better suited for long running workloads. Dedicated instances are the most expensive of the group and are instances that run on hardware dedicated to a specific customer.

85. D. Dedicated instances are the most expensive of the group and are instances that run on hardware dedicated to a specific customer. This is a perfect fit for organizations that have strict security and/or privacy requirements. On-demand are cost effective as you pay by the hour and they can be shut down at any time. You are only billed for the time that they are active. Spot instances are great, low-cost options for running jobs that are tolerant of being stopped at any point in time. Reserved instances offer significant cost savings but are better suited for long-running workloads.

86. B. Reserved instances offer significant cost savings over on-demand when you know that you are going to use your instances for a period of time. Reserved instances done for a three-year period, for example, can result in significant cost savings. On-demand are cost effective as you pay by the hour and they can be shut down at any time, but they are more expensive than reserved instances. Spot instances are great, low-cost options for running jobs that are tolerant of being stopped at any point in time. Dedicated instances are the most expensive of the group and are instances that run on hardware dedicated to a specific customer.

87. C. Since you used your organization's standard AMI, you will need to install the Amazon ECS agent first. You will also need an IAM role for authentication with the Amazon ECS service endpoint and network access to the ECS service endpoint. The AWS SSM agent is utilized by AWS Systems Manager to manage systems. Installing antivirus and configuring the host firewall are all good things to do, but they are quite often baked into a standard image, or managed in some other way. They are not required to start using ECS.

88. B. Since this application is written in C# and is event driven, AWS Lambda is a perfect fit. Consider an upload to Amazon S3. AWS Lambda could be invoked when an object is uploaded and can start its workflow. An Amazon EC2 instance would work; however, it would not be as cost effective as AWS Lambda would be. AWS Elastic Beanstalk is meant to run full web applications, not event-triggered applications, and AWS CloudFormation isn't designed to run applications at all.

89. C. Amazon Lightsail is a perfect fit for this type of scenario where a single server with an OS and a development stack are all that is desired. Developers can be granted permissions in Amazon Lightsail so that administrators don't need to do anything at all. AWS CloudFormation requires administrative overhead to create templates and deploy stacks. AWS Elastic Beanstalk requires some administrative overhead to configure everything properly. Amazon EC2 would require a great deal of administrative overhead as you would need to pick the OS and manually install the development stack.

90. A, C. When using Lightsail, you have the choice between Amazon Linux and Ubuntu for the operating system.

91. D. Since Amazon Lightsail supports WordPress, it presents the best option for the developers and can be used with minimal administrative overhead. Elastic Beanstalk requires more administrative effort than Lightsail does. An Amazon EC2 instance would allow you to install WordPress but would require a significant amount of administrative effort. The Elastic WordPress service sounds cool, but it doesn't actually exist.

92. A. The Connect option in the Amazon Lightsail Console gives you access to the console of the guest operating system. While Session Manager can be used to access an instance without the need for SSH software, it requires a little work to set up. Remote Desktop will not work. Amazon Lightsail only supports Linux operating systems, and they do not have an X server running. You don't need to install an SSH client.

93. C. AWS Batch is purpose built to schedule and run batch jobs as well as account for dependencies between jobs. AWS Lambda is not a good solution as it is tied to triggers (in this case, static timing). Amazon EC2 instances could be used in place of the virtual machines you have on-premises, but there is no gain in doing this. SQS could help with communication between the jobs but would not be able to do the needed work by itself.

94. B. Job definitions specify how your job should be run, including identifying resources needed like CPU and memory, storage, etc. A job is used to define a single unit of work in AWS Batch. A job queue is used to store jobs until they are scheduled to run. The scheduler is the brains of the outfit and determines when jobs should be run.

95. C. A job queue is used to store jobs until they are scheduled to run. A job is used to define a single unit of work in AWS Batch. Job definitions specify how your job should be run, including identifying resources needed like CPU and memory, storage, etc. The scheduler is the brains of the outfit and determines when jobs should be run.

96. D. The scheduler is the brains of the outfit and determines when jobs should be run. A job is used to define a single unit of work in AWS Batch. Job definitions specify how your job should be run, including identifying resources needed like CPU and memory, storage, etc. A job queue is used to store jobs until they are scheduled to run.

97. A. A job is used to define a single unit of work in AWS Batch. Job definitions specify how your job should be run, including identifying resources needed like CPU and memory, storage, etc. A job queue is used to store jobs until they are scheduled to run. The scheduler is the brains of the outfit and determines when jobs should be run.

98. B. By default, the AWS Batch job queue uses the FIFO algorithm to process jobs.

99. D. With AWS Batch, the default job size is 20 KB. This is a hard limit and can't be changed.

100. A. The Managed Compute Environment is managed by AWS, and provisioning of instances and management of said instances is done by AWS. An Unmanaged Compute Environment is managed by the customer. Neither Elastic Compute Environment nor Scheduled Compute Environment are real compute environments available in AWS.

101. B. An Unmanaged Compute Environment is managed by the customer; provisioning and management of the instances is done by the customer and not by AWS. The Managed Compute Environment is managed by AWS, and provisioning of instances and management of said instances is done by AWS. Neither Elastic Compute Environment nor Scheduled Compute Environment are real compute environments available in AWS.

102. C. AWS Batch uses containers to execute batch jobs. To take advantage of AWS Batch, you must install the Amazon ECS (Elastic Container Service) Agent on your compute resources. There is no such thing as an AWS Batch Agent. While Amazon Inspector Agent and AWS Systems Manager Agent are actual things, they are not required to be installed to support AWS Batch.

103. C, D. The Fargate launch type removes the need for you to provision the support infrastructure for your containers. The EC2 launch type creates a cluster of Amazon EC2 instances that are used to run your containers. The other launch types in the question are not valid.

104. B. By specifying FARGATE in the requiresCompatibilities parameter, you can set the launch type to Fargate. The "image" parameter is used to specify the image that you want the container to be built from. executionRoleArn is used to specify the role that should be used to execute the task.

105. C. You can use the Amazon ECS CLI, AWS Management Console, AWS CLI, or the AWS SDK to manage and provision resources in Amazon ECS. The Amazon EB CLI is used to manage Elastic Beanstalk but is not used to directly manage ECS.

106. B. The command to install Docker on Amazon Linux 2 is
`sudo amazon-linux-extras install docker`. Without `sudo`, you will run into permissions issues trying to install. `sudo install docker` will not work, and Linux is case sensitive, so it is important to understand that `docker` and `Docker` would not be treated the same.

107. D. If the user account is added to the docker group on the Amazon EC2 instance, then that user account will no longer need to use `sudo` in front of all Docker commands. In this case, the default user ec2-user needs to be added to the docker group; however, any user account could be added to get this effect. Adding the ec2-user to the root group would create an overly permissive account and is certainly not a best practice. Changing the ownership of the Docker files could actually bring Docker down.

108. A. Occasionally a reboot is needed after granting permissions to the user accounts so that they can access the Docker daemon without `sudo`. Adding your administrator's account to the root group gives them far more access than what is needed. Restarting the Docker service will not fix the permission issue. Reinstalling Docker will not resolve the issue.

109. B. The EXPOSE line in the dockerfile tells Docker which ports you want the containers to listen on. By changing the 80 to 443, you have met the request of your security team. Your security team wants 443 and not 80, so you would want to remove it from the dockerfile altogether; re-ordering it won't make any difference. While removing EXPOSE 80 from your dockerfile will make your security team happy, it will not result in a very usable container.

110. C. When you log in interactively with docker login, you use an authentication string that is visible in the process list; the process list is displayed using ps -e. The pen tester could install a key logger but that is not very likely as most organizations do not allow the installation of malicious software. While the pen tester may have been sniffing the network, you are authenticating with an authentication string, not a username and password. If you leave off the -p and are prompted for your password, the authentication string would not have shown up in the ps -e command.

111. B. By dropping the -p from the docker login command, you will be prompted for the password to connect. Since you are prompted for the password, it will not show up in the process list. Running the docker login command as root user is too permissive and will still show up in the process list. With sudo in front of the docker login command, it will still show up in the process list. Restarting the container might clear the process list, but the authentication string is good for 12 hours, so an attacker could simply reconnect, or would watch the process list for when you reconnect.

112. B. Images are stored in repositories, and repositories are kept within a registry. Authorization tokens are used to authenticate and can be retrieved with the get-login command. An image is used to provide the operating system and dependencies for your application to run.

113. A. Images are stored in repositories, and repositories are kept within a registry. Authorization tokens are used to authenticate and can be retrieved with the get-login command. An image is used to provide the operating system and dependencies for your application to run.

114. D. An image is used to provide the operating system and dependencies for your application to run. Images are stored in repositories, and repositories are kept within a registry. Authorization tokens are used to authenticate and can be retrieved with the get-login command.

115. C. Authorization tokens are used to authenticate and can be retrieved with the get-login command. Images are stored in repositories, and repositories are kept within a registry. An image is used to provide the operating system and dependencies for your application to run.

116. D. You would need to enable VPC peering on the Lightsail account page, and from there Lightsail will configure everything for you. Direct Connect and VPN gateways are for external connections to your AWS resources and are not applicable here. VPC endpoints are available for specific services but would not work in this case.

117. A. Amazon Lightsail supports solid-state drives only. The other drive types in the question are valid EBS volume types, but they are not supported in Amazon Lightsail.

118. B. Each Amazon Lightsail instance can support up to 15 disks.

119. C. Each disk attached to an Amazon Lightsail instance can be a maximum of 16 TB in size.

120. B, E. To enlarge your disk, you need to take a snapshot of the disk you want to make larger, then create a larger disk from that snapshot. You don't need snapshots of all the disks, just the disk that you want to enlarge. You can't enlarge a disk directly from the Amazon Lightsail Console. You can't enlarge a disk directly through the CLI.

121. B. The Lightsail load balancer is able to balance traffic across instances in other availability zones and will automatically scale when traffic loads increase. Network Load Balancers and Application Load Balancers require more administrative overhead to get them to work, as does Route 53.

122. C. Using Amazon Lightsail's built-in certificate management utilities makes the most sense as they will request and renew certificates for you as well as add the certificate to your load balancer. The other two certificate options in this question require more manual effort to make them work. Ignoring your security team is never a good thing to do, so I wouldn't recommend it.

123. A. You need to enable session persistence on the Lightsail load balancer so that it will direct the user to the correct instance. While you may hear the term *sticky cookies* in reference to load balancers and persistent user connections, the appropriate AWS terminology is *session persistence*.

124. D. You will need to add a CNAME record to your DNS zone at your DNS hosting provider to validate that you own the domain for which you are trying to issue certificates.

125. A. Lightsail certificates can support up to 10 domains or subdomains, and since Lightsail does not support the use of wildcard certificates, this is the best option.

126. B. The Upgrade to EC2 feature is the simplest way to convert from Lightsail to an EC2 instance. You simply export a Lightsail snapshot and use the Upgrade to EC2 wizard to convert it. You do need to set up the networking infrastructure to support your new EC2 instance. Manually creating an EC2 instance and installing your application results in higher administrative overhead, as does creating a CloudFormation template from which to create an EC2 instance.

127. C. Hotfix updates are not a valid type of platform update. Major, minor, and patch updates are all valid types of platform updates.

128. A. To take care of the source bundle automatically, change the Application Versions settings to delete the source bundle from S3 when the application version is removed. While an AWS Lambda function could work in this way, it is simpler to use the built-in versioning tools.

129. B. Since the lifecycle settings are set to 5 versions and you want to keep 10 versions in S3, your best choice is to manually remove the source bundles from S3. The AWS Lambda function would potentially remove too many bundles, leaving you with fewer than 10.

130. C. AWS recommends using a blue/green deployment when upgrading from Amazon Linux to Amazon Linux 2 as there may be certain things that are not backward-compatible. It would not be recommended to manually upgrade all of the instances as you may discover the upgrade has caused your application to crash.

131. A. The instance security group serves as a stateful firewall; by ensuring it only allows TCP/443, you have locked down the instance to HTTPS. HTTP uses TCP/80, which is what you want to avoid. HTTPS does not use UDP/443 or UDP/80.

132. B. The best response is to use a load balancer security group to lock down traffic to only TCP/443. HTTP uses TCP/80, so you will want to use TCP/443 to support HTTPS.

Domain 4: Storage and Data Management

1. C. Amazon Elastic Block Store (EBS) is a block storage service. Changes made to an existing file will only change the blocks containing data that has changed.

2. A. Amazon Simple Storage Service (S3) is an object storage service. Changes to a file require the upload of an entirely new file (object).

3. B. Amazon Elastic File System (EFS) is a managed file storage service. It allows you to create filesystems that can be attached to Amazon EC2 instances.

4. B. The instance store used with Amazon EC2 instances is ephemeral. It is destroyed whenever the instance is stopped or terminated.

5. B. The only type of storage that can deliver the IOPS needed by the application is Provisioned IOPS SSD, which can support 64,000 max IOPS per volume.

6. D. Cold HDD is the lowest-cost storage available in AWS and is a great choice for workloads that are not accessed frequently.

7. C. For workloads with high throughput needs such as data warehouses and log processing systems, the Throughput Optimized HDD is a great fit.

8. A. The General Purpose SSD is a good fit for this use case. It's a great balance between performance and cost and is good for dev and test instances.

9. B. All tiers of storage in S3 offer 99.999999999% durability (11 9s). So durability would not be a factor that you would need to look at when deciding on which storage tier to use.

10. C. All of the storage types listed are tied to a region except AWS Snowball. AWS Snowball is designed to transport large amounts of data (think petabytes) from your datacenter to AWS.

11. D. EBS volumes can't span availability zones. The volume can only be attached to an Amazon EC2 instance that is in the availability zone where the EBS volume resides. None of the other choices are correct.

12. A. The formula for this calculation is 50 IOPS per provisioned GB. You would need a 150 GB drive to support 7500 IOPS. A drive of 400 GB would allow you to provision the maximum amount of IOPS.

13. C. To mount an EBS volume, you would use the command
`aws ec2 attach-volume --volume-id <volumeid> --instance-id <instanceid> --device /dev/<drivename>`.

14. D. The best way to make the data available to the other instance is to create a snapshot of the EBS volume and then use the snapshot to create an EBS volume in the other availability zone and attach it to the other EC2 instance. Snapshots are stored regionally, so they work great for crossing availability zones. You can't copy the volume to another availability zone, nor can you download an EBS volume from the console. While you could create an AMI and use that since AMIs are stored regionally, this would only work if you wanted to copy the whole instance. In this case, you only wanted to copy the EBS volume.

15. A, D. With EBS volumes, you have a choice between either client-level encryption, which is done by the operating system, or volume-level encryption, which is managed by AWS.

16. A. Client-level encryption is done by the operating system and requires you to manage your encryption keys. For organizations with strict security requirements, client-level encryption is the best fit.

17. D. Volume-level encryption is managed by AWS, which makes it the simplest from an administrative standpoint. Since each volume gets its own encryption key, and those keys use the AES-256 algorithm to perform encryption, you can be sure that you are using strong encryption.

18. B. AWS KMS offers key management capability and should be used when you want to audit key use. AWS KMS works in concert with AWS IAM and AWS CloudTrail to provide greater visibility into key use and key protection.

19. B. Amazon EFS acts like a filesystem and can be attached to multiple EC2 instances, so it is the best choice. Amazon EBS can only be attached to one EC2 instance at a time. Amazon S3 is object storage solution and does not act like a filesystem. Instance stores are ephemeral storage that is available for some EC2 instance types. They can't be moved to another instance or attached to multiple instances.

20. C. Amazon S3 bucket names can be up to 63 characters long, so the 50-character name you want to use will be allowed so long as it is unique.

21. A. Amazon S3 bucket names can't contain underscores. They can contain lowercase characters, numbers, periods, and dashes.

22. B, D. Amazon S3 buckets can be either virtual-hosted-style or path-style. Virtual-hosted-style includes the bucket name as part of the domain name in the URL. Using path-style, the bucket name is not part of the domain name in the URL. The other two options were made up for this question.

23. D. All tiers of Amazon S3 have the same durability. Amazon guarantees 99.999999999 (11 9s) durability for all Amazon S3 storage classes.

24. A. S3 Standard and Amazon Glacier both offer 99.99% availability; however, S3 Standard is the better choice since the data is accessed regularly.

25. B. Choosing S3 Standard-IA makes the most sense here. It is less expensive than S3 Standard, is still highly available as your data is replicated across three or more availability zones, and is a great fit for data that is not accessed frequently.

26. D. Amazon S3 Glacier is an excellent fit for archiving data. It is less expensive than the other S3 tiers and will allow retrieval with the needed time span. Its data is replicated across three or more availability zones, so it is highly available.

27. C. The best fit in this case would be S3 One Zone-IA. The data is stored in one availability zone only but can be accessed immediately and is the least expensive option that meets the requirements.

28. A. S3 Standard offers 99.99% availability; none of these other options do.

29. B. S3 Standard-IA offers 99.9% availability; none of these other options do.

30. C. S3 One Zone-IA offers 99.5% availability; none of these other options do.

31. D. S3 Glacier Deep Archive is the best fit. Its retrieval times are into the hours; however, it is the least expensive option for long-term archival.

32. C. By enabling MFA Delete, you are able to protect against accidental deletions. Since the question asked about authorized users specifically, you don't need to make changes in IAM. Versioning doesn't protect against accidental deletion; it just provides a mechanism to recover a file if it were deleted.

33. A, D. By moving data that is 30 days old to S3 Standard-IA, and then to S3 Glacier after 90 days, you are saving money while still meeting the requirements set.

34. C. This is a perfect example of when you would want lifecycle policies. A lifecycle policy in S3 can automatically move data between the various storage classes and then finally delete data as well.

35. C. Amazon CloudFront caches your content closer to your customers. You can have your website in S3 in one region, and CloudFront can serve it out worldwide.

36. B. While the snapshots are stored in Amazon S3, they are not directly accessible. You must use the Amazon EC2 API to work with the snapshots.

37. C. Amazon EFS offers many of the same features you would expect from your file servers and can grow dynamically as you accumulate more data. Amazon S3 doesn't act like the file servers you currently have. Amazon EBS can only be used by one Amazon EC2 instance at a time. The question stated that you want to avoid creating file servers, so that removes option D.

38. C. AWS DataSync is built for this use case. It allows you to sync your existing filesystems with your Amazon EFS filesystem and can work over the Internet or via an AWS Direct Connect/AWS VPN connection. The other options require more effort or are simply not feasible, and AWS will never have a third-party product like Robocopy as an answer on one of its exams.

39. C, D. For Amazon EFS, you can choose either Standard or Infrequent Access. The other two options don't belong to Amazon EFS.

40. A. You can use lifecycle policies in Amazon EFS to move data from Amazon EFS Standard to Amazon EFS IA. In Amazon EFS, these are called age-off policies; expiration policies are used in Amazon S3.

41. B. Files smaller than 128 KB in size will not be moved by Amazon EFS Lifecycle Management.

42. B, C. VPC security groups can be used to specify which systems or IP ranges are allowed to access your file shares. IAM policies can be applied to the filesystem.

43. C. Amazon EFS Access Points allow you to use an operating system user or group to access a particular shared directory as their root directory. You can further enforce this by adding an IAM policy on to the access point.

44. B. SSE-C allows you to maintain control over your keys while still allowing Amazon S3 to handle the actual encryption process. This simplifies administration as you don't need to implement a client-side encryption library; you can instead leverage the tools provided by AWS.

45. A. Since there is no requirement to keep control over the keys, SSE-S3 is going to be the best fit in this case. The level of administrative effort is kept low as well, since AWS manages the keys for you.

46. C. SSE-KMS uses the AWS KMS service to manage the encryption of your keys and provides an audit trail for who has accessed your key and which object or objects were accessed by the key. Whenever there is an encryption question and auditability is a requirement, you will want SSE-KMS.

47. D. The Amazon S3 Encryption client allows you to maintain control of your keys and take advantage of client-side encryption libraries.

48. C. Amazon Macie can be used to discover sensitive data and will send alerts if there is reason to believe an unauthorized access has occurred or there has been data leakage.

49. D. Access Analyzer for S3 is able to examine your bucket policies and remediate buckets that are overly permissive.

50. B. By using S3 Intelligent-Tiering, you are getting the best of both worlds. You aren't having to set up lifecycle policies, and you are saving money on storage as it will automatically move stale data to less expensive storage. With S3 Intelligent-Tiering, you have two tiers for storage; you have one tier that is set up for frequent access, and one tier set up for infrequent access. It is able to intelligently move data between the tiers automatically.

51. B. Much like lifecycle policies, files under 128 KB will remain in the frequent access tier rather than be moved.

52. C. S3 Standard-IA is designed for long-term storage and has a minimum storage duration of 30 days. While your data was only stored for 10 days before being deleted, you were charged for the full 30 days as that is the minimum duration.

53. B. Standard retrieval in Amazon S3 Glacier will usually be complete within 3–5 hours.

54. A. Expedited retrieval in Amazon S3 Glacier will usually be complete within 1–5 minutes. While you have been asked to keep the costs down, if the data is truly needed as soon as possible, then this is the way to go.

55. C. Bulk retrieval in Amazon S3 Glacier will usually be complete within 5–12 hours.

56. D. If you need to get a restore from Amazon S3 Glacier faster than initially requested, you can use the S3 Restore Speed Upgrade. This will require you to choose a faster restore speed, and you will be charged for both retrieval requests.

57. B. S3 Glacier is designed for long-term storage and has a minimum storage duration of 90 days. Your data was stored for 30 days, which you would have been charged for, and then you were charged a pro-rated 60 days for the early deletion fee.

58. B. Standard retrieval in Amazon S3 Glacier Deep Archive will usually be complete within 12 hours.

59. C. Bulk retrieval in Amazon S3 Glacier Deep Archive will usually be complete within 48 hours.

60. C. Transferring over the Internet is not a recommended method to migrate from tape backup to Amazon S3 Deep Archive. Using AWS Tape Gateway or AWS Snowball or transferring over AWS Direct Connect are all recommended solutions for data migration from tape.

61. C. S3 Glacier Deep Archive is designed for long-term storage and has a minimum storage duration of 180 days. Your data was stored for 90 days, which you would have been charged for, and then you were charged a pro-rated 90 days for the remainder of the minimum storage duration.

62. A. Amazon Athena makes it possible to query data in Amazon S3 using standard SQL queries.

63. D. Amazon S3 notifications can be tied into Amazon SNS, Amazon SQS, or AWS Lambda. Amazon CloudWatch does not have the same level of integration into S3 that the other three do.

64. B. The best answer here is to enable S3 Transfer Acceleration. When this is enabled on your S3 bucket, your offices connect to the Amazon CloudFront edge location nearest them, which routes the traffic to your Amazon S3 bucket.

65. C. A Storage Class Analysis is able to look at access patterns to determine if there is data that should be moved to a less frequent access tier of storage. It can look at whole buckets, or more specifically at prefixes and/or object tags.

66. A. Using S3 Batch Operations will allow you to automate this process easily with very little administrative effort.

67. D. When you enable Amazon S3 Cross-Region Replication, you are able to replicate the contents of your Amazon S3 bucket to another region. You can choose a region that guarantees your data has at least 350 miles between each copy of the data. For instance. you could replicate between us-west-1 and us-east-1.

68. A. For static files, Amazon S3 is the best choice for an origin server.

69. C. For dynamic files, an Amazon EC2 instance running some kind of web server is the best choice for an origin server.

70. C. You should set up an CNAME record with your domain name and point it to the CloudFront distribution address.

71. B. Amazon CloudFront improves performance by caching the content of your site closer to your end users. It intelligently routes them to the nearest edge location to them.

72. B. Amazon CloudFront is at its best when it is being used to cache static content like images, videos, software downloads, etc. Dynamic content that changes often does not benefit as much from caching. In fact, it can cause a problem if the old version is cached and you need the new version to show up.

73. A. Origin redundancy in Amazon CloudFront allows you to add a "backup origin." You can specify what should trigger the usage of the backup origin and can choose a combination of HTTP 400 and/or HTTP 500 response codes.

74. B. In the Amazon CloudFront Console, you can choose to whitelist allowed countries or blacklist countries you want to block. In the scenario posed in the question, you would want to blacklist the desired countries in the Geolocation tab.

75. C. You can create customized error pages in Amazon CloudFront that include your logo and different messages (if desired) for different types of HTTP 400 or HTTP 500 errors.

76. D. Amazon CloudFront looks for new versions of files 24 hours after the last time the file was checked. You can set the expiration to 0 to make it check the file right away. However, it is important to change it back to 24 hours (or whatever your setting is) as the 0 will cause it to request a new version of the file from your origin server every time there is a request. This is a popular exam topic.

77. B. Invalidating the file in Amazon CloudFront will ensure that the ad is removed from future requests for the page that the ad was on. This is the closest thing to an immediate removal you have in Amazon CloudFront. Deleting the file in Amazon S3 will not result in immediate removal; you will have to wait for the ad's file to expire on Amazon CloudFront.

78. C. Field-level encryption can be used to further secure sensitive fields like those asking for credit card numbers. As the name suggests, it must be enabled for individual fields. The input is encrypted with a public key and only authorized applications have access to the private key needed to decrypt the data.

79. B. AWS Certificate Manager has integrations into CloudFront so it is the best choice. AWS Certificate Manager can take care of certificate renewals for you as well.

80. A. By default, you have access to AWS Shield Standard. You can pay to upgrade to AWS Shield Advanced if desired. AWS Shield provides protection from DDoS attacks.

81. C. The AWS WAF is purpose-built to detect web application attacks. It can be put in place to protect your web applications that use Amazon CloudFront.

82. C. You can modify the request headers to prove that traffic bound for your origin servers came from Amazon CloudFront.

83. D. All you need to do here is allow CloudFront to forward cookies to your origin servers. So long as this is allowed, you can continue to use the cookies for dynamic content on the website.

84. B. When you use a URI query parameter in an HTTP GET request, the parameter starts after a "?" and ends with a "&" character.

85. C. Amazon S3 doesn't put a limit on file size, but Amazon CloudFront has a limit for single files, which is 20 GB. That would explain why you can upload the file to Amazon S3 with no issue and why it is not being delivered by Amazon CloudFront.

86. D. The best answer here is going to be AWS Snowball. It is designed to transfer petabytes of data and is an expedient solution.

87. B. To prepare your source host to transfer data to the AWS Snowball device, you will need to install the AWS Snowball client. This handles the encryption and compression of the data as well as the transfer to the AWS Snowball device.

88. B. For large ongoing transfers, Amazon recommends AWS Direct Connect as it is a dedicated high-speed connection. AWS Snowball is only meant to be used for an initial data transfer; in fact, you can only keep the device for 90 days.

89. B. Of the possible answers, the only one that will work would be S3 Cross-Region Replication. AWS Snowball doesn't allow transferring of data to different regions, and the other options don't work to move data from one region to another.

90. C. The best answer to give them is that the data on the AWS Snowball device is encrypted with an AES-256 bit key and that the private key is not stored on the AWS Snowball device, it is managed by AWS KMS.

91. A, C. The AWS Snowball device uses a combination of a tamper-resistant enclosure and a TPM chip to ensure that the hardware, software, and firmware have not been tampered with in any way. AWS will also inspect the device when it arrives at its datacenter to ensure that nothing has been tampered with. Encryption will protect the data but won't prevent tampering. Inspection stickers can show that someone may have opened a device but will not prevent tampering,

92. A. You should have some knowledge of the basic regulatory situations. In this case, hospitals have personal health information (PHI) and must be compliant with the Health Insurance Portability and Accountability Act (HIPAA). Since AWS Snowball is HIPAA-eligible, you would just need a Business Associates Agreement (BAA) with AWS. The Gramm-Leach-Bliley Act (GLBA) is a privacy law and does not deal with medical information specifically; it is more commonly used in financial institutions.

93. A. To set up AWS Snowball, you need the AWS Snowball client as well as the job manifest file and the job manifest unlock code. There is no unlock code for the AWS Snowball client.

94. C. AWS Snowball can be used to export large amounts of data from an AWS datacenter, just as it can be used for import.

95. B. While you can export Amazon S3 data to the AWS Snowball device, you must first restore data from Amazon S3 Glacier to Amazon S3 before you can export it to the AWS Snowball.

96. D. The valid lifecycle policies in Amazon EFS are AFTER_7_DAYS, AFTER_14_DAYS, AFTER_30_DAYS, AFTER_60_DAYS, and AFTER_90_DAYS.

97. C. To enable lifecycle management for Amazon EFS via the AWS CLI, you would use the command `aws efs put-lifecycle-configuration`.

98. B, C. To safeguard your data in Amazon EFS, you can use the AWS Backup Service or the EFS-to-EFS backup solution. Enabling lifecycle management doesn't safeguard data; it simply helps reduce cost. EFS-to-S3 backup doesn't exist.

99. A. Data at rest in Amazon EFS is protected by AWS KMS if you create the filesystem to use encryption.

100. D. Data in transit from and to Amazon EFS is automatically encrypted, and the keys are managed by Amazon EFS.

101. D. The customer master key (CMK) must be in an enabled state or the users will not have access to the contents of the filesystem. The process is seamless to users; they don't need to know how to decrypt data.

102. D. The deletion of a CMK is irreversible so you can't do it immediately; you have to schedule the deletion. You can schedule it for anywhere from 7–30 days. If you must get rid of it more immediately, you can revoke or disable the key.

103. A. Remember that AWS CloudTrail is used to audit API activity, not performance activity. Amazon CloudWatch can be used to monitor performance activity.

104. B. You can use tags with Amazon EFS. In this case, a tag named Department could be used to identify the owner of various folders and files.

105. A. You would use the command `aws efs create-tags` to create tags in Amazon EFS.

106.   C. The simplest way to retrieve the tags that have already been created in Amazon EFS is to use the AWS CLI and type **`aws efs describe-tags`**.

107.   B. If you want to restrict which hosts can access a filesystem, the simplest way to do this is to create a mount target security group.

108.   C. When you create mount points for Amazon EFS, it is recommended to create them in each availability zone as this will reduce the amount of cross-availability zone access, which incurs additional cost.

109.   D. You would use `aws efs describe-mount-targets` to retrieve the list of current mount targets.

110.   A. Using the AWS CLI, you can use the command `aws kms enable-key-rotation` to enable key rotation in AWS KMS.

111.   D. From the moment the automatic rotation of keys is enabled, the key will be rotated every 365 days.

112.   C. To prove to an auditor that key rotation is enabled, you can use the command `aws kms get-key-rotation-status` followed by the key ID.

113.   B. You should disable the CMK for a period of time to see if it really is not being used. If you delete it, there is no way to recover it, and you will have potentially lost access to your data.

Domain 5: Security and Compliance

1.   C, D. Deny and Allow are the only two options for the Effect element. A wildcard (*), Permit, and Notify aren't valid options.

2.   B. AWS SSO is a managed service that allows you to grant users to an AWS account using their Active Directory credentials. Cognito doesn't support this. SAML is a markup language, not an AWS service. AWS Organizations allows you to centrally manage multiple AWS accounts.

3.   A. An inline policy is embedded in a principal and thus applies to only that principal. The other policy types can apply to more than one principal.

4.   E. IAM will retain five versions of every customer managed policy.

5.   C. Assuming a role that has access to the `TerminateInstances` action allows you to terminate the instance with the least security risk. Logging in as the root user poses a greater security risk because the root user has access to all aspects of the AWS accounts. Using the CLI command won't work if the IAM user doesn't have the permissions to terminate the instance. Logging into the instance and shutting it down from the command line will stop the instance but won't terminate it.

6. A, D. AWS is responsible for patching the hypervisors that run a customer's EC2 instances. AWS is also responsible for patching the operating systems of RDS instances. Patching the operating systems and applications running on a customer's EC2 instance is the customer's responsibility.

7. D. Creating an inbound network access control list (NACL) rule to explicitly deny the traffic and then applying that NACL to the subnets the web servers are in will prevent traffic from the IP range from reaching the servers. Creating outbound rules to deny the traffic won't prevent inbound traffic. It's not possible to explicitly deny traffic either inbound or outbound using a security group. Using the operating system's built-in firewall won't prevent traffic from reaching the server.

8. B. You must get permission from AWS before performing any penetration testing against your EC2 instances. It's not the responsibility of AWS to patch your EC2 instances. There's no need to give the third party credentials to your AWS account.

9. C. The customer is responsible for ensuring files stored in S3 are encrypted. Although AWS offers server-side encryption, it's up to the customer to enable it. The customer, not AWS, is responsible for controlling access to customer master keys (CMKs) stored in KMS. AWS, not the customer, is responsible for rotating S3-managed keys.

10. A, B. The customer is solely responsible for configuring the two available S3 security access controls: bucket policies and access control lists.

11. A, C, D. Bucket policies, identity-based IAM policies, and access control lists can all be used to grant access to a non-public file stored in S3. Identity-based policies can't be used to grant public, anonymous access. Resource groups are not an access control method.

12. A, C, F. To grant anonymous access to a file stored in S3, you must create the bucket policy specifying a * (wildcard) for the principal and include the bucket name in the policy resource element.

13. B. You must specify the resource element along with the bucket name and file name. Specifying the bucket name followed by a wildcard would allow access to all files in the bucket.

14. E. By specifying a source IP address in the condition element, you can apply the policy statement only to users coming from that IP address.

15. B. The action `s3:DeleteObjectVersion` deletes a file, regardless of whether versioning is enabled. `s3:PutObject` creates a file. `s3:DeleteObject` and `s3:RemoveObject` aren't valid actions.

16. D. The condition operator `DateLessThan` returns true if the date and time at policy evaluation precedes the date and time specified in the key's value. In this case, the value is `2021-01-01T00:00:00Z`, which is the ISO 8601 representation of January 1, 2021 at 0:00 Universal Coordinated Time (UTC). The `aws:CurrentTime` key requires the time to be specified in ISO 8601 format. `DateBefore` is not a valid condition operator. The `aws:epochTime` key requires the time to be specified in Unix epoch time.

17. B. Object lifecycle expiration actions automatically delete files in S3 after a specified period of time without requiring you to grant any special permissions. Lambda functions and CloudWatch Events Rules can be used to delete objects in S3 but would require creating roles and granting them permissions to S3. Object lifecycle transition actions don't delete files. There's no such thing as a bucket lifecycle expiration action.

18. C, E. The most secure way to grant access to DynamoDB is to create an IAM role with the appropriate permissions and link that role to the instance using an instance profile. Using an access key identifier and secret access key would require storing those long-term credentials where they could potentially be stolen. DynamoDB doesn't support resource-based policies.

19. A. SQS is the only service listed that uses resource-based policies.

20. D. The Principal element isn't required in an identity-based policy because the policy itself applies to a principal. The other elements are required.

21. C. The Condition element is not required in a resource-based policy. The other elements are required.

22. A. IAM policies are stored only in JSON format.

23. A, B, C. To create a new IAM policy, you can import it from an AWS managed policy, import an existing policy document using either the AWS CLI or the AWS Management Console, or use the Visual editor to create a policy from scratch. You can't import a policy document from an S3 bucket. When you create an IAM user, it has no default policy attached.

24. C, E. The web server on the instance is configured to listen for HTTP (TCP port 80) traffic, so its security group should allow inbound HTTP traffic, but not HTTPS. The load balancer needs an outbound rule to permit HTTP traffic to the instance. The presence of the "gateway timeout" error indicates that the load balancer already has an inbound rule for HTTPS, so there's no need to add one. Because the load balancer is configured to listen only for HTTPS traffic, there's no need to add an inbound rule to its security group to allow inbound HTTP traffic.

25. A, C, E. For this to be successful, HTTPS traffic needs to flow through the network load balancer to the instance's secondary interface. Hence, you must create a security group allowing inbound HTTPS access and attach it to the network load balancer and the instance's secondary interface, since that's where the web service is listening for traffic. The instance's primary interface is reserved for SSH management traffic and has nothing to do with the web service. There's no need to create an outbound security group rule because security groups are stateful.

26. D. NACLs are stateless and require an outbound rule to explicitly allow return traffic on an ephemeral port. Because the ephemeral port range varies by operating system, creating an outbound NACL rule allowing all traffic is sufficient. Security groups are stateful and thus don't require an explicit outbound rule to permit return traffic.

27. A. Whitelisting is the practice of denying all permissions by default and granting only those specifically required. Blacklisting is the opposite. Greylisting is a technique to avoid spam emails. Blackmailing is a form of extortion.

28. B, C. Blacklisting is the practice of allowing all actions for all services and on all resources while denying access only to specific actions or resources.

29. B. CloudTrail may contain the contents of the policy if CloudTrail has been configured to log API events for SNS. CloudWatch Events doesn't store any API events. IAM doesn't store resource-based policies. SNS doesn't keep backups of policies.

30. C. An egress-only Internet gateway allows outbound-only IPv6 access to the Internet. NAT gateways do not support IPv6. A NAT instance could be configured to support IPv6 but would not be as simple as using an egress-only Internet gateway. There's no such thing as a NATv6 gateway in AWS.

31. C. A permissions boundary could be configured to limit the user's EC2 access. The region isn't relevant as the permissions policy doesn't have any conditions, and IAM is a global service. ACLs aren't relevant either, as the permissions policy and user are in the same AWS account. The user's SSH key pair is only for logging into the instance once it's launched and has no bearing on their permissions to launch it. The permissions policy allows access to all resources, so the specific AMI the user is attempting to launch is irrelevant.

32. A. The statement ID, or Sid, is the only optional element of those given. The action and resource elements can be given as wildcards to signify all, but they must be included in the policy.

33. B. A trust policy defines who is allowed to assume a role. A permissions policy defines the permissions of the principal.

34. D. RDS allows you to use a customer managed customer master key that you can rotate every 30 days. DynamoDB also lets you use your own KMS keys, but it's not a relational database system. MongoDB doesn't let you use KMS keys. KMS is the service that manages the encryption keys, but it isn't a database service.

35. C. Cognito allows you to grant application users temporary access to services in your AWS account. Directory Service allows integration with Microsoft Active Directory. Instance profiles grant applications running on an instance—not users—access to AWS resources. There's no such service as Security Ticket Service.

36. A, B. STS provides short-term credentials consisting of an unencrypted access key ID, a secret access key, and a token.

37. B. IAM roles make API calls using an access key that starts with AROA. If it were another AWS service, the access key would have begun with ASIA. If it was an IAM user, the key would have started with AKIA or ASIA. An IAM group is not a principal.

38. C. You can have up to 1000 IAM roles in an AWS account.

39. B. An IAM user can have only two access keys assigned concurrently.

40. A. You can assign only two keys to a user concurrently regardless of whether the keys are active or inactive.

41. D. An AWS account can have up to 5000 users, so creating an IAM user for each employee isn't feasible. The limit on roles per account is 1000, so assigning a role to each user isn't an option either. Using multiple AWS accounts is a possibility but requires more effort than the final option: automatically assigning temporary security credentials to each employee.

42. B. Disabling STS in all other regions except us-east-1 will prevent instances in those regions from obtaining temporary credentials, even if they have the instance profile role. Because IAM is global, deleting the instance profile role or attached trust policy will affect instances in the us-east-1 region as well. It's not possible to disable the EC2 service.

43. C. You can attach up to 10 managed policies to an IAM principal.

44. C. A managed policy can have up to 6144 characters.

45. A. The sum of all inline policies embedded in an IAM user is 2048 characters.

46. B. The sum of all inline policies embedded in an IAM group is 5120 characters.

47. D. The sum of all inline policies embedded in an IAM role is 10,240 characters.

48. A. An instance profile can have only one role associated with it.

49. C. The maximum session duration for a role is 12 hours. The minimum can be as little as 15 minutes.

50. B. The default credential lifetime for an IAM role is 1 hour.

51. D. The policy grants access to read actions against all resources in S3. Because IAM uses an implicit deny framework, any actions not specifically allowed will be denied, so the user won't be able to delete an S3 bucket or terminate an EC2 instance. The user also won't be able to read EBS snapshots stored in S3 since those snapshots must be accessed via EC2 and not directly from S3. The user will, however, be able to read files even if they're encrypted using SSE-S3.

52. A, B. In the case of a failed login, CloudTrail Events will hide the username and password fields to avoid accidentally exposing a password. The account ID and error message text will be logged.

53. A. Because the application encrypts the data, it's also responsible for decrypting it. DynamoDB and KMS play no role because they're not involved in the encryption process. The Lambda service provides the compute power to run the application but doesn't actually perform encryption or decryption.

54. C, D. Because users already have department tags, the easiest way to grant them access according to their tags is to create a single managed policy and use the Condition policy element. For example, including the following element under a policy statement would apply the permissions in the statement only to those with a department tag with a value of marketing:

```
"Condition":{"StringEquals": {"aws:ResourceTag/department": "marketing"}}
```

55. D. You can attach an ACM-generated certificate to an application load balancer. You can't attach it to an RDS instance, S3 bucket, or EC2 instance.

56. A, C. The way to achieve this with the least effort is to import the certificate into ACM, create an application load balancer (ALB), and use the certificate with the ALB. Creating a network load balancer won't work because it can't terminate TLS connections. Importing the certificate into each EC2 instance is possible but would require greater effort.

57. C. If the EBS volume is encrypted, the snapshot will always be encrypted. Encrypting the filesystem won't encrypt the snapshot. There's no option to enable snapshot encryption. You can't select the S3 bucket to store the snapshot in.

58. A, B. Terminating the instance and launching a new one is a valid next step. Logging into the instance using SSM Session Manager is also a possibility. Importing an existing SSH key pair into the instance is an option only after you've gained access to the instance. You can't RDP into an Amazon Linux 2 instance.

59. B. Because KMS generates and stores the contents of the master key and doesn't allow customers to ever see it, AWS is solely responsible for protecting it from release.

60. B, D. A data key is encrypted using a master key and can be *up to* 1024 bits in length. KMS stores the data key encrypted and can export it encrypted. KMS will not export the key in plaintext.

61. D. Because the data key is encrypted using the customer master key, there's no need to take any action. Without the customer master key, no one can use the encrypted data key to decrypt the contents of the database. Rotating a customer master key doesn't re-encrypt any data encrypted by the data key.

62. C. You can't delete a KMS key immediately, but you can schedule its deletion to occur within 7 to 30 days.

63. A, B. Once you schedule a key deletion you can't use the key during the waiting period. And once the key is deleted, any data encrypted using it will be permanently lost. KMS doesn't prevent the deletion just because an AWS service is using the key. You can cancel a scheduled deletion.

64. A. Keys that you import into KMS can be deleted immediately. There is no waiting period.

65. B, D. To immediately rotate a key, you need to create a new key and then point the application to the new key. Optional automatic key rotation precludes the need to create a new key or update the application, but it occurs only once a year and can't be triggered manually.

66. A, B. Enabling automatic key rotation will cause KMS to annually rotate the keys that it generated. You must manually rotate imported keys, which entails creating new ones and updating the applications to point to them. Aliases make this process easier. Instead of updating the application to reference the key by its ARN or key ID, you reference the key by its alias. You then update the key's alias to point to the new key's ID.

67. B. A disabled key can't be rotated automatically. Manually rotating a key requires creating a new key and using it in place of the original one, and disabling the original key has no effect on this process. A disabled key can be deleted. Disabling a customer master key doesn't delete any data keys.

68. B. The imported key could have been set with an expiration. Upon expiration, the key material is deleted, rendering the key unusable. Imported keys can't be automatically rotated. The instance role permissions aren't likely an issue because attempting to access the table directly via the S3 API also fails, even with the proper permissions.

69. B. Keys in a custom KMS key store are stored in a CloudHSM cluster. They can't be automatically rotated or imported. AWS managed keys can't be stored in a custom key store.

70. A, C. To export a private key from CloudHSM, you must create a wrapping key, then export the private key using the `exportPrivateKey` command. The `exportPubKey` command is only for public keys. Sharing the private key isn't necessary to export it.

71. C. The monthly SLA for KMS is 99.9 percent.

72. C. The monthly SLA for CloudHSM is 99.95 percent. Note that this is higher than the KMS SLA of 99.9 percent, as KMS depends on CloudHSM for its custom key store.

73. A, C. ACM will automatically renew a public certificate if two conditions are met: First, the certificate must be associated with an AWS service such as an application load balancer. Second, ACM must be able to validate domain ownership using email or DNS validation. Email validation is only good for 825 days, but DNS validation will remain valid as long as the appropriate records exist in the domain's DNS. Manually renewing the certificate will renew it once but will not cause ACM to automatically renew the certificate indefinitely.

74. D. Because ACM is a regional service, you'd have to create a new certificate in the other region. You can't use the existing certificate. Elastic load balancers don't offer cross-region load balancing. The question implies the use of an application load balancer, so creating a network load balancer in the other region wouldn't fulfill the requirement.

75. A, B, E. There are three possible causes: First, the user may have IAM permissions boundaries set that prevent access to KMS or S3. Second, the S3 bucket policy may not grant the user access to any objects in the bucket. Finally, the key policy may not allow the user to use the key. There's no such thing as an object policy. The settings in the user's IAM policy permissions are correct according to the question.

76. C, D. DynamoDB can encrypt data using only AWS managed KMS keys, which are never stored in CloudHSM. Of course, encrypting data prior to writing to it to DynamoDB is always an option.

77. C. KMS uses FIPS 140-2 validated hardware security modules. It integrates with CloudHSM but only for custom key stores. KMS keys can be used with any application, not just AWS services. KMS is a regional service, not a global service.

78. B. AWS owned CMKs are used by multiple AWS customers. AWS managed CMKs and customer managed CMKs are for use by only one customer. There's no such thing as a data CMK.

79. D. You can have up to 10,000 customer master keys per region.

80. B. Usage of KMS keys, whether they're in a custom store or the default key store, are tracked in CloudTrail logs. They're not kept in CloudWatch Events or VPC Flow Logs. There are no CloudHSM logs or CloudTrail metrics.

81. D. The maximum size of a key policy document is 32 KB (32,768 bytes).

82. A, B. KMS custom key stores use CloudHSM in different availability zones. Alternatively, you could create your own CloudHSM cluster in multiple availability zones. Using multiple regions wouldn't provide redundancy for keys since keys are specific to a region. Storing duplicate keys wouldn't necessarily provide high availability if the keys are stored in a CloudHSM cluster in just one availability zone.

83. C. Whether a principal can assume a role is determined by the role's trust policy. Removing the IAM PassRole permission from a user might prevent them from launching an instance that uses the role, but it won't prevent the user from assuming the role themselves. Removing unnecessary permissions from the role, although a good idea, also won't stop a user from assuming the role. There's no such thing as a user trust policy.

84. D. The simplest solution is to duplicate the service-linked role, adding the permissions you need. Because service-linked roles are controlled by AWS, you can't add policy permissions to a service-linked role or modify its trust policy.

85. A, D. The practice of assuming one role and then assuming another role is called role chaining. Role chaining is allowed but limited to a maximum duration of one hour. While operating under a role, you have only the permissions of that role.

86. B. You can't assume an IAM role while operating as the root user. You must use an IAM user instead. There is no CLI session limit, the root user credentials can be used with the CLI, and the root user has full access to all AWS services.

87. A, B. The user needs the `sts:AssumeRole` permission with Role X's ARN given as a resource. The user doesn't need the `iam:PassRole` permission. There is no `iam:AssumeRole` API call.

88. C, D. A trust policy is a resource-based policy and therefore does require specifying a principal.

89. B. The principal can't be a wildcard in a trust policy. It can be an AWS service or a principal in the same account or another account. The effect in a trust policy statement can be Allow or Deny.

90. C. EC2 throttles outbound traffic on TCP port 25, the port commonly used for the Simple Mail Transfer Protocol (SMTP). Only the root user can make a request to have this throttle removed. The root user isn't required to view the canonical user ID or delete an IAM user. The root user can't assume an IAM role.

91. B. When multiple AWS customers use the same service provider, there's a possibility that a malicious customer could provide your AWS account number and the ARN of a valid role, thus tricking the service provider into accessing your resources. Configuring the trust policy to require the service provider to also provide a unique external ID when assuming the role can mitigate this. It also eliminates the need to alert when someone assumes the role without specifying the external ID. The external ID is not a principal. There's no need to rename the role since that would also change the role ARN, which the service provider already knows.

92. A. The instances should be associated with an instance profile role that has the proper permissions. The agent uses STS to obtain temporary credentials to connect to SSM, so there's no need to configure credentials explicitly. The agent requires outbound, not inbound, HTTPS access and doesn't require SSH access at all.

93. A. DynamoDB server-side and KMS encryption encrypts the entire table. If you want to encrypt only a subset of the table, such encryption must take place outside of DynamoDB.

94. C. The database instance's security group must allow inbound access from the EC2 instance. The database instance won't initiate a connection to the EC2 instance. There's no need for the two instances to be in the same VPC or subnet.

95. B. MariaDB listens for incoming connections on TCP port 3306, so the database instance's security group must be configured accordingly. The database doesn't need to initiate any outbound connections.

96. C. The MySQL audit plug-in can be configured to log all queries. CloudTrail can log only API calls against AWS resources. The pgaudit plug-in is only for the PostgreSQL database engine. MySQL Workbench is a database design tool.

97. B, D. To use SSL with Oracle, you must disable native network encryption and add the Oracle SSL option group to the instance. Transparent data encryption is for encrypting data at rest and has nothing to do with SSL.

98. B. AWS handles all aspects of security between the master and the replica, including security group configurations. The data on a read replica is encrypted only if the master is encrypted. Likewise, if data on the master is encrypted, the data on the replica must also be encrypted.

99. A. AWS handles all security between the master and replica. In the case of cross-region replication, in-transit data is always encrypted. RDS doesn't use KMS for in-transit encryption. KMS is used only with encryption at rest.

100. B. Because resource-based policies apply to a resource, they can restrict the access of users who don't have an AWS account, such as anonymous users. Resource-based policies are not necessarily more restrictive, they can't be used to restrict the root user, and they don't replace identity-based policies.

101. D. A bucket policy can be up to 20 KB in size.

102. C. The canonical user ID is a 64-character string that can be used to identify an AWS account in an S3 bucket policy. Creating an IAM role and providing the ARN would permit the vendor to grant that role access, but they'd still need either your AWS account number or canonical user ID. Asking the vendor to create for you an IAM user with permissions to the bucket would get you access to the bucket, but you wouldn't be able to store your EBS backups there since you wouldn't be using your own account. An IAM permissions policy can't be used to grant another account access to an S3 bucket.

103. D. All regions support Signature version 4. Regions created before January 30, 2014, support Signature versions 2 and 4. There is no version 1 or 3.

104. B. The signing key is used to sign requests. The secret access key is used to create a signing key, which is valid for up to 7 days. A policy key is not an encryption key, but a condition that can be specified along with the request. S3 requests don't use public keys.

105. D. The command `aws s3api list-buckets` is the only one that will list the canonical user ID. `aws s3 list-buckets` is not a valid command.

106. A, B. Aurora offers only MySQL and PostgreSQL and supports IAM database authentication for both.

107. A, C. The root user or an IAM user can create a CodeDeploy deployment. CodeDeploy doesn't authenticate using Git credentials and it doesn't allow anonymous access.

108. C. The user needs to have the `GetDeploymentConfig` permissions to get the deployment configuration for the application they're deploying. They don't need permissions to update the deployment group, view other deployments, or modify the application.

109. B. You can have up to 10 GitHub tokens per region.

110. D. The AWS CLI requires you to explicitly acknowledge that a template will create an IAM resource. In this case, the error indicates that the template assigns the resource a custom name. The AWS CLI checks for this prior to making a request to the CloudFormation service, so it doesn't first check permissions or whether the template would update an existing resource.

111. A. The AWSCodeDeployDeployerAccess managed policy grants access to create and deploy application revisions. The rest are permissions policies to be used with roles but don't grant permission to create or deploy application revisions.

112. B, D. CodeDeploy deploys EC2/on-premises applications from an S3 bucket, so the instances need access to list and get buckets and files from S3. They don't need access to the CodeDeploy or Auto Scaling services.

113. C. CodeDeploy agents earlier than version 1.0.1.854 don't support the SHA-2 hash algorithm required by CodeDeploy. Upgrading the agent will resolve the error. The error indicates that the agent is reaching the CodeDeploy service, so adding a security group rule or restarting the instance won't make a difference. The error doesn't indicate a permissions issue.

114. B. An S3 bucket policy could restrict a principal's access to the revision. An S3 ACL could also block access to it, but ACLs operate at the account level, and the fact that you were able to read the application revision indicates that an ACL is not the issue. The question indicates that you verified the permissions of the instance profile role, so permissions boundaries aren't the problem. The appspec.yml file is included in the application revision bundle, so a misconfiguration there can't be the problem.

115. C. The error appears only if the instance profile role is missing or if it doesn't have the appropriate permissions. The error comes from the CodeDeploy agent running on the instance, so the instance must be running.

116. B. When the CodeDeploy agent sends a request to the CodeDeploy service, it signs the request with a signature that is valid for a small window of time. The error indicates that the time on the instance and the time of the CodeDeploy service don't match.

117. A, D. You can set a password policy to enforce password expiration and require an administrator to reset expired passwords. A policy can't require MFA or set a maximum length.

118. B. Users with passwords older than 90 days will have to change them at their next sign-in. Password policies don't affect access keys.

119. A. IAM doesn't offer lockout policies that lock out a user after a number of failed login attempts. All of the other choices are available options for a password policy.

120. B. A token obtained from a regional STS endpoint is valid in all regions. It's not necessarily smaller or valid for a longer time than one obtained from the global STS endpoint.

121. A. You can't disable STS in the us-east-1 (N. Virginia) region. You can disable it in all others.

122. A, D. Once a region is disabled, EC2 instances running in it continue to incur charges. You can't make changes to resources in a disabled region. You need to enable the region and then terminate the EC2 instances. STS has no bearing on whether the region is enabled or disabled.

123. B. The account:EnableRegion and account:DisableRegion actions are required to enable or disable a region. The others aren't valid actions.

124. B, C, E. All but three endpoints can be disabled: The global endpoint (sts.amazon.com), us-east-1 (N. Virginia) (sts.us-east-1.amazonaws.com), and ap-east-1 (Hong Kong) (sts.ap-east-1.amazonaws.com).

125. B. Web identity federation allows a user to log into an external identity provider, receive an authentication token, and exchange it for temporary AWS credentials.

126. B. Cognito can create IAM roles to define permissions for users. STS provides temporary credentials in exchange for a Cognito token but doesn't control user permissions. OpenID Connect is an authentication framework used by some identity providers. Resource Access Manager lets you share a few of your AWS resources with other AWS accounts.

127. C. AWS recommends using Cognito instead of a TVM. Cognito supports web identity federation, but the question doesn't indicate that it's needed. Web identity federation can also be implemented without Cognito.

128. B. The condition in the role's trust policy will require a valid MFA token to assume the role. Applying an identity-based policy won't be effective because once a user assumes a role, they no longer operate under the permissions of their user principal, but of the role. Disabling the users' access keys won't prevent them from assuming the role. You can't configure a password policy to require MFA.

129. A, C. You can grant only specific users access to change their password by creating and applying an identity-based policy that grants them permission to perform the `iam:ChangePassword` action against their own IAM user resource, which is specified by its ARN in the format `arn:aws:iam::account-id:user/${aws:username}`. A password policy allowing users to change their own passwords would apply to all users. It's not possible to implement a password policy requiring users to create a random password, and even if it were, it wouldn't be necessary for allowing users to change their own passwords.

130. B. When assuming a role, you can specify a managed session policy to restrict the permissions granted to the session. Access control policies apply only to cross-account access. An IAM permissions boundary is an identity-based policy, which in this case would apply to the role and hence would impact every application that assumes the role. There's no such thing as a session control policy.

131. A, D. Service control policies and session policies can only limit permissions. Access control lists and trust policies can grant permissions.

132. D. A service control policy can restrict access granted by identity-based and resource-based policies, so it could restrict access to the AppBucket bucket by limiting the permissions granted by the bucket policy and the role's permissions policy. Simply modifying the bucket policy would still leave access via the role's permissions policy. A session policy and permissions boundaries can't limit access granted by a resource-based policy.

133. B. You would need to specify the excepted instance as `NotResource`. There's no need to use the `NotAction` element. You can't use `Condition` to specify an instance. Principal and `NotPrincipal` have no effect in an identity-based policy.

134. B. `AssumeRole` and `GetSessionToken` are the only actions that support MFA.

135. A. `GetSessionToken` is the only action that doesn't support session policies.

136. B, C. A PEM-encoded certificate body and private key are required to import a certificate. You can optionally provide a certificate chain. You don't have to provide a certificate signing request.

137. D. The certificate must contain a public key, which can be 1024-, 2048-, or 4096-bit RSA or Elliptic Prime Curve 256-, 384-, or 521-bit. The certificate can be self-signed. The private key can't be encrypted.

138. B. GuardDuty analyzes VPC flow logs, CloudTrail logs, and Route 53 DNS query logs to look for malicious network activity that could be an indication of malware. Inspector scans instances for vulnerabilities but doesn't detect suspicious activity. AWS Shield Standard and WAF protect AWS resources from threats outside of AWS.

139. B, D. Using AWS Secrets Manager to store the connection string and configuring the application to programmatically retrieve it can help protect the string from exposure. Using RDS or encrypting the string won't protect it from exposure.

140. A, D. Storing the API key in AWS Secrets Manager is the most secure option, as it encrypts secrets at rest. A Lambda function can integrate with Secrets Manager to automatically rotate the key. You can't store an API key in KMS. Securely storing and rotating the key in DynamoDB is possible but would require more effort than using Secrets Manager.

141. B. It takes GuardDuty 7 to 14 days to establish a baseline for certain finding types, including the Behavior:EC2/TrafficVolumeUnusual finding. GuardDuty findings are updated in real time. You don't need to configure VPC Flow Logs in order to use GuardDuty to monitor network traffic ingressing or egressing a VPC.

142. C. Inspector checks instances for listening TCP ports that don't receive any traffic during the assessment run. GuardDuty, Macie, and Web Application Firewall would not have discovered this.

143. D. Amazon publishes notifications about new Windows AMIs to the ec2-windows-ami-update topic. The ec2-windows-ami-private topic is for when Amazon makes obsolete Windows AMIs private. The other two aren't valid ARNs.

144. B. AWS publishes the latest AMI ID as a Simple Systems Manager (SSM) public parameter that you can query by the AMI's alias, which in this case is Windows_Server-2019-English-Full-Base. The `aws ec2 describe-images` commands would yield a list of AMI aliases for Windows Server 2019, but not the latest AMI ID.

145. B. The software without data execution prevention (DEP) rule generates findings only for Linux instances. The other rules generate findings for Linux and Windows instances.

146. C. Lambda function invocations are stored in CloudWatch Metrics. Deleting the log group for a function has no effect on metrics, but it does result in the log stream being deleted. You can't restore a deleted log group, and even if you could, creating a metric filter for function invocations would not generate a retroactive metric. CloudTrail event logs would contain function invocations, but counting them would require more effort than just checking CloudWatch Metrics.

147.   A, B, D.   The solution requiring the least effort includes creating an IAM role that can be assumed by a user in another account or by a non-AWS user via an identity provider. An SQS queue policy grants the role access to the queue by specifying the role as a principal. Specifying the wildcard (*) as a principal for either the queue policy or the role's trust policy would give everyone access to the queue.

148.   B.   Each build environment runs in an isolated Docker container. Isolation is not achieved by using separate compute instances, access control lists, or separate VPCs.

149.   B,C.   To connect a CodeBuild environment to an RDS instance in a private subnet, you must connect the environment to the VPC the instance is in. The RDS instance doesn't have a public endpoint. You can't configure port forwarding on a NAT gateway.

150.   A.   To grant CodeBuild permissions to pull a Docker image from ECR using its own credentials, you need to add the service principal to the repository's policy. Adding permissions for a user won't have any impact on the permissions of the service. A SID is just an identifier and doesn't grant permissions.

151.   B, C.   AWS SSM can reference secrets stored in AWS Secrets Manager. The easiest solution is to add the secret to AWS Secrets Manager, name it "password," modify the application to reference the SSM parameter name "/aws/reference/secretsmanager/password." Modifying the application to query AWS Secrets Manager directly would require more work, as would manually rotating the password.

152.   D.   Appending the --with-decryption flag will decrypt the string. Just having access to the encryption key isn't enough. The aws kms decrypt command won't decrypt the encrypted value.

153.   B.   AWS Managed Microsoft AD is the only PCI DSS–compliant service for integrating on-premises AD-aware applications with AWS. LDAP is a protocol, not an AWS service.

154.   A, C.   AWS Directory Service for Microsoft AD and AD Connector both support MFA. Simple AD doesn't. IAM is not a part of AWS Directory Service.

155.   B.   Simple AD is a stand-alone Active Directory–compatible server that can store up to 20,000 objects and supports group policies. AWS Directory Service for Microsoft AD supports group policies but is more complicated to configure. AD Connector redirects requests to an existing Active Directory but can't act as a stand-alone AD server. Amazon Cloud Directory doesn't provide any AD services.

156.   A, D.   Inspector will scan applications installed using a package manager such as yum or Windows Installer. It won't scan applications that were compiled on or copied to the instance.

157.   C.   Inspector scans for vulnerabilities using an agent installed on your instances. Inspector can perform network assessments without an agent. GuardDuty, Macie, and Firewall Manager are agentless.

158. B. Lambda is a serverless compute service that makes it easy to deploy and upgrade applications written in a variety of languages, including Python. You provide the application code, and Lambda provides the rest. EC2 requires you to manage the operating system the application runs on. Elastic Beanstalk automates deployment of your application on EC2 instances, but it requires you to create a manifest to define the runtime environment. By default, it makes the application publicly available. ECS requires you to create and deploy containers for your application to run in.

159. A. The most efficient approach is to use AWS Systems Manager to apply the patch. There's no indication that autoscaling is being used. You can't apply an AMI to an existing instance. It's not the responsibility of AWS to patch EC2 instances.

160. A. The RDS Console displays the current patching status of RDS instances. Because RDS instances aren't EC2 or on-premises instances, they can't be patched with SSM Patch Manager and won't show up in SSM Compliance Manager. Artifact allows you to download security and compliance documents for AWS services.

161. B. AWS Config tracks the configuration status of resources over time and can show the relationships between resources. You could use CloudTrail logs to derive this information, but it would require more effort. CloudTrail events don't contain information for events more than 90 days old, and even if they did, this would require more effort than using AWS Config. SSM Compliance Manager can be used to analyze which AMIs instances you are currently using, but it won't show this information from 99 days ago.

162. A, D. Systems Manager Inventory can run periodically to detect which applications are installed on EC2 instances. AWS Config can track these state changes over time. Systems Manager Automation can be used to perform changes to your AWS resources but doesn't perform any inventory collection on instances. CloudWatch Events performs actions on a schedule or in response to events in your AWS environment.

163. A, C. GuardDuty can monitor for port scans, and when it generates a finding, it can trigger a CloudWatch Events rule to send a notification using Simple Notification Service. There's no need to use Lambda or Simple Email Service.

164. C. The Inspector agent must be installed on instances for Inspector findings to show listening processes. Running a host assessment won't generate a finding that shows this information. If the instances are stopped, the agent won't be running. An inbound security rule isn't needed because the agent initiates the connection to the Inspector service.

165. B. AWS Shield Advanced automatically alerts you to application layer (layer 7) attacks. WAF requires you to create your own rules to identify and mitigate layer 7 attacks. Firewall Manager is a management interface for WAF and AWS Shield Advanced, but it doesn't provide protection by itself.

166. B. You can grant permission to the DRT to create WAF web access control lists to mitigate an attack. The DRT doesn't proactively mitigate layer 7 attacks, nor does it stop them at the source. The DRT can't conclusively identify the source of an attack.

167. B. CloudFront is the most effective option for absorbing DDoS attacks as it processes requests at edge locations, keeping the malicious traffic away from your AWS resources. Elastic load balancing occurs within your VPC, and a DDoS attack could overwhelm your VPC resources. Many DDoS attacks can exceed hundreds of gigabits per second, so using 10-gigabit EC2 network interfaces also isn't the most effective option. There's no service called AWS AirBag (yet).

168. B. You can use WAF to create rules that count the number of requests from a particular country. You can get visibility into the origin of requests using CloudFront, but it requires more effort.

169. A. Macie specifically monitors CloudTrail event logs for suspicious activity against your S3 buckets. There's no charge for analyzing the first 100,000 events. GuardDuty provides more broad protection by analyzing resource access patterns across your AWS account. You could monitor S3 access by streaming CloudTrail data logs to CloudWatch Logs, but this would require analyzing the logs yourself. Likewise, you could use Lambda to perform this analysis, but this too would require a great deal of effort.

Domain 6: Networking

1. C. The public IP address of an instance is stored in the instance metadata. User data is defined at instance launch and doesn't define the instance's public IP address. The `ifconfig` command won't display the public IP address because it's not assigned to the interface.

2. A. Sending an HTTP GET request to 169.254.169.254/latest/meta-data/public-ipv4 will return the instance's public IP address. Sending a request to 169.254.169.254/1.0/meta-data/local-ipv4 or 169.254.169.254/latest/meta-data/local-ipv4 will yield the instance's private IP address. 169.254.169.254/latest/dynamic/public-ipv4 isn't a valid URL.

3. B, D. A virtual private gateway and customer gateway are required to set up a VPN connection. An Internet gateway isn't necessary. Although a default route to the virtual private gateway is allowed, it's not required.

4. C, D. Configuring ELB health checks to monitor the web service and then using that health check in the Auto Scaling group will ensure that any instance on which the web service fails will be replaced. Using an EC2 health check will only look at the system status and instance status, but not the status of the web service. There is no UDP health check.

5. B. Enabling session stickiness can result in uneven distribution to instances. Once a client is routed to an instance, it receives a session cookie and subsequent requests are routed to the same instance until the session cookie expires. Disabling cross-zone load balancing wouldn't cause the issue in this case because the instances are evenly distributed across availability zones. The instances don't have public IP addresses because they're in private subnets.

6. A, B. A NAT instance or NAT gateway can be used to allow an instance in a private subnet access to the Internet. A VPC peering connection or VPC endpoint can't achieve this.

7. C. The instance not having a public IP address would prevent it from downloading updates, so assigning an elastic IP could fix the issue. The fact that the instance is in a public subnet indicates that an internet gateway and default route are already in place. There's no need for a NAT gateway because the instance is in a public subnet.

8. B. The egress-only Internet gateway allows outbound-only IPv6 access. An Internet gateway allows both outbound and inbound IPv4 and IPv6 access. NAT gateways and NAT instances don't allow IPv6 at all.

9. B. The geoproximity routing policy can route users to a resource based on their distance from a geographic location. A geolocation routing policy routes users according to the specific geographic region they're in. A latency record routes users to the region with the lowest latency, but this may not necessarily be the closest to them. There's no such thing as a region routing policy.

10. A, C. The best solution is to create an Auto Scaling group in each region, using the same group size to ensure an even number of instances. Next, configure an elastic load balancer in each region. Then configure a Route 53 weighted routing policy to evenly distribute requests to each load balancer. Using cross-region load balancing may not ensure high availability because the load balancer listener will exist in only one region. Lambda doesn't use instances.

11. B. The latency routing policy routes users to the AWS region with the best network performance. Geoproximity considers the user's location but not network performance. Failover routing considers whether a resource is healthy but doesn't consider network performance. A weighted routing policy attempts to distribute users to resources according to a configured ratio, such as, for example, 50% to one elastic load balancer and 50% to another.

12. A, D. A simple basic resource record or a multivalue answer resource record without a health check will always return the public IP address of the instance. A simple alias resource record can't point directly to an instance. A simple resource record doesn't use health checks.

13. B. The source/destination check must be disabled on the NAT instance. Configuring a NAT gateway could resolve the problem but would require more effort. A NAT instance needs a public IP address but doesn't require an elastic IP address. The default route in the private subnet is configured correctly.

14. C. A CIDR block can have a prefix length between /16 and /28 inclusive.

15. C. AWS assigns IPv6 VPC CIDR blocks with a /56 prefix length.

16. B. Adding a secondary VPC CIDR of 172.31.1.0/24 is the easiest option. You can't add a secondary CIDR that overlaps with the existing CIDR as 172.31.0.0/16 does. You also can't change the VPC CIDR. Creating a new VPC for the additional application instances is possible but would require more effort than just adding a secondary CIDR.

17. B. The number of subnets you can have in a VPC depends in part on the size of the VPC CIDR. A VPC CIDR and a subnet CIDR can be between /16 and /28 inclusive. The number of availability zones, the number of VPCs, and the number of NACLs aren't limiting factors.

18. B. Creating three subnets, each in a different availability zone, will maximize IP address space utilization and achieve the highest level of reliability. A subnet can't span multiple availability zones. Creating three subnets in one availability zone would not provide high availability. Creating two subnets in one availability zone and one subnet in a different availability zone would provide a highly available configuration but would not be the most efficient use of IP address space.

19. B, D. Simply giving the instances a public IP address and permitting inbound HTTPS access is sufficient and requires minimal effort. Using a VPN is a possibility but would require implementing NAT to overcome the IP addressing conflicts and would entail a lot more effort.

20. A. An elastic network interface must have only one primary private IP address. It can have a secondary private IP address, but it must be from the same subnet as the primary. An ENI can be associated with multiple elastic IP addresses. It doesn't have to be attached to an instance but can be created separately.

21. B, C. Assigning a secondary elastic network interface or launching the instance in a private subnet both prevent EC2 from automatically assigning a public IP address to the instance. Assigning an elastic IP address to the instance and then unassigning it will result in the instance receiving a new public IP address. It's not possible to remove the primary elastic network interface from an instance.

22. A, C. The symptoms raise the possibility that the instances are configured with IPv6 addresses but can't reach the IPv6 Internet due to a missing IPv6 default route. Creating the route may resolve the problem. Alternatively, disabling IPv6 in the VPC would also resolve the problem, as the instances would no longer attempt to communicate using IPv6. Because the instances can reach other (ostensibly IPv4 resources), an Internet gateway must already be present. An egress-only Internet gateway isn't necessary because an Internet gateway can pass both IPv4 and IPv6 traffic.

23. B. A route table performs the same function as a router in a traditional network. Associating a route table with a subnet is like connecting a router to a traditional network. In a traditional network, creating a default route is done on a router after the router's been connected to the network.

24. D. VPCs don't support multicast traffic, so the migration isn't possible. VPCs do support RFC 1918 addresses.

25. A. The traffic between the VPCs must traverse the Internet, and so instance B will see instance A's public IP address as the source. If VPC peering or a VPN were being used, instance B would see the private IP address. An Internet gateway doesn't have a public IP address but enables an instance to obtain one. Even if a NAT gateway was present in instance A's VPC, instance A would still directly go through the Internet gateway and not use the NAT gateway.

26. B, D. NACLs apply to a subnet, while security groups apply to an elastic network interface.

27. A. A NAT gateway is an elastic VPC resource that hides the public source IP address of an instance from hosts on the Internet. A NAT instance can also do this, but it's not elastic; that is, it doesn't scale automatically. An Internet gateway hides the private source address, not the public address. A virtual private gateway is used to establish a VPN connection and doesn't perform NAT.

28. B. VPCs with overlapping CIDR blocks can't be peered. VPCs do support IPv6 and don't support transitive peering. You can have only one peering connection between any two VPCs.

29. D. IPv6 isn't supported for inter-region VPC peering. DNS resolution works, and the VPCs don't need to have RFC 1918 CIDRs. An MTU of 1500 or less is supported.

30. A. You must add routes to the appropriate route table in each VPC, specifying the VPC peering connection as the target. There's no need to configure NAT, assign public IP addresses to instances, or enable DNS resolution.

31. D. Changing the instance type requires stopping the instance, thus releasing its public IP address. Rebooting the instance or removing the default route won't change the public IP address. It's not possible to remove the primary elastic network interface from an instance.

32. B. Enabling DNS support in the VPC is sufficient to enable DNS resolution. Enabling DNS hostnames will only assign public DNS hostnames to instances with public IP addresses. There's no need to transfer the domain name to Route 53. It's not possible to assign an elastic IP address to an instance since it's in a private subnet.

33. B. S3 transfer acceleration uses edge locations to speed up transfers between S3 and the Internet. CloudFront distributions deliver content to end users from edge locations. S3 cross-region replication transfers objects between S3 buckets, not between S3 buckets and the Internet. Elastic load balancing has nothing to do with S3.

34. A. An elastic IP address will incur costs only if it's not associated with an instance. NAT gateways and elastic load balancers incur costs regardless. Elastic network interfaces are free.

35. B. You can connect Lambda functions to EC2 instances using an interface VPC endpoint. Lambda doesn't offer a gateway VPC endpoint. The API gateway service is for creating your own APIs. VPC peering is for peering two VPCs that you control. Lambda functions execute in a VPC controlled by Amazon.

36. A, D. An interface endpoint exists in only one availability zone and supports only IPv4 TCP traffic. It doesn't support IPv6 or UDP.

37. B. You can restrict access to a gateway endpoint using security groups and the S3 prefix list ID. You can't use a prefix list with a NACL. S3 bucket policies and IAM permissions policies will restrict access to S3 across the board, not just via the endpoint.

38. D. An IPv4 CIDR is always required in a VPC, even if you plan to use only IPv6. Enabling DNS hostnames or configuring an egress-only Internet gateway aren't required to use IPv6. You can't assign a link-local IPv6 address to a VPC. AWS automatically assigns a global unicast IPv6 address upon your request.

39. C. A route table contains routes that determine how network traffic is directed. Security groups and NACLs control whether traffic is allowed or blocked but doesn't affect the direction of traffic. An Internet gateway enables Internet access for a VPC.

40. C. A /28 will give you 16 possible IP addresses, 5 of which AWS reserves, leaving you with 11 usable IP addresses.

41. D. AWS reserves five IP addresses in each subnet: the first four and the last.

42. C. Reserved addresses include 10.0.0.0–10.0.0.3 and 10.0.0.255. You can use the rest.

43. C. RDP uses TCP port 3389, which is permitted by the security group and NACL. The Linux host is able to RDP to other hosts. That leaves the Windows firewall as the only possible culprit.

44. B. A transit gateway is an elastic resource that can be used to connect a VPC to customer gateways, other VPCs, and Direct Connect gateways. A transit gateway's route table can be configured to control how traffic is allowed to flow. VPC peering only connects two VPCs. A virtual private gateway only provides a site-to-site VPN connection between a remote site and a single VPC; VPC endpoints provide a private (non-Internet) connection between a VPC and AWS services.

45. D. A Direct Connect link to AWS provides consistent latency. It doesn't necessarily provide higher bandwidth or reduced cost over an Internet VPN connection. Direct Connect doesn't provide data encryption.

46. B. Direct Connect can improve the security of this configuration by bypassing the public Internet. All AWS services, including S3, use HTTPS for their public endpoints. A VPN connection can't be configured between a remote site and S3. A VPC endpoint only connects a VPC to an AWS service via a private network, bypassing the Internet.

47. A, D. Whenever a VPC is connected to an external network, the IP address ranges mustn't overlap. Also, routing must be configured so that resources in the datacenter and VPC can reach each other. Encryption is useful for securing data, but it isn't required for proper connectivity. IAM policies are unrelated to network connectivity.

48. B, D. Direct Connect is available in two ways: a dedicated connection between your equipment and AWS at a Direct Connect location or a hosted connection from an AWS Direct Connect Partner. AWS doesn't install Direct Connect connections at customer sites. You can't create a VPN connection to a Direct Connect location.

49. B. A public virtual interface allows you to use public AWS endpoints over a Direct Connect connection. A private virtual interface is used for connecting to a VPC. A transit virtual interface is only for use with an Amazon VPC Transit Gateway. There's no such thing as a peer virtual interface.

50. A. You must advertise at least one public IP prefix to use a public virtual interface. A public ASN isn't required. You can use a public ASN if you have one; otherwise, you can use a private ASN between 64512 and 65534. Jumbo frames aren't supported on public virtual interfaces, and even if they were, enabling jumbo frames wouldn't be required.

51. C. A hosted connection with a 100 Mbps port costs about $0.06 per port-hour. A 50 Mbps hosted connection isn't big enough, and there isn't a 80 Mbps hosted connection. A dedicated connection always costs more than a hosted connection.

52. B, C. To increase your bandwidth, you have two options. You can create a new 2 Gbps connection and remove the 1 Gbps connection. Or you can create a new 1 Gbps connection and combine it with the existing 1 Gbps connection in a link aggregation group (LAG) to achieve a combined bandwidth of 2 Gbps. All connections in a LAG must have the same bandwidth. You can't upgrade a connection's bandwidth.

53. A. The default MTU is 1500 bytes.

54. C. You can have up to 10 VPN connections to a VPC.

55. B. AWS assigns you a /125 IPv6 CIDR that you and AWS must use to set up an IPv6 BGP peering session. You may not specify your own IPv6 addresses. You may also have a simultaneous IPv4 BGP peering session.

56. B. Using jumbo frames can decrease network overhead by allowing more data to be sent across the connection in a single frame. The other options don't decrease network overhead.

57. B. You can advertise up to 100 routes over each BGP session over a private virtual interface.

58. A. If you advertise more than 100 routes over a private virtual interface, the BGP session will go down. The Direct Connect link will not go down.

59. A. BGP MD5 authentication settings must match both on the Direct Connect side and on your router. You don't need to apply community tags to BGP prefixes. Direct Connect doesn't support MP-BGP. BGP uses TCP port 179, not UDP port 179.

60. C. You can advertise up to 1000 prefixes over a public virtual interface.

61. B. Specifying the peer AS number or your own AS number incorrectly can cause a session to fail. Having prefixes to advertise isn't a prerequisite for establishing a BGP session. BGP uses TCP port 179, not 197. Direct Connect supports the NO_EXPORT BGP community, and even if it didn't, that wouldn't stop the session from establishing.

62. C. Your only option is to block the prefixes on your router. AWS can't suppress specific prefixes for a private virtual interface. Deleting the subnet isn't an option because it would require deleting the instances in that subnet. You also can't remove the prefix from the VPC route table without deleting the subnet.

63. B. VPN CloudHub allows you to use a VPC for transit between two connected sites. The other options are feasible but require substantially more effort.

64. A. Direct Connect will always be preferred, regardless of AS PATH length.

65. A, C. Summarizing the prefixes into fewer than 100 or advertising the default route are both feasible options. You can't advertise more than 100 prefixes per BGP session. You can establish only one BGP session per virtual interface.

66. A. You can choose a /30 CIDR block anywhere in the 169.254.0.0/16 (link-local) range, so 169.254.0.0/30 would be a valid choice. 169.0.0.0/16 isn't a /30. 10.0.0.0/30 and 10.0.0.0/16 don't fall within the 169.254.0.0/16 range and aren't allowed.

67. B, C. CloudHub connects on-premises networks (via a VPN or Direct Connect link) and VPCs in only one region. Direct Connect Gateway connects on-premises networks and VPCs in any region.

68. C. The community 7224:9300 propagates routes to all AWS regions. 7224:9100 propagates routes only to the connected AWS region. 7224:9200 propagates routes to all AWS regions in the same continent. 7224:8100 is a community that AWS applies to outbound routes that originate in the connected AWS region.

69. B. Applying the 7224:7300 community gives it a higher local preference on the AWS side. Applying the 7224:7100 community gives it a lower precedence. Using AS PATH prepending on the prefix from the datacenter would make it less preferred.

70. A. The community tags must be the same on prefixes to load balance them across different connections. Local preference and router ID don't have to be the same.

71. D. You can use a private ASN on a public virtual interface, but AS path prepending won't work. Private ASNs are between 64512 and 65534. You can't own a private ASN.

72. A,D. Valid VLAN ranges are 1 through 4094.

73. B. The easiest way to advertise IPv6 prefixes is to establish an IPv6 BGP session. You can't establish more than one IPv4 BGP session per virtual interface. You can't advertise IPv6 prefixes over an IPv4 BGP session. Creating an IPv6 VPN tunnel is an option, but not the one that requires the least effort.

74. A. The ASNs of the transit gateway and Direct Connect gateway must be different. The association between the two doesn't use VLANs. The gateways don't have to be in the same account.

75. C. The ConnectionLightLevelTx metric indicates the health of the egress fiber from the AWS side. ConnectionLightLevelRx indicates the health of the ingress fiber from the AWS side. Both metrics are available only with 10 Gbps port speeds.

76. B. You can create one transit virtual interface per LAG.

77. B. You can have up to 4 connections per LAG.

78. D. You can assign a global unicast IPv6 address to an instance after launch. Link-local IPv6 addresses aren't routable. Attaching an additional network interface and assigning it a public IPv6 address is fine, but it requires more work than necessary. There's no need to terminate the instance and launch a new one.

79. B. Instances don't have IPv6 DNS hostnames, so you'd need to create a publicly resolvable AAAA record pointing to the IPv6 address. An A record is for IPv4 addresses only. The instance's security group has no bearing on being able to resolve the instance's IPv6 address.

80. C. fe80:db8:1234:1a00::1/64 is a link-local IPv6 address. Elastic IP addresses are IPv4, not IPv6.

81. B. The instance's public IPv4 address is released when the instance is stopped. The others are retained.

82. D. The external DNS hostname would be `ec2-203-0-113-25.compute-1.amazonaws.com`. The IP address octets are separated by dashes, not dots.

83. B, C. An instance launched into a default VPC will be launched into a public subnet, have a public IP address, and have outbound access. Its primary private IP address will have a /20 CIDR, not a /16.

84. A. The private hostname is ip-10-9-13-37.ec2.internal. In the US East 1 region, the hostname suffix is ec2.internal, while in other regions it follows the format region .compute.internal.

85. B. If enableDnsHostnames is set to true, then instances with a public IP address will receive a public DNS hostname. If enableDnsSupport is enabled, the Amazon DNS server is enabled. The other two options aren't valid attributes.

86. B. If enableDnsSupport is set to true, then instances in a VPC can use the Amazon DNS server to resolve the Amazon-provided private hostname of another instance in the VPC. If enableDnsHostnames is set to true, then instances with a public IP address will receive a public DNS hostname.

87. D. The first four addresses and last address of a subnet are reserved and can't be assigned to an instance.

88. A. The route table tells the VPC's implicit router how to reach the datacenter subnets. Because the virtual private gateway terminates the VPN connection with the customer gateway, the virtual private gateway should be the route target.

89. B. The error indicates that you've established connectivity to the instance but didn't supply the right credentials. For credentials, Windows RDP uses a password, not an SSH key.

90. D. Using the SSM `AWSSupport-TroubleshootRDP` automation document to enable RDP and disable the Windows firewall is the troubleshooting step that requires the least effort. It can also tell you what port RDP is listening on, in case it's not using the well-known TCP port 3389. Doing the same with a PowerShell remoting session may be an option but would require adding additional security group and NACL rules.

91. A. An instance screen shot of a Windows instance can reveal whether the instance is at the logon screen (and hopefully ready to accept RDP connections) or at another screen where it wouldn't be ready to accept RDP connections, such as the recovery console screen, the boot manager screen, the Windows update screen, the Getting Ready screen, the Chkdsk screen, or the Sysprep screen. The EC2 system log, CloudTrail logs, and AWS Config logs won't provide valuable information for troubleshooting Windows RDP issues in this case.

92. A. Changing the time zone can cause the instance to temporarily lose its IP address for up to several hours. Upgrading the PV driver may cause a temporary loss of connectivity, but only for up to 15 minutes. The Windows Plug and Play Cleanup feature won't remove the EC2 network device except in Windows Server 2012 R2. Enabling TCP offloading may cause TCP connectivity problems but won't affect all network connectivity.

93. A. AWS uses the addresses 169.254.169.250, 169.254.169.251, and 169.254.169.254 for Windows activation.

94. D. Because the EC2 instance initiates the connection, the database instance's security group must allow inbound access from the EC2 instance. The EC2 and RDS instances don't need to be in the same VPC.

95. C. Removing all outbound rules for the instance's subnet's NACL will stop all outbound traffic from the instance. Removing security group rules that allow outbound access or adding an outbound NACL rule denying access to TCP port 22 wouldn't prevent an inbound SSH connection or cause it to drop. You can't add a deny rule to a security group.

96. D. The errors indicate that you're reaching the instance but it doesn't recognize your credentials as valid. Entering the wrong passphrase for the private SSH key or using an SSH key that grants other users or groups read/write permissions will result in the SSH client not even attempting the connection. This leaves an incorrect username as the only possible answer.

97. C. The error indicates that the SSH client won't permit the connection because the private key's permissions are too open. Executing the command `chmod 0400 .ssh/private_key.pem` would resolve this. Deleting the private key or creating it wouldn't resolve this issue. The SSH public key is stored on the instance, not on your workstation.

98. A. The SSH server may be disconnecting the session after a period of inactivity. To avoid this, you can enable keepalives on your SSH client. Enabling, not disabling. TCP keepalives will also work. Setting the ClientAliveInterval on the server to 0 or running a continuous ping won't prevent the server from disconnecting an idle session.

99. A. You need to allow ICMPv4 Echo Requests inbound to the instance. An ICMPv6 Echo Reply is what the instance would send in response to the ping. Elastic IP addresses are IPv4 addresses, so there's no need to add rules for ICMPv6.

100. D. An outbound NACL rule that denies ICMPv4 Echo Replies would block the response to the Echo Request. ICMP and UDP are different protocols.

101. A. You can create a CloudWatch alarm to recover an instance when it fails its system status check.

102. B. Up to three instance recovery attempts are allowed per day.

103. B. Of the options, only VPC Flow Logs can track whether traffic is allowed or denied.

104. A, B. VPC Flow Logs can be configured to log flows for a VPC, a subnet, or an elastic network interface (such as one attached to an elastic load balancer or instance). VPC flow logging can't be configured per host or per placement group.

105. D. A VPC Flow Logs record contains a 5-tuple that includes source address, source port, destination address, destination port, and protocol. A VPC Flow Logs record doesn't include an indicator to explicitly distinguish an IPv4 flow from an IPv6 flow, nor does it contain the number of packets in the flow.

106. A. NODATA is written to the end of a flow log record when there's no traffic to log during a 10-minute capture window. If there were too much traffic to log, SKIPDATA would appear instead. There's no reason to conclude that any traffic is not getting logged or is getting blocked.

107. B. The most cost-effective option is to enable VPC flow logging for rejected traffic and save the logs in an S3 bucket.

108. C. To add an alternative domain name to a distribution you must specify a valid TLS certificate issued by a trusted CA, and the certificate must contain the alternative domain name. Some CAs may limit the number of domain names per certificate. The alternative domain name must be in all lowercase.

109. B. The distribution requires a certificate that is valid for both domain names. The default CloudFront certificate is only good for the domain name *.cloudfront.net. There's no need to verify your ownership of the www1.example.com domain name to add it to the distribution, but you may need to verify your ownership of the domain name to obtain a certificate from a certificate authority.

110. D. Adding the S3 bucket as an origin is the most scalable approach. You can use an ELB or instance as an origin, but in this case the assets are stored in an S3 bucket, not on the instances. A streaming distribution is for streaming media, not static web assets.

111. B. The media player files must be served via a regular HTTP distribution. Only the video files should be served via an RTMP distribution.

112. D. RTMP uses TCP port 1935 by default. CloudFront RTMP distributions don't support RTMFP, which uses UDP port 1935. The fact that some users can view the videos indicates that the distributions for the media player and video files are configured correctly.

113. B. RTMPT tunnels RTMP over TCP port 80. RTMP distributions can't be converted to HTTP/HTTPS distributions. CloudFront doesn't use security groups.

114. A. RTMP distribution URLs begin with `rtmp://` and the domain name begins with s (for streaming). HTTP distribution URLs begin with `http://` or `https://` and the domain name begins with d (for distribution).

115. C. A CloudFront edge location doesn't fetch a file from an origin until it receives a request for that file. It doesn't preemptively fetch files from an origin.

116. A. Route 53 doesn't charge to resolve records that point to an alias target, such as a CloudFront distribution. The record type must be an A or AAAA record, not a CNAME record. Decreasing the TTL would result in more queries and higher cost. There is no such thing as a zone reservation.

117. D. You must create an AAAA record in order to provide IPv6 resolution.

118. D. Alternate domain names that contain a wildcard must begin with *.

119. B. You can accomplish this by setting the origin path to `/production`. You don't need to specify the bucket name in the origin path. There's no need to restrict access to the bucket. You can't create a CNAME record for the apex of a zone.

120. B. CloudFront supports HTTP, HTTPS, and WebSocket. It doesn't support UDP-based protocols or Real Time Streaming Protocol (RTSP). RSA is a cipher, not a network protocol.

121. A. An origin access identity allows CloudFront to access a bucket while restricting public access to it. A bucket policy that grants read permissions to the * principal would make the bucket public. You can't grant CloudFront access to a bucket using an ACL except by making it public. You can't put a password on a bucket.

122. B, D. The simplest solution is to move the audio files to an S3 bucket and create a streaming distribution. The custom player files can remain on the instances, and you can prevent direct access to the instances by placing them in a private subnet.

123. D. A public web server that's open to the Internet can be a custom CloudFront origin. This includes a public S3 bucket configured for static website hosting.

124. B. The instance's security group is blocking traffic from the NLB, but not from other instances in the subnet. If the NACL were the problem, all instances in the subnet would be failing the health check. NLB health checks only check for TCP connectivity, not for TLS certificate validity.

125. C. You must reference instances in a peered VPC by IP address.

126. D. You can specify any RFC 1918 or RFC 6598 addresses in a target group. You can't specify a publicly routable IP address.

127. B. Only application load balancers support the Lambda target type. There is no such thing as a Lambda load balancer.

128. A. The network load balancer preserves the client's source IP address. The application load balancer doesn't preserve the client's source address but provides it in the X-Forwarded-For HTTP header. Route 53 weighted resource records only resolve domain names to addresses.

129. C. The error usually indicates that the load balancer received an unexpected response from the target, such as a TCP reset or TCP FIN. The "Bad Gateway" error is generated by the application load balancer, so receiving the error indicates users are able to connect to it.

130. B. The "Gateway Timeout" error occurs when the target doesn't respond.

131. C. The HTTPCode_ELB_5XX_Count metric tracks the number of server errors generated by an application load balancer, such as "502 Bad Gateway" and "504 Gateway Timeout." HTTPCode_ELB_4XX_Count tracks the number of client errors such as "404 Not Found."

132. B. You can configure an application load balancer to store logs in an S3 bucket.

Domain 7: Automation and Optimization

1. A. A metric contains a timestamp and a value. It may also contain a unit of measure and dimension. A metric exists within a namespace, which acts as a container for metrics.

2. A. EC2 collects CPU utilization metrics every minute.

3. B. Detailed monitoring sends metrics to CloudWatch every minute. Basic monitoring sends metrics every 5 minutes. There is no regular or high-resolution monitoring, but metrics can be stored at regular or high resolution.

4. C. High-resolution metrics can be stored with up to 1-second resolution. Regular resolution metrics are stored at no less than 1-minute resolution. Averaging the metric values over a minute and storing the data would imply not storing the individual data points. Timestamping each metric 1 minute in the past is allowed, but you'd still need to do so at high-resolution to avoid losing a data point.

5. C. The available statistics in CloudWatch include Sum, Minimum, Maximum, Average, Sample Count, and Percentile.

6. D. Data points stored at 1-hour resolution are deleted after 15 months.

7. C. The Sum statistic adds the metric values in a given period, so it would be the most appropriate.

8. C. CloudWatch uses dimensions to identify metrics that have the same name and are within the same namespace. Metrics being in the same namespace entails that they're in the same region.

9. B. CloudWatch can store regular-resolution metrics at no less than 1-minute resolution. Therefore, updating a metric at 10:00:30 and then again at 10:00:59 will result in CloudWatch storing only the second value.

10. D. To graph the exact data points, specify the Sum statistic and set the period equal to the metric's resolution, which is 1 minute.

11. D. The instance being stopped and restarted would explain the momentary lack of CPU utilization data. If the instance was terminated, then the alarm would not have been able to reenter the OK state because the metric is tied to the instance. If the CPU utilization went above the alarm threshold, then the status would have been ALARM, not OK or INSUFFICIENT_DATA. An alarm can't be paused.

12. B. You have to specify the size for an EBS volume, and expanding it is a manual task. It's therefore wise to monitor your EBS volume utilization to ensure you don't run out of space. Lambda, S3, and EFS are all elastic services that automatically provision additional capacity as needed.

13. B. An Auto Scaling group can automatically scale EC2 instances horizontally based on a metric. Launch configurations and launch templates are used to define the characteristics of the EC2 instance launched. An elastic load balancer doesn't launch or terminate EC2 instances.

14. A, C. In addition to providing elastic scaling and integration with an Auto Scaling group, you can terminate the HTTPS connection on an application load balancer instead of on the instances, potentially freeing up CPU resources on each instance. You can't terminate an HTTPS connection on a network load balancer. Using latency records won't provide any advantage because they only route users to the region with the lowest latency. In this case, both instances are in the same region.

15. D. Using the Standard storage class for frequently accessed files is ideal. Standard-IA has a slightly lower availability and a higher cost for GET requests. Moving the files to Glacier would also negatively impact availability. Enabling versioning wouldn't reduce costs but might increase costs. There's not much else you can do to reduce costs except to delete unneeded files from the bucket.

16. B. AWS Budgets can alert you via email if your bill exceeds a specified amount—a good indicator of excessive resource utilization. CloudTrail records events, and CloudWatch Events can be used to alert you to specific events, but neither will give you a good indication of resource utilization. AWS Config is good for monitoring changes but likewise isn't good for tracking resource utilization. Cost Explorer can't send notifications.

17. A. Enabling automated snapshots will enable point-in-time recovery, which archives database logs to S3 every 5 minutes. Multi-AZ synchronously replicates data from the primary instance to a standby instance, but failover to the standby instance is automatic if the primary fails. Amazon Aurora doesn't use MySQL but does have a MySQL-compatible option. A read replica is for scaling reads, but because replication is asynchronous, it's not ideal as a backup.

18. A. The volume queue length metric measures the total number of read and write operation requests waiting for completion. If this has increased and remains high, it's a good indication that the volume isn't able to sustain enough IOPS. Because it's a gp2 volume, the number of IOPS depends on the size allocated for the volume. You can't provision IOPS explicitly using gp2 storage, but you can with io1 storage. The number of EBS snapshots has no impact on EBS performance, because snapshots are stored in S3.

19. C, D. AWS Config and CloudWatch Events can monitor S3 for new buckets and alert you when they're created or deleted. CloudTrail can log the API events but won't do any alerting. S3 server logging won't log bucket creation events.

20. C. EBS data lifecycle manager automatically takes snapshots at a specified interval and retains only the latest. It's configurable; for example, you could have it take a snapshot every 6 hours and retain only the latest 120 snapshots.

21. B. Memory-optimized instances have dedicated bandwidth for EBS storage. Standard instances are not EBS optimized. Burst-capable instances are for test workloads and don't have dedicated bandwidth. There is no network-optimized instance class.

22. B. RDS will retain automatic snapshots for 7 days by default. You can choose a retention period between 1 day and 35 days.

23. D. Unlike automatic snapshots, RDS will retain manual snapshots indefinitely.

24. A. CloudTrail logs can be stored in S3 buckets or CloudWatch Logs. By default, S3 and CloudWatch Logs don't delete any files or logs automatically. Therefore, any logs CloudTrail stores will remain indefinitely.

25. A, B. Retention periods are set per log group. To have separate retention periods for different log streams, the streams have to be in different log groups. Exporting CloudTrail logs to an S3 bucket can preserve the existing logs but won't affect retention moving forward.

26. B. The period should be greater than or equal to the resolution of the metric. In this case, you want the alarm to trigger as soon as the metric crosses a threshold, so you should set the period to 5 minutes.

27. A, D. Setting the period to 1 minute and the datapoints to alarm to 5 out of 5 will evaluate the metric every minute and trigger the alarm if it remains crossing the threshold for 5 consecutive minutes.

28. B, D. The instance being stopped would preclude EC2 from sending any CPU utilization metrics. If the alarm period were set to something greater than 4 hours—such as 6 hours or a day—then that would also explain the `INSUFFICIENT_DATA` state.

29. B, C. You can effectively monitor the average CPU utilization and the instance's running status by creating a single alarm to only monitor CPU utilization as long as you treat missing data as breaching. If the instance is stopped, the evaluation period of the alarm will be missing data and treating that missing data as breaching will trigger the alarm. You can't create a single alarm to monitor multiple metrics.

30. D. Using CloudWatch to graph the `BucketSizeBytes` metric will give you the data with minimal effort.

31. D. The EC2 service console will show you your account's EBS service limits. CloudWatch won't, and there is no EBS service console. Sending a request to AWS support would probably work, but it isn't the easiest way.

32. D. If you run an instance on a dedicated host, you can see how many physical sockets and cores the host has. You can't do this if the instance is a dedicated instance.

33. D. There is no practical limit to the number of files you can store in S3. The KMS key limit applies to the number of customer master keys, but you can use the same key to encrypt each file in S3.

34. C. AWS reserves the first 4 addresses and last IP address of a subnet. That leaves you with 251 usable addresses.

35. B. Strongly consistent reads deliver the most up-to-date data from a table. There is no such thing as a strongly consistent write. Provisioned throughput has to do with performance, not with the contents of the data being read.

36. B, D. One RCU gets you a strongly consistent read per second of an item up to 4 KB in size, or two weakly consistent reads per second of 4 KB each.

37. D. 100 WCUs will let you write 100 items that are up to 1 KB each every second.

38. C. You can have up to approximately 120,000 in-flight messages in a standard SQS queue.

39. B. You can have up to 20,000 in-flight messages in a FIFO queue.

40. B. Glacier offers the lowest storage cost per GB. EBS gp2 storage is the most expensive per GB.

41. B. S3 standard charges nothing for data transfer up to 1 GB per month. S3 One Zone-IA and Standard-IA charge US$0.01 per GB.

42. B. Cost Explorer lets you analyze your costs and usage for the preceding 13 months.

43. C. You can access the query engine that powers Cost Explorer via the API for a cost of US$0.01 per request.

44. C. You can create up to two AWS Budgets custom budgets for free. Every subsequent custom budget costs US$0.02 daily.

45. B. The Simple Monthly Calculator lets you specify the exact resources you plan to run in a region and gives you an estimated monthly cost.

46. C, D. Spot Instances can be terminated by AWS, and Lambda functions have a timeout of 15 minutes, so they're not appropriate for a long-running process.

47. D. Each instance family is limited to a certain number of vCPUs per region. You can run as many on-demand instances as you want until you reach the vCPU limit. There is no memory limit.

48. E. If you have a 2400 vCPU limit for standard instances, you can simultaneously run 2400 t2.small instances on demand.

49. C. ECS will let you run the application in Docker containers at a lower cost than on EC2 instances. Auto Scaling can help reduce costs by scaling in and out based on demand, but the real cost savings will be in using containers rather than multiple EC2 instances. Lambda can't run Linux applications. Since the application is SQL-backed, DynamoDB can't help since it's not a SQL database.

50. D. Convertible reserved instances will give you a lower cost, and you can exchange them later if you ever need to switch to a different instance type.

51. C. All upfront, partial upfront, and no upfront are your only payment options for an instance reservation. On demand isn't a reserved instance payment option.

52. B. For a 1 Gbps connection, a dedicated connection is actually cheaper than a hosted VIF. A hosted connection is only for sub-1Gbps connections. There is no such thing as a VPN Direct Connect connection.

53. A. You can create a budget to track all of these things except EC2 CPU utilization.

54. C. Cost allocation tags can take up to 24 hours to appear in the console. You don't need to be using AWS Organizations, and you don't have to activate AWS-generated cost allocation tags. Cost allocation tags are retroactive.

55. C. Each Snowball Edge appliance offers about 100 TB of storage. A Snowball appliance costs more and offers up to about 80 TB of storage. A Direct Connect connection is the costliest option.

56. B. Standard-IA storage is the lowest cost option. Creating a lifecycle policy to transition files to Standard-IA will leave a 6-month gap before the files are moved to the lower-cost storage. Versioning will store more data, increasing costs. S3 Intelligent-Tiering incurs a monthly monitoring and fee per object.

57. C. Scheduled Auto Scaling is the cheapest option since it will add more instances only during the Christmas season. Dynamic Auto Scaling (of which a step scaling policy is an option) could add more instances outside of the busy season, thus incurring more costs. Instance reservations are good for a contiguous period of time such as six months or a short time interval such as a certain day of the month. With reservations, you pay regardless of whether you launch any instances.

58. C. Containers offer better memory utilization than instances. Although containers launch faster than instances, this doesn't lead to significant cost savings. Containers don't offer better CPU utilization. Containers are more complex to configure than instances.

59. A, D. A Windows application that must run continuously every weekday is a good reason to purchase an instance reservation. Running a highly available application in containers on an EC2 instance (using ECS) is also a good candidate for an instance reservation. Spot Instances are most cost-effective for batch jobs.

60. A, B. You can select a Spot Instance duration of 1, 2, 3, 4, 5, or 6 hours. After that, the instance terminates.

61. B. A scheduled Spot Instance request can automatically generate a Spot Instance request daily for a specified duration, such as 4 hours. A persistent Spot Instance request will create a new Spot Instance request as soon as the instance from the previous request terminates. A one-time Spot Instance request will launch an instance only once, not daily. An instance reservation will cost more than using Spot Instance requests.

62. B. You only need two Direct Connect connections, one per datacenter. These can connect you to all subnets in all regions.

63. B. VPN CloudHub allows you to use a VPC for transit between two connected sites. A transit gateway lets you route traffic between VPCs and a VPN. The other options are feasible but cost more.

64. D. When the spot price rises above your maximum price, the instance terminates. The instance's workload completing or canceling the request won't necessarily terminate the instance. Increasing the target capacity won't do it either.

65. C. Setting an overall target cost per hour lets you control your absolute cost for Spot Instances. Reducing total target capacity can reduce costs, but if you don't specify a maximum cost per hour, you can't control your overall cost. Using on-demand instances is always more expensive than using Spot Instances. Stopping instances instead of terminating them when interrupted costs more because there's a cost associated with storing an instance's EBS volume(s).

66. C. In provisioned capacity mode, DynamoDB charges you based on the read and write capacity units provisioned.

67. D. In on-demand capacity mode, DynamoDB charges you based on the read and write request units used.

68. D. Replicating reads and write to another region doubles the amount of reads and writes, thus doubling your cost.

69. A. The DELETE operation costs nothing. The rest incur a nominal cost.

70. A, D. Inbound data transfers to RDS or S3 and via Direct Connect cost nothing. Inbound data transfers through an elastic load balancer or NAT gateway factor into the total cost.

71. A. You can store VPC flow logs in S3 or CloudWatch Logs, but S3 is the cheapest option.

72. A, C. Sending CloudTrail logs to S3 and using S3 Select to search them is cheaper than using CloudWatch Logs. CloudTrail event history stores only 90 days of events.

73. A. All things being equal, the application load balancer is the cheapest resource.

74. B. Logging S3 data events using CloudTrail will do the trick. Enabling S3 server logging may not log every request. S3 GET requests are data events, not management events. S3 is not a global service.

75. B. AWS costs vary by region.

76. A. Since you've already registered the domain name, the most cost-effective option would be to keep it with the current registrar and create a public hosted zone for the domain in Route 53.

77. D. CloudFront offers 50 GB data transfer out for the first year in the free tier.

78. C. If you need to serve content to browsers that don't support server name identification (SNI), you can use CloudFront's Dedicated IP Custom SSL. This will give you a dedicated IP address per SSL/TLS certificate at one Edge location. The monthly cost of this is $600.

79. B. CloudFormation lets you provision resources as needed and delete them quickly when you're done, potentially saving you money. Resources created with CloudFormation cost the same as if you created them manually, and there's no extra cost to use CloudFormation. CloudFormation doesn't entail using Lambda.

80. C. EC2 Auto Scaling Dynamic scaling policies add or remove instances based on a metric related to demand, such as the number of web requests or CPU utilization.

81. C. A public IP address attached to a running EC2 instance is free. If the instance is stopped, it loses its public IP address. An elastic IP address attached to a stopped instance incurs a small charge. Route 53 public hosted zones are never free.

82. C, D. It's free to use CodeDeploy to deploy to EC2 instances. You can automate the process with CodePipeline, which lets you have one free active pipeline per month. CodeBuild isn't free. CodeCommit is a Git repository with options under the free tier but isn't necessary in this case since the developers will be pushing updates to an S3 bucket.

83. C. CodeDeploy can perform a rolling application upgrade on one or more instances at a time. Using CloudFormation to do the upgrade would require doing an all-at-once switchover. AWS Systems Manager could also be used but would require more manual effort. CodeStar doesn't do application deployments.

84. A. You can define the AMI ID as a Systems Manager parameter and reference it in your CloudFormation template.

85. C. The most cost-effective solution is to create an AMI with the changes and then deploy it to all regions. This will require copying the AMI from one region to another, but there are no data transfer costs associated with doing this.

86. B. SNS is the cheapest option. SES is designed for sending and receiving bulk emails but isn't specifically designed for sending notifications. SQS and CloudWatch Alarms can't send emails. They use SNS.

87. B, C. Creating an Internet gateway and default route and assigning an elastic IP address is the most cost-effective option. A NAT gateway will incur charges. Using AWS Patch Manager to download the updates will still require the instance to have Internet access.

88. C. The cheapest option for hosting a static website on AWS is to use S3.

89. C. Kinesis allows multiple consumers to read the same message from a single producer. SQS allows only a single consumer to read a message. Amazon MQ is not elastic. SNS is not a messaging service.

90. D. ACM can renew certificates automatically if they're associated with an AWS service such as elastic load balancing.

91. A. CloudFront can replicate the videos to the Asia Pacific edge locations, resulting in fast delivery to users in Japan.

92. D. Configuring the target group's health check to check the status of the web service on each EC2 instance less than every 10 seconds will remove the problem instance from load balancing.

93. A. You can use BYOIP with network load balancers, EC2 instances, and NAT gateways. When you bring your own IP addresses to AWS, you can assign them to these resources as elastic IP addresses.

94. C. You need a Business or Enterprise support plan to access the Health API.

95. B. SSE-KMS with AWS-managed CMK is the cheapest option. There is no such thing as SSE-ACL.

96. A. Using CloudWatch Events to stop and start the instances on a schedule is the most cost-effective approach. Terminating the instances and re-creating them will lose each developer's customizations. Using instance reservations is a good idea, but they're time-limited and would need to be manually renewed.

97. C. RDS is the most cost-effective solution. Redshift is designed for data warehouses, and Redshift Spectrum is for data stored in S3.

98. A. Multi-AZ is the only option for synchronous database replication.

99. B. Read replicas give you asynchronous replication to another instance. Automated snapshots back up the entire instance but don't offer asynchronous replication of just a single database.

100. A. AWS VM import/export is designed to export on-premises virtual machines to EC2 instances.

101. B. If the maximum Spot price you've set consistently meets or exceeds the on-demand price, the instance will run indefinitely.

102. B. You can request Spot Instances in the launch template or launch configuration.

103. C. Using AWS Systems Manager Patch Manager to patch the instances—both the current ones and any instances launched in the future—is the most cost-effective and easiest approach. Just flipping to the new AMI may not work; You don't know unless you first test your workload with it. You can't update a launch configuration.

104. A, D. Creating a role with access to the DynamoDB table and using an instance profile role to grant the instance the ability to assume the role is free. AWS Secrets Manager isn't free. Hardcoding credentials into the application isn't secure.

105. C. Upgrading the instance type and creating a read replica are comparable options pricewise but upgrading is much quicker in part because it doesn't require reconfiguring the application to use a read replica.

106. B. Amazon Aurora will dynamically expand its storage cluster to grow with your database.

107. D. The most cost-effective option is to enable VPC flow logging for allowed traffic and save the logs in an S3 bucket.

108. B. Uploading the file to an S3 bucket and making it public is the cheapest and quickest option.

109. D. AWS Storage Gateway—File Gateway offers an SMB or NFS interface to store files on S3.

110. C. AWS Storage Gateway—Volume Gateway can function as an iSCSI target and back up the data to S3.

111. C. Expedited retrievals are the most expensive.

112. D. Convertible reserved instances do not include a capacity reservation.

113. C. The minimum required utilization for a scheduled instance is 1200 hours per year.

Domain 8: Practice Test

1. C. ClusterService is a dimension, not a metric.

2. A, C. Filesystem corruption or running out of memory can cause an instance to fail its status check.

3. B. The command aws ec2 describe-instance-status will show instance and system status for an instance as well as its running status.

4. B. The AmazonEC2ReadOnly has the permissions the admin needs to view EC2 instance status.

5. A. The agent runs on various flavors of Linux and Windows Server. Sadly, it doesn't run on Unix variants like BSD or Solaris.

6. A. You can use the CloudWatch Logs agent to send Windows event logs to CloudWatch Logs.

7. C. CloudWatch Logs uses HTTPS to secure data in transit. HTTPS doesn't use SSL, only TLS.

8. A. CloudWatch Logs uses KMS to secure data at-rest.

9. B. The Service Health Dashboard shows the status of all AWS services, not just the ones you use.

10. B. GuardDuty analyzes VPC traffic for security threats. It doesn't require configuring VPC flow logs, and VPC flow logging doesn't perform any security analysis. Inspector performs security assessments against EC2 instances.

11. B. EC2 Instance Connect lets you achieve command-line access to an EC2 Linux instance without using your own SSH client. Telnet is insecure.

12. B. RedShift uses PostgreSQL. EMR uses Hadoop. There's no service called Minerva.

13. C. Predictive scaling will automatically scale instances based on the past 14 days' performance. There's no such thing as lifecycle scaling.

14. A. Auto Scaling groups will spawn more instances to handle the load. An application load balancer won't help because the instances are in different regions.

15. A. A launch template is versioned and can be edited. It can't be used with ECS, and you can't tag a specific version. A launch template doesn't require an AMI ID, but if you use it to launch an instance, you must provide an AMI ID at launch time.

16. C, D. A launch configuration requires an AMI ID and can't be edited.

17. B. Multi-AZ synchronously replicates data from the primary instance to a standby instance and fails over to the secondary instance if the primary fails. Amazon Aurora doesn't use MySQL but is MySQL-compatible. A read replica uses asynchronous replication.

18. B. Simple Queue Service (SQS) provides reliable delivery of messages to applications.

19. C. A sent message is deleted automatically after 4 days.

20. D. You can configure an SQS queue to retain sent messages for up to 14 days.

21. A, B. S3 and DynamoDB are good options for storing temporary files. SQS can't store files greater than 256 KB, but it can store a pointer to DynamoDB or S3. Lambda and SNS aren't storage services.

22. E. SQS is for message queuing, not for storing session state. The rest can be used for storing session state.

23. C. An availability zone name may not map to the same physical location across AWS accounts. To see AZ name to location mappings for an account, use the AWS CLI command aws ec2 describe-availability-zones --region *region-name*.

24. B, D. An ALB with path-based routing fits the bill. NLB doesn't provide path-based routing.

25. A. The US-West-1c zone for your friend's account is probably mapped to a different location than it is for your company's account. Because there's no apparent problem in the AZ you're using, there's no need to take action. As the saying goes, "If it ain't broke, don't fix it."

26. D. Create a bucket policy to grant the user access to the file. There's no need to make the file public or disable SSE-S3 encryption.

27. B, C. The web server's security group should allow inbound traffic to TCP port 444. The load balancer needs an outbound rule to permit TCP port 444 traffic to the instance. The presence of the "gateway timeout" error indicates that the load balancer already has an inbound rule for HTTPS, so there's no need to add one.

28. A. IAM is designed to store long-term credentials. STS is for generating short-term credentials. Secrets Manager is designed for storing short-term application secrets such as API keys, which should be rotated regularly. KMS stores encryption keys, not credentials.

29. A, D. Adding the appropriate permissions to the IAM role is all that's necessary. Creating a bucket policy and granting the role access would also work. You can't add permissions directly to an instance profile, only an instance profile role. Creating a new IAM role with just the S3 permissions and attaching it to the instance profile would result in losing the DynamoDB permissions.

30. B. KMS custom key stores use CloudHSM clusters.

31. B. You can export a private TLS certificate from ACM. The rest you can't export.

32. B, D. The SSM agent must run and have outbound Internet access to check in with SSM.

33. A. The 64-character string is a canonical user ID, which you can use instead of the account ID to grant the client access. You also need the ARN of the IAM principal.

34. B. AWS reserves the first four addresses and last IP address of a subnet. The range of the CIDR is 10.0.0.0–10.0.0.15 inclusive. Subtracting 5 IP addresses leaves you with 11 usable.

35. C. The root user has access to all resources, and its access key isn't blocked by default and doesn't expire. Having the wrong time on your machine will result in an invalid signature exception.

36. B. VPC flow logging is the only option given the short time frame. GuardDuty takes 7–14 days to establish a baseline. Inspector doesn't monitor VPC traffic. There isn't a CloudWatch metric that tracks all VPC traffic, so you can't create such an alarm.

37. B. You can create a simple resource record that resolves to the instance's private IP address. There's no need to use a private hosted zone. An alias record would return the public IP address of the target resource, which can't be an EC2 instance.

38. B, D. You need to accept the peering connection on VPC B and configure the appropriate routes, NACLs, and security groups. There's no need to create a transit gateway or create an additional peering connection.

39. A. You need to allocate an IPv6 CIDR for the VPC to use IPv6. There's no need to put the instance in a public subnet. There's no such thing as an IPv6 gateway in AWS. Internet gateways support IPv6. An IPv6 egress-only gateway allows only outbound IPv6 traffic to the Internet.

40. A. Direct Connect provides consistent latency, also known as low jitter. It doesn't provide encryption, authentication, or packet capture facilities.

41. A, D. Session stickiness and path-based routing can result in an uneven distribution of traffic to instances. Cross-zone load balancing attempts to evenly distribute traffic to instances across availability zones.

42. B. An instance must have a global unicast IPv6 address in order to be reachable via IPv6. You can't disable IPv4 on an instance, in a subnet, or in a VPC. There's no such thing as an elastic IPv6 address. An egress-only Internet gateway is essentially a NAT gateway for IPv6.

43. A. If enableDnsSupport is enabled, the Amazon DNS server is enabled. If enableDnsHostnames is set to true, then instances with a public IP address will receive a public DNS hostname. The other two options aren't valid.

44. B. Removing the rule allowing inbound SSH access will shut down any existing SSH sessions and prevent more. Inbound NACL rules don't allow you to specify a destination, only a source. Shutting down the instance may affect other instances.

45. C. The URL begins with `https://` and the domain name begins with d, indicating a CloudFront HTTP distribution. RTMP distribution URLs begin with `rtmp://`.

46. D. A Lambda function can't be a CloudFront origin. The other options can.

47. A. Adding the instance's private IP address to the target group is sufficient. You can't add a public IP address to an NLB target group. There's no need to create a VPN since the NLB and instance are already in the same VPC.

48. C. The "503 Service Unavailable" error can indicate that there are no healthy or registered instances. Since there are registered instances, the most likely explanation is that all the instances are unhealthy.

49. D. The Average statistic with a 30-minute period will average all the values over the period.

50. C. Increasing the number of provisioned IOPS will reduce the volume queue length, which is a metric, not a configuration parameter. The number of snapshots doesn't impact EBS performance because snapshots are stored in S3. Increasing the disk size won't change the number of provisioned IOPS.

51. D. EFS uses the Network File System (NFS) protocol. FSx isn't a protocol but an AWS service.

52. A. The Volume Gateway lets you mount volumes using iSCSI.

53. B. The File Gateway lets you mount file shares using NFS.

54. C. You must enable MFA Delete using a bucket policy. You don't have to turn on versioning, but doing so adds an extra layer of protection by retaining "deleted" object versions. A hardware token isn't required since you can use a virtual software token as well.

55. B, D. You can launch an instance from the AMI, make the needed customizations, and then take a snapshot of the instance. You can then create an AMI from the snapshot.

56. B. There is such a thing as the SBE instance type, and the Snowball Edge appliance can launch these instances from an AMI.

57. A. Because versioning is enabled, S3 will only create a delete marker. There's no need to specify the encryption key to delete an object version.

58. D. A delete marker causes the object to disappear from the bucket. Deleting the delete marker causes the object to reappear. Strange but true!

59. B. The Expedited option lets you access data in 1–5 minutes. Bulk retrieval takes 5–12 hours. The others aren't valid options.

60. D. AWS Storage Gateway permanently stores data in S3 buckets. It can use local volumes for temporary storage.

Index